THE MAN WHO BUILT
LONDON TRANSPORT

THE MAN WHO BUILT LONDON TRANSPORT

A Biography of Frank Pick

CHRISTIAN BARMAN

David & Charles
Newton Abbot   London   North Pomfret (Vt)

British Library Cataloguing in Publication Data
Barman, Christian
   Frank Pick.
   1. Pick, Frank   2. London metropolitan area –
   Transit systems – Biography 3. London Transport -
   Biography
   388.4'092'4   HE311.G72L6

ISBN 0–7153–7753–1

Library of Congress Catalog Card Number 78-74074

Set by Trade Linotype Limited, Birmingham
printed in Great Britain
by Redwood Burn Limited, Trowbridge
for David & Charles (Publishers) Limited
Brunel House   Newton Abbot   Devon

Published in the United States of America
by David & Charles Inc
North Pomfret   Vermont 05053   USA

Old Father Chaos in these wild Spaces, reigns
absolute, and upholds his Realms of Darkness.
He presses hard upon our Frontier.

Shaftesbury, *The Moralists*, 1709

The cycles of trade depression which afflict the world warn us
that business relations are infected through and through with the
disease of short-sighted motives. The robber barons did not con-
duce to the prosperity of Europe in the Middle Ages, though
some of them died prosperously in their beds. Their example is a
warning to our civilisation. Also we must not fall into the fallacy
of thinking of the business world in abstraction from the rest of
the community . . . The behaviour of the community is largely
dominated by the business mind. A great society is a society in
which its men of business think greatly of their functions.

Alfred North Whitehead, *Adventures of Ideas*

CONTENTS

1

IN THE BEGINNING:
1878–1914

Answers and Questions

On Thursday 3 January 1935 a letter arrived at my office in Davies Street where I carried on a modest practice as architect and industrial designer. It was quite short, only three lines. 'Will you come and see me? I would like a few words with you.' The writer then suggested that if I were free I might care to call at his office at five o'clock on the following Monday.

I suppose I was entitled in 1935 when I went to call on Frank Pick at his request to feel that I had known him for some four or five years. We had met and corresponded over a variety of problems; he had thought fit to ask my advice on odd matters like nominations for the Royal Institute of British Architects' medal for London street architecture and the interior design of the Cunard Liner 534, or *Queen Mary* as she was later to be called. He had allowed me to print in the *Architectural Review*, during my short spell as editor, a rather remarkable lecture he gave to the Art Workers' Guild. And yet in saying that I had 'known' him I am conscious of not using quite the right word. Did anyone really know him? Certainly I had never met a man about whom so many people held so many different views. His effect on others was powerful, sharp, disturbing, and it was never the same on different persons. 'Cold, ruthless, a dictator of the worst type.' 'One of the kindest men I have known.' 'Horribly superior; a prig, really.' 'He can be incredibly humble.' 'Intolerant, never listens; he knows all the answers.' 'The perfect listener; no one is more ready to admit you're right if you really are.' 'A great administrator, inspiring to work for.' 'A bully and a bore.' 'He depends on clever people around him.' 'No idea how to delegate.' 'Moody, impulsive, no idea of fairness.' 'He can be hard, but no one was ever more just.' Who was right? Were any of them right?

With some people you will find that a clearly defined persona consistently maintained in life seems to break up and dissolve after death so that they become more and more of a puzzle as new aspects of their character are revealed of which you suspected nothing at the time you knew them, or thought you knew them. Those who once held the same views about their character find themselves taking different and often conflicting views. With other people the personality, enigmatic in life, grows clearer and simpler in death. The judgements of those who knew them instead of drifting apart are brought closer in retrospect; the different images mix and coalesce till only a single sharp image remains. Not so with Pick. His death changed nothing. He had been dead for nine years when his old colleague A. A. Menzler spoke about him in a paper he read to the Institute of Public Administration. Menzler, a brilliant statistician who later became the President of the Institute of Actuaries, knew Pick well. He said:

> His distinguishing characteristic was a forthright directness, yet coupled with a fundamental shyness which made close personal association with him in a daily task almost impossible to achieve. Save on the rarest occasions, Pick was an inhibiting personality who caused people to play for safety. He was very impatient if anyone told him something that he knew or apprehended already, as was almost always the case, or with which he instinctively disagreed. It required great courage and resolution to stand up to Pick, and most of us just could not do it.

Among the friends to whom Menzler sent a copy of his paper was Steen Eiler Rasmussen of Copenhagen, author of *London: The Unique City*. Rasmussen was puzzled by what he read. In a letter to Menzler he said:

> I saw Frank Pick regularly whenever I visited London. The portrait you have given of this great personality is very different from my recollections of him. It is only now, several years after his death, that I hear it required great courage and resolution to stand up to Pick. I was a young man when I first met him and I have always known him as a friend with whom I could discuss anything. I was surprised to find that he always had plenty of time to speak with me, either at 55 Broadway or in his club. The first time I visited London I found it most difficult to

10

come in personal contact with English colleagues. They were more formal than most Danish people are. Frank Pick was to me the one exception. We were friends from the first day, and he was to me and my wife more free and frank than most Englishmen I have met.

One of Pick's neighbours in Wildwood Road in the Hampstead Garden Suburb was Sir Arnold Plant, the economist; he lived at no 19, two doors away. Plant and I were talking about him one day, some years after his death; Plant was trying to give me his impression of Pick's personality. He asked me if I knew the passage in Lord Franks' pamphlet *Central Planning in War and Peace*, in which the author describes different types of organisation in zoological terms:

Because it is hard inside and soft outside the vertebrate is flexible and able to adapt itself rapidly to change in the environment. Its bony structure gives unity and strength; the flesh and blood which clothe the bones, range and diversity of response to circumstance. The crustacean, soft inside and hard outside, is prevented by its carapace from quick and varied responses to the world. The points at which it is in contact with the environment are for the most part hard surfaces insensitive to change.

Plant thought the descriptions could equally well be applied to types of individual and to him the word 'crustacean' seemed to sum up both Pick's qualities and his defects. I thought I could see some truth in his analogy. There is a kind of person who manages to meet the impacts of the external world by falling back step by step from one line of defence to another. Behind every barrier there always lies another, there is always room for one more retreat. Seldom, if ever, is the innermost person really reached. With Pick you never got this feeling of defence in depth, the form of defence that according to Franks is made possible by 'quick and varied responses to the world'. But did Plant really mean to say that Pick as a person lacked the 'unity and strength' which are the prerogative of the vertebrate? Or that other quality, sensibility, in other words that he was a thick-skinned type? It did not seem possible. The only explanation surely was the one given to me by Edward Rawdon Smith, another Underground man, who complained in a letter he once wrote me that 'few men have been more misunderstood and few have seemed to invite misunderstanding more.'

11

This multiplicity of contrasting views was found not only in people's impressions of Pick's personality but in their judgement of his work, of his manner of conducting his business, of what he stood for as a public man. I am reminded of a talk I had with an old colleague of his, Sir Ernest Clark. At the end of World War II Clark had resigned the Governorship of Tasmania and returned to England; he felt that eighty-two was a reasonable age at which to retire. One day, about a year before he died, he was sitting in the long library he had made in the attic of his house in Seaton in Devonshire talking to me about the late 1920s when he had been a director of the Underground group of companies. He saw the Underground as a new kind of public service business; there had never been anything like it before; and if Pick had not created it single-handed – that would have been out of the question – it was nevertheless he who had made it work, who had made it what it was. How gratifying, I thought, to hear this eminent administrator echoing my own thoughts. But then, as we went on talking, I soon found that his grounds for making such a statement had little in common with mine. The achievement that had made an impression on Clark was concerned with management techniques. Running a tube railway was a new and unfamiliar job; though London's tubes had been in existence for a number of years before Pick took them on, nobody had yet found out how to work them successfully. The tram people had had a go, and so had the railway people, but the tube was neither a proper railway nor a tram and there were many new problems to be solved of which these experts had had no previous experience. They could be foolish little problems but something had to be done about them just the same. He quoted the train brakes as an example. When the tube lines were first extended to the surface the drivers would find that the brakes did not act with the same efficiency on these open parts of the track. No question of safety was involved and when the trouble was first noticed it was not regarded as important. But as the lines grew longer, great pains had to be taken to keep up average speeds, and quickness of movement both on entering and on leaving stations became very important. For some years the rain-wetted rail continued to defeat their efforts. It was Pick who, by a mixture of imagination and sheer persistence, had driven the experts to find a way out of this difficulty. But getting the tubes to work properly was only a small part of the story. There were no real precedents for anything and least of all was there any precedent for the main job of blending or integrating the different forms of transport into a single service, of getting three managers, each interested only in the performance of his own trains, trams or buses, to think and act as one. It was, thought Sir Ernest Clark, a problem in business leadership whose solution was an event comparable to an important scientific discovery. I saw that though we agreed that there was something extraordinary and possibly unique about London Transport we had, in fact, been talking about quite different things. I recalled a remark that Herbert Morrison had made to me: 'The trouble about Pick is that to him London is just a market for transport. He is without any social conscience, the business is everything.' The words were spoken in all seriousness about a person of whom another Clark, Kenneth Clark, once said that 'in a different age he might have become a sort of Thomas Aquinas'.

For some days after that conversation in January 1935 I spent many anxious moments thinking about the proposal that Pick had made to me. It would mean an abrupt breaking-off in the middle of much interesting work, some of it with friends of long standing. On the other hand his proposal was certain to open some fascinating prospects. And then there was Pick himself. Gradually, as my thoughts continued to circle round his personality, round his ideas, his involvement in common interests, as they dwelt on the business of moulding and shaping an important enterprise to the pattern of those ideas, of those interests, and on the manner in which he seemed to be going about it, I was overcome by a desire to find out what sort of person Pick really was. I wanted to get to understand him.

Early Years

From the records we learn that Frank Pick was born on 23 November 1878 in Spalding, Lincolnshire, the eldest of the five children of Francis and Fanny Pick. Francis kept a draper's shop in partnership with one Joseph Dinsdale whom he had got to know when the two of them were employed in a shop in Barton-upon-Humber, the town where he had also met Fanny Clarke, his future wife. When the men went into business on their own account they moved to Spalding where they bought an old house called Bridge House; it took its name from an old bridge across the river Welland. Frank, as he got older, would often recall those early Spalding days with his favourite sister Ethel, who was a couple of years younger than himself. One thing she always remembered was the way he could see in his mind's eye a picture of the Welland, and how, with that picture as he recalled it, there would come a spasm of childish fear. He would see a great brute of a river lashed into angry movement by the tides of the North Sea that lay fewer than ten miles from the house in which he lived. He would see a kitchen in which the floodwater of the Welland stood several inches deep upon the floor so that little bridges or gangways had to be built with planks supported on bricks. Small, brittle waves would agitate the river's surface as the tidal bore came driving up; and suddenly there was a group of men marching in the dark, carrying between them a short ladder on which lay stretched a body with a white sheet pulled over it, and he would hear the loud cries of the drowned man's wife who followed behind. It was only after the family moved to York that he got to know other sorts of rivers. As you watched the river Ouse moving in its leisurely way under the bridges there were times when you felt it was just a tired old river pacing list-lessly behind the bars of the great locks at Naburn, exiled from its freedom, from the green jungle of the sea, toothlessly amiable, looking at you with stupid eyes. But there were days when it became a radiant, friendly creature, moving gracefully about the town like a beautiful woman walking in the house, folding back shutters, bringing light and gaiety into sunless rooms. On the other side of the town the river Foss ran dressed in arrowheads and pondweed and tall green rushes. Pike, roach and eels would circu-late mysteriously under water lilies that shone like beaten gold. Here were new kinds of rivers; these were not secret enemies of which you could not help feeling always afraid. But the raging Welland was never quite forgotten.

There was a firm belief in the Pick family that to live meant to gather knowledge, and to gather knowledge meant not being afraid of hard work. Frank had early formed the habit of settling down to long evenings of study that he kept up till the very end of his active life. It was not the kind of habit that went with being a good mixer. While the other boys played games he preferred to sit under a tree with a book; the posture was one in which school friends were apt to remember him best in after years. He was conscious, too, that the son of a local draper and chapel man was liable to be regarded by the other boys as one standing not altogether on the same social footing. Great barriers divided this class from the professional and upper middle classes, from members of the Anglican Establishment, and the barriers here were made the more exclusive by the fact that York was both a cathedral city of archiepiscopal rank and the headquarters of Northern Command; officers of crack regiments with their families held an important place in local society. When Sir Ernest Clark said that 'in this cathedral city nonconformists were dirt' his statement may have been a shade overemphatic but is probably not very far from the truth. And, though York was not an industrial city in the same sense as Manchester or Birmingham, these social distinctions nevertheless followed the same geographical pattern. It would never have occurred to anyone who deemed himself to be higher than the shopkeeper class actually to live within the town. No doubt this sense of segregation helped to make the townspeople more conscious of their special virtues. A strong sense of order and neatness was one of these. Sober, industrious, imbued with a deep respect for the serious things in life and a deep distrust of that which is frivolous or useless, this little society was knit powerfully together in the discipline of an ethos they recognised as their very own.

Though at school Frank was regarded as unsociable he nevertheless set great value on his friendships. A short essay he wrote at the time tells how:

As in a garden one morning we are conscious of a new flower we had not noticed before, so is the birth of a friendship. Yet for many mornings the plant was there with a multitude of others as a seed, as a tiny shoot, as a green stem then crowned with buds, and only at the last when the sheath bursts and the petals unfold is it distinguished from the others for its beauty and fragrance and become a thing apart, a joy for evermore, a friend. In a sense there is no such thing as the choice of a friend. He whom we would choose must also be willing to be chosen. It is not a question therefore of what is offered to us, but of what we offer to others. It is not so much the qualities of a friend that we need to be anxious about as our own qualities. For to whatever we offer to that there will be response. Give and it shall be given to you again, good measure, pressed down and running over.

One of the things that helped to keep friendships alive was the giving of gifts. Those that Frank gave were quite unlike the kinds of presents you got from other people. He had a great fondness for little midget objects, tiny carved animals, doll's house china; the front edge of the shelves on which his books stood was lined with what his sisters laughingly heard him call his 'tinies'. If an object was strikingly or unexpectedly little, as though you were looking at it through the wrong end of a toy telescope, that was a quality that in itself was both endearing and productive of laughter. His family long remembered how, when he was a small child at Spalding, he used to wander into the bakery next door to his father's shop and watch the baker at his work. If the baker was in a good mood he might knead for the child a little toy pig with currants for eyes. The little animals with their message of love and laughter were the earliest presents he could remember being given. Later, he himself started to give to those around him small presents of extreme simplicity, quite inexpensive, but chosen with care and invariably accompanied by a note that invested the object with some mysterious quality of intimate personal thought. Always in whatever he gave there would be found some artistic quality that had caught his fancy, though this quality might amount to nothing more than an appearance of cleanness or neatness. Brothers and sisters and friends would come first, though the grown-ups were never forgotten. For his sisters he would choose little brooches or pottery jugs to hold flowers, for his brothers more practical things such as wallets or notebooks, but invariably smaller than the size you were accustomed to seeing.

Bit by bit in his bedroom he started to build up his museum. It was necessary that some of the space in the wardrobe should be given up to the keeping of clothes; a large part of it however became a collector's cabinet, the central point in the private gallery. From the river beach he had gone to the seashore at Filey and Carr Naze, from which came many interesting exhibits; presently other collections were started, moths and butterflies came to join the shells and fossilised ferns. But running a museum was not only a matter of acquiring new objects; if you were to do it properly you had to study the great problems of arrangement. The art of museum display was a subject that never ceased to hold his interest throughout his life. In moments of relaxation at home or abroad, in London or Finland or on the North African coast, he would wander about the local museum, not so much to see what they had got there as to see what they had done with it. He must have been in his late teens when he paid his first visit to London. There were many museums there, perhaps too many. What was to be made of so much accumulated wealth? He came away baffled and exhausted. He wrote:

> There were a mile of stuffed animals, a mile of fossils and bones, a mile of bottled invertebrates, so many cubic feet of minerals, so many acres of paintings, a mile of engineering models and castings, a mile of Asiatic *objets d'art*, a mile of manuscripts, sundry miles of archaeological relics and so on, till the legs weary with walking round the endless galleries and the eyes ache with constant gazing on the changing panorama . . . Space is destructive of the capabilities of observation.

When Francis Pick, Frank's father, was nearing the end of his schooldays he had hoped that he might one day be able to take up the profession of law. But he had reckoned without his father Charles, a yeoman farmer. Charles Pick was a sociable, pleasure-loving fellow and in those easy-going days of expanding populations and high corn duties he was able to live like a gentleman, riding about the farm or following the hounds, and spending much of his time and also a good deal of his money at the card table, assiduous with the port. Having got rid of his patrimony, and later of his wife's also, Charles died in his early forties, leaving his widow Jane with eight children of whom one was still to be born. They were living at that time on a farm at Moulton, near Spalding. After the birth of her last child Jane had to get busy maintaining her considerable young family. She was helped by two better-off brothers of her husband's to open a small school and laboriously brought up her sons and daughters. How sharp was the contrast between Charles Pick and the maternal grandfather, Thomas Clarke, most of whose life had been spent working alongside his two brothers in his father's smithy! This Thomas had been no ordinary blacksmith. A dedicated Wesleyan lay preacher, he used to disappear every Sunday to walk or drive long distances over the circuit that was in his charge. He took especially seriously his responsibility for ministering to the sick and dying and would spend many nights at the bedside of these members of his scattered flock. They liked him to read to them for he was a well-read man with a large collection of books, an attractive speaker and reader. He was a deeply religious man, too, beloved by the people in whose service he wore himself out. Of such a kind were these two men, the two grandfathers. It was fortunate for their children that both of them had had the good sense to marry strong, level-headed women who kept their families safe and whole under the stresses of a difficult home life; the wives lived to be well over eighty, surviving the husbands by many years of industrious widowhood. There is something about the contrasting characters of these men that makes one think of two vital influences trying to pull the future in different directions but succeeding only in conspiring to make it go the one way. If their two strains did anything to influence the personality of the boy Frank they must have worked like the poles of a magnet – one positively, by attraction, the other negatively, by repulsion.

Francis Pick's interest in the law business, though it had so unfortunately been thwarted, had yet at no time been altogether given up. As not infrequently happens with sons of frustrated fathers, Frank as he got older found the full force of it concentrated on him. The boy was made to feel that he was not like the other members of the family; it was something like primogeniture but the other way about: he was different not in that more was given to him but in that more was required of him. Presently at the Salem Chapel he started to develop the fastidious social conscience that was like a sort of inner response to these promptings. The father had been brought up in the established faith, the mother as a Wesleyan; they had compromised on Congregational worship. When the Pick family moved to York in 1883 the chapel, then just over half a century old, was enjoying the afterglow of its finest period, the eleven-year pastorate of John Hunter, one of the outstanding religious personalities of the time. Hunter had left York shortly before the Pick family arrived but Frank must have heard him there later as a visiting preacher. His memory was still fresh in Pick's mind when Pick was living in London and just before World War I, when Hunter paid occasional visits to London, Pick with his wife would go to some trouble to attend his services, then held in the Aeolian Hall. There was a streak of positivist radicalism in Hunter, and his liturgies and prayers have many references to social duties that must have had a powerful influence on Frank. Using the words of Hunter's confession he would say: 'For the strength which we have wasted; for the gifts we have not cultivated; for the opportunities which we have neglected . . . for our selfish comfort amid the wrongs, oppressions and sorrows of life; for our undue and exclusive regard to our own interests; for our lack of brotherhood and neglect of the service of humanity; have mercy upon us, O God.' He would pray that the Lord would regard with His favour 'the commerce of our country; that men everywhere may be in their transactions upright and honourable, in their workmanship conscientious and thorough'. He would offer thanks 'for all the blessings of civilisation, for wise government, for education and all the privileges we enjoy through literature, science and art', being careful always to add that 'for every opportunity of serving our generation according to Thy will we praise Thee, O God'.

Two short essays written by Frank at this time are of special interest because they show how beneath that calm, collected exterior there lay a capacity for deep emotion that like some explosive charge could be set off at a touch. But the evidence suggests that there was only one thing that could produce that flash of feeling, though many names might be given to it: injustice, cruelty, oppression, inhumanity, social wrong. Even at that time he was consumed by what Henry Nevinson once called 'the Englishman's rage for justice'. The fact that he had grown up in expectation of a life's work in the profession of law must have helped to strengthen that feeling, but its roots stretched very deep. He cannot have been more than nineteen or twenty when he started to write, on the backs of some sheets from a Standard Life Assurance calendar, an account of a foxhunt he had been watching. He made three separate starts with this essay; each of the pieces opens with the same sentence: 'there is a pleasant fascination about a foxhunt.' After some sober descriptive paragraphs the writing breaks off and a new start is made. You can see him putting down the sentences coldly, firmly, writing with his head, in an effort to push back, by the careful objectifying of an experience, the things he really wants to say. But the rebellious heart refuses to be subdued, and so yet another fresh start is made: 'There is a pleasant fascination . . .' This time the restraining head breaks down, the writing gets bolder, blacker, rougher:

The fox had reached the road and was met by the high wall, made higher still here by standing on a green and brambled bank. The fox scarce knew what to do in its terror and turned this way and that, hastening its end. The hounds were closing up and their harsh barking grew more and more confused and loud. In a paroxysm of terror the fox sprang at the wall and failed, its feet bleeding with the rough bricks and brambles and the roughness of the chase. Concentrating all its fast-ebbing strength it again sprang up the wall; its feet caught on the coping but with a fearful howl it fell back once more. The ills caused by the fox are little compared to the ills caused by the hunting of the fox. You men and women of England, and you children who are on the threshold of life, with sensitive feelings and tender consciences, your parents have brought you here, suppose our God, Who is far higher above us than we above the fox, was but to keep us in order to preserve us as you call it for His sport, and His notions of sport were but improved notions of ours, and we were tortured and agonised to death? Fit thoughts and aims of the worst of fiends and devils, you would say; and so when you, the gods of earth, thus treat your humbler companions shall I not call you fiends, too – fiends incarnate?

There is another essay which he wrote at the time of the Boer War. The subject is *Imperturbability*. He is writing about the Roman *aequanimitas*, using the word first of all in its original sense of justice, consistency, impartiality. He quotes authorities like Bentham and Maine and goes on to examine the current uses of the word to describe calmness, evenness of temper. Suddenly the argument switches to the subject which was uppermost in his mind at that moment:

But when our mighty Empire in an unjust and unrighteous cause buckles on its armour to fight a nation which, small though it be, is found thrice-armed with a passionate enthusiasm for its fatherland, how can there be left to those whom inconsistency in diplomacy and policy has not robbed of the dream of eternal justice an imperturbable spirit?

It had been long understood that Frank should make the attempt to go on to Oxford. Having sat for a scholarship at Magdalen he got no more than a *proxime accessit*. He felt the blow more deeply than most boys would. Presently he was articled to George Crombie, a well known York solicitor who had his office in an eighteenth-century house in Stonegate. Frank went to work in Crombie's office in March 1897; he had been there eighteen months when he settled down to read for a degree. In January 1902 he managed to pass the final examination of the Law Society with second-class honours. The work in a solicitor's office, however, held but little attraction for him and he never went so far as to apply to be admitted. But he still carried on with his studies: the long evenings between high tea and eleven or twelve o'clock would mostly be spent up in his bedroom, alone with the works of Holland, Pollock, Maine, Dicey, Austin. He would drive himself on. Turning from one work to another to collate and compare, he would stop only to enter abstracts, quotations, comments, in a thick writing book bound in maroon calf that was found among his papers after his death. He used different sizes of handwriting as a printer would use different sizes of type: the smallest, his footnote writing, was microscopic. It is clear from these notes that – with one significant exception – the one writer in all this company whose work left a permanent impression on his mind was Henry Maine. Frank had already shown signs of a strongly developed historical sense; most of his hobbies were concerned with the past history of the earth and of mankind. Maine was the first to write about law like an anthropologist, his principal work was the window through which Frank looking out on the landscape of Darwinian evolution first saw the fullness of its tremendous expanse. The other writer was John Austin. If his law studies were a major educational experience in his life, the central core of that experience was undoubtedly Austin's *The Province of Jurisprudence Determined*. 'I was trained in the strict Austinian school', was the kind of remark he would sometimes make in later years as an excuse for what might seem to some an excessive love of mental discipline, of the careful analytical approach to a question.

In 1902 he took his degree of Bachelor of Laws with first-class honours in the University of London. It was perhaps a somewhat unusual preparation for the business to which he was presently to turn his hand.

His brothers and sisters were a little puzzled at first when they found Pick taking a job with the railway. Ethel, the elder sister, would recall: 'I never knew him to take any special interest in railways: he never had a toy train or engine in his boyhood days as both his brothers had.' True, the North Eastern was one of the very few local employers known to be looking for young men of the graduate sort to be brought in as trainees. Could there perhaps have been also a little prompting from his father? According to Ethel the railways to the father were a kind of hobby: he would enjoy spending an occasional hour with his copy of a time-table to look up trains, stopping points, changes, connections, platform numbers. 'We used to call him our Bradshaw.' The North Eastern's well known interest in statistics no doubt had also something to do with the choice of a career; Frank had inherited his father's 'splendid head for figures' and when he joined the company statistics indeed became his first business. The railway's costs were known at the time to be going up at an alarming rate. Working expenses which had required only 43 per cent of gross revenue in 1860 were now swallowing 65 per cent, half as much again. The standard of timekeeping had been slipping badly, too, largely because of the steady increase in the number of freight trains which now brought in some two-thirds of the total gross earnings. When Pick joined the company in the spring of 1902, he started work in a newly established department known as the traffic statistics office. After a year or so in this headquarters post he was moved around to a couple of local offices, first Sunderland and next Newcastle, spending some seven or eight months in each place. Then, at the end of 1904, he was recalled to York, where he became a personal assistant to the general manager, Sir George Gibb. He carried on working in the general manager's private office till the beginning of 1906 when Gibb, who had left his job by then to start another career, invited Pick to come to London to continue working for him in his new employment with a business popularly known as the Underground Group.

About the time when Pick went to work with the North Eastern, the railways of Britain had their first experience of the erosion of what we now remember as the age of steam. The electricians had scored big successes in the United States and were now hard at work in most of our large cities. It was natural that the war should be fought with special ferocity in London, where the prizes to be won were so much greater than elsewhere. Here it was going on in two different fields: trams in the streets and, deep below ground, a new kind of train marvellously free from smoke and dirt. The principal victim was London's own independent steam railway, one of the biggest of its kind in the country. It was not long before the Metropolitan District Railway, as it was called, fell into serious trouble. It was saved from going under by American electric tram people, who found the means to convert the old steam railway to electricity and at the same time managed to purchase a few authorised schemes for little electric underground lines which would provide the District Railway with useful branches. There was just one more problem now: the problem of management for the new network about to be created. Sir George Gibb would be the ideal man. His North Eastern was being run with outstanding efficiency and had done better than most other railways in standing up to the electricians. And, moreover, Gibb was more conversant with London's problems than any other manager: when the Royal Commission on London Traffic was set up he had been chosen as the only railwayman member. His knowledge of American developments, too, was wide and detailed; after his first visit to the United States on behalf of the North Eastern he had again spent some time there as one of a party of five members of the Royal Commission. There was little hope of finding in this country a person better qualified to fill this critical post.

In the spring of 1906 Pick arrived in London to resume his work in Gibb's office. But he was not destined to continue in that office for very long. As work on the Underground's second tube, the Great Northern, Piccadilly and Brompton, was nearing completion, the American board of directors felt the time had come to strengthen the management by the appointment of a general manager. Since the main reason for their decision was the need to restore the confidence of the American bankers, this would mean importing a person from the United States. At the beginning of January 1907 there came a piece of news that looked as though it might lead to a quick solution of their problem. The Public Service Corporation of New Jersey announced the promotion of a bright young divisional manager to the important post of general manager of its entire system of transport. This young man, Albert Stanley, now aged thirty-two, was known to have rendered outstanding service in his present post. What made the news so especially interesting was a casual mention of the fact that the fellow was of British birth.

The greater part of Stanley's life had been spent in Detroit, Michigan, where he had arrived with his English parents as a small boy eleven years old. He was born on 8 August 1874 in a little terrace house in Madeley Street in the Rosehill district of Derby where his father, Henry Knattriess, worked as a coach painter. This was the time of the great depression when a new word, the word 'unemployed', used as a noun, was first adopted into the English language, the black decade in which nearly a million of the unfortunates so described crossed the Atlantic as government-assisted steerage passengers in search of work. When little Albert and his parents had been in Detroit a few years his father arranged to change the family name to the more English-sounding Stanley.

Detroit at that time was a city with a population only a little greater than that of Derby. Different parts of the city were served by seven tram undertakings not counting two or three smaller fry. At the age of fourteen Albert got a job working in the stables of one of the seven, the Detroit Citizens' Street Railway Company. After spending a year working as a messenger, he found himself promoted to a clerical post in the schedules department. The business of converting the horse trams to electrical traction was now in full swing, accompanied by the inevitable process of amalgamation. In January 1900 the promoters who had been responsible for launching the Citizens' Street Railway formed a new holding company to acquire the other undertakings; Stanley was appointed superintendent of this company with responsibility for the whole of Detroit's tram system. Four years of steady upward progression had finally landed him in this post of general manager, from which it was the business of the Underground's emissary to tempt him away.

In February 1907 Stanley was appointed general manager of the Underground Group. Many years later when reminiscing about those first weeks in London Stanley, or Lord Ashfield as he had become, would compare his arrival in the offices there to the letting loose of an electric eel in a tank of somnolent fish. 'There was a constant state of turmoil and uncertainty from the moment he entered the building', said H. W. Lamprell who was working there at the time. 'You never knew whose head was coming off next.' But though indeed you 'never knew' it did occasionally happen that something would point to a particular head as being in special danger. The danger to Pick's was plain to see. The general manager appointed by Yerkes to take charge of the electrified District Railway had thrown in his hand in the spring of 1906 and his successor, an old railway colleague of Gibb's, had proved a sad disappointment. And, moreover, the two tubes now in operation were still without the benefit of any real oversight from the centre. The fact that Pick, working in the managing director's office, had found himself drawn into the vacuum thus created could hardly be blamed on him. It was an ambiguous situation that left Lamprell and his colleagues 'a little uncertain just where his responsibilities began or ended'. But there was no uncertainty in Stanley's mind. Gibb, anxious to be helpful, was willing that Pick should be transferred to Stanley so that Stanley might have the benefit of Pick's experience. A young man called Evan Evans was employed by one of the tube companies; many years later when he had risen to the position of operating manager of London Transport's railways he still remembered how Stanley appeared to have judged it necessary that Pick should be conditioned by a process of 'putting down'. One day Evans walked into Pick's room and saw to his astonishment Pick sitting behind an empty desk holding his head in his hands. 'I don't know why I'm here,' said Pick, 'I have got nothing to do.'

The next move was described by Stanley many years later in a newspaper interview. He called a meeting of his principal officers and told them the terrible news. The company had managed to survive but it would not survive for very long if the losses were allowed to continue at the current rate. To make it clear that the responsibility lay firmly on all those present, he told each one of them to hand in his resignation in writing to take effect in six months. After that he had a few words to say to individual officers, and rather more than a few to one particular young man who had made a nuisance of himself by continually finding fault with the Underground's publicity. The young man's name was Frank Pick. Stanley had decided that Mr Pick should be made to assume responsibility for this work. The announcement caused some surprise among Pick's colleagues. A lawyer by training, whose main concern had been with statistics, seemed to them a most peculiar choice for a post of this sort. Having delivered his ultimatum, Stanley felt he could safely proceed with the next stage in his work on the Underground's new image. He had restored that which Gibb had taken away; the problem now was not to restore but to add and enlarge. The real improvement would come when the company was able to buy additional rolling stock; already he could see in his mind's eye the incredible record figure of forty-four trains an hour serving the Hampstead tube in the peak hours and the ten-car trains on the District Railway that were to be hailed a couple of years later as the longest multiple-unit trains in the world. But the first thing was to do their utmost with what they had. A few weeks later there started to appear in the local newspapers a steady flow of announcements

25

about more frequent trains, longer trains, extra-fast trains that whipped through a number of stations without stopping, longer station stops made necessary by the rising tide of impatient passengers, measures taken to prevent dangerous overcrowding. The announcements may not seem so very remarkable to us to-day but in those early years of the century Londoners found them somewhat strange. The railways and other transport undertakings around London were living in a fiercely competitive world and were convinced that the one sure way to beat your competitors was to keep them guessing. If customers, too, were left in the dark, it was something you just had to accept. Stanley was not unaware that there are some sorts of enterprises that have to be carried out in the dark but he also knew that the making of a success is not one of them.

To Keep in Touch

The Underground's publicity at the time when Pick took over had been largely confined to simple announcements conveying the same sort of information that would be sent out to newspaper editors. The company had been earning a substantial income from the sale of poster space; Pick's first thought was that more and better posters might be used by the Underground itself for the purpose of developing and elaborating this information. 'Underground to Anywhere!' cried the first poster, displayed in May 1908; a few days later 'Book here for Central London Railway: New Through Bookings' appeared on all stations except those of the Central London. When another poster proclaimed 'Four trains per hour to Richmond on Sunday afternoons', the message was effectively driven home with a painting of the Richmond riverside. Pick had started to feel his way among the artists. The first one with a name familiar to the public was John Hassall, a successful commercial designer famous for his simple, robust humour, his cheerful disreputable faces. His work had helped to popularise well known brands of cocoa, condensed milk, furniture-polish and Irish whiskey. The title of his poster is 'No Need to Ask a P'liceman'. An elderly rustic couple ask their way from a low-comedy policeman; the policeman, with raised eyebrows and a saucy George Robey stare, answers them by jerking his thumb over his shoulder to point to the large Underground map displayed outside the station behind his back. Little by little the public were made to see that the Underground's system meant more than just a means of getting about that was easy, convenient, fast, reliable, safe. For anybody who was strange to London, uncertain of the way, uncertain of the time it would take to get there, the posters were there to say: Walk this way, the Underground will take care of you. An Underground liftman standing beside his open gate calls 'Let us Give you a Lift'; the Underground stations are chessmen on a board beneath which is printed 'Your Next Move'; another time the mood switches to the poetical but it is poetical with tongue in cheek: the Underground railways are soaring female figures that bear above their heads a crepuscular London skyline gathered under the ball and cross of St Paul's.

In September 1908 the six months' period of grace allowed by the new general manager came to an end and another meeting was called as had been arranged. Stanley had the pleasant duty of announcing that, thanks to their combined efforts, the current deficit was being kept well below the forecast. And indeed at the end of the year it was found to be less than one-quarter of the estimated figure. A few months later there came some interesting news for Pick. Stanley had found him determined to continue to be a nuisance; that sharp inquisitive mind was still making it impossible for him to restrict himself to his appointed duties. What had happened was that Pick had seen a little too clearly the limitations inherent in even the most effective publicity. In the long run the one sure way to get more business, and keep it, is to make the product itself more attractive. Were the services giving satisfaction to the new customers, and to those other customers also whose travel had perhaps been made a little less comfortable by the irruption of the new? Just as a year or two earlier he had spoken up as a critic of the advertising department, so he had now became a critic of those who ran the services. Pick however was not just a denigrator. Nothing is more common in business, and nothing can be a greater nuisance, than the man responsible for sales whose criticism of the products he is given to sell means only that he is trying to cover up the poverty of his own perform-ance. But Pick's work thus far had proved highly successful and, moreover, he was not in the habit of finding fault with a thing without having some clear ideas about what might be done to make it better. And so once again it was decided that he should himself take a hand in the activities in which he was showing so keen an interest. At the end of April 1909 a new department was

27

set up, the Traffic, Development and Advertising Department, of which he was appointed head under the simplified description of Traffic Officer. From now on, part of the responsibility for the quality of the service would fall squarely upon him.

Pick's zeal in promoting good communication with passengers showed no falling-off as he took this larger task. On the contrary, the Underground was becoming ever more articulate, more confirmed in its habit of keeping its customers continuously in touch. Anyone who wants to follow stage by stage the process of development and improvement on the Underground railways between then and the outbreak of World War I has only to turn up the record files of the posters and Press advertisements of the period. There are the engineering works, the new station at Paddington, the first escalator in London, the Mansion House subway, the new Earls Court junction, and then, a few months before the war, the reconstructed Charing Cross station, whose escalators were at last effectively to link together the three lines that crossed each other here at the dominant nodal point of the Underground system. Seen in retrospect the advertisements form a running commentary as continuous as the file of a newspaper. A typical line, the Bakerloo, which in 1907 had provided 50,000 seats a day in each direction, was offering 54,000 in 1908; in 1909 the figure was 57,000; in 1910, 60,000; in 1911, 66,000 – an increase of one-third in four years. The extra accommodation was well received by the public, not only because it meant less overcrowding but also because trains were running in greater numbers so that waiting times, too, were cut. Speeds crept up at the same time: the journey from Baker Street to Waterloo took 18 minutes in 1907, $17\frac{1}{2}$ minutes in 1908, 17 minutes in 1909, $16\frac{1}{2}$ minutes in 1910, $15\frac{1}{2}$ minutes in 1911. The fast non-stop trains on the District Railway proved a powerful attraction and helped to account for the rise of £1,000 in the average weekly takings for 1919 over those of the previous year. Announcements told of non-stop theatre trains, a 90-second interval service in the business peak hour, better Sunday services, improved connections with the trams at Hammersmith and in the Edgware Road. Constantly there was impressed upon the people who travelled a picture of restless energy; what was good enough today would not be good enough tomorrow. The Underground's system was not a machine, it had intelligence, vitality; it was something that could only be compared to a living organism.

Pick knew when he took up poster publicity that he would be moving into a somewhat disreputable world. It was not so much the posters themselves that were at fault, it was the way they were scattered over London's buildings. In our day the poster has come under the double restraint of Acts of Parliament and of a discipline voluntarily accepted. Its effect in those not-so-distant days is as hard for us to imagine as the effect of that older nuisance – the obstruction of city streets with what a fourteenth-century statute elegantly describes as 'garbage, dung and filth'. Poster advertising was an aggressor. Even as late as the 1920s its behaviour still caused the sort of concern that teenager behaviour is liable to cause in our time. When William Morris inveighed against 'the daily increasing hideousness of the posters'; when William Richard Lethaby cried that 'the public must be protected from a form of violence which seeks to attract your attention by slapping you in the face'; when Patrick Abercrombie, writing about town and country planning, pointed angrily to 'the very large number of offenders' guilty of 'the enormity of advertisement abuse', they were voicing the feelings of thousands of bored, resentful fellow-citizens. The railways had become a special object of this resentment, not because of any positive wickedness on their part but simply because it was in and about the railway stations and their approach roads that the poster plague was seen at its most virulent. As Lethaby complained, not only had the stations themselves been turned into slatternly looking hoardings, they had become a sort of breeding ground disfiguring whole neighbourhoods with the ugly symptoms of their disease. The disfigurement was made all the more noticeable by the contrast seen on the blank walls of the newly opened tubes which would take a little time to fill up. When the Bakerloo stations were first opened to the public *The Times* printed a letter from a delighted passenger who had found to his amazement that it was possible for him 'to alight at the station required without having to hunt through all the soap, pills, whisky, milk, etc., to find the name of the station' and begged the company to accept his congratulations on its splendid act of self-denial.

In Pick's programme of ruthless scavengery there was not however any room for self-denial. The underground was not in a condition to allow the advertising revenues to be simply thrown away. His colleague Walter Gott remembered how Pick managed to convince Stanley that 'fewer advertisements well spaced out and displayed in an orderly fashion would bring twice as much revenue as the old method of filling every available space with a mass of different shapes and sizes'. It was a bold forecast to make but when the job was finished Pick was proved to have been very nearly right. His first approach to the new 'orderly fashion' was the proper siting of the one thing the passenger was always looking for, the station name-sign. The name-signs took up a great deal of wall space but, as with the posters themselves, it could not be said that the space was used to the best advantage. The Underground builders had followed the common railway practice of putting up a small number, never more than four to a platform, of very large name plates with letters some eighteen inches high. In some stations the letters, moulded in relief on the wall tiles, were a permanent part of the architectural fabric. Pick came to the conclusion that it would be helpful to passengers if there were more name plates of smaller size. The ideal arrangement would be to space them a carriage length apart so that passengers throughout the whole length of a train would have an equal opportunity of seeing one. He arranged for some experiments to be made on District Line platforms.

After a trial run, however, it was felt that something a little more forceful would be needed and experiments were then carried out with sheets of paper overprinted in bright red colour cut out in a near-semicircular shape. The red segments were pasted on the white background panel, one above and one below the name-plate to make a full disc pattern. This time he was more satisfied; the bright red disc made all the difference to the name-plate, which now became quickly recognisable for what it was. The problem now was to find the correct height at which to fix them. In all the experiments the first consideration was always to make the names clearly visible to passengers in the trains and so he placed them at a level just above the heads of the people standing on the platform. But this arrangement was not a success: the names were too high up and indeed if you happened to be travelling as a straphanger there was little chance of your seeing them. Some of the name-plates were then brought down to about the eye-level of passengers seated in the train. A year or two later, the whole of the District station platforms were being equipped with tall standard background panels of white enamelled steel, made with a plain red disc in the middle; the station name-plates were fixed on top of this disc.

Having marked out the standard distance between one name-plate and another Pick decided that the right way to treat the walls was to form a continuous strip or band of advertising running from one name-plate to the next. Each strip was laid out in a grid pattern, based on the printer's double crown sheet, 30in deep by 20in wide. The strips were two units deep and there was a range of four lengths of panel consisting, respectively, of four, eight, twelve and sixteen of these units. To make sure that the layout was properly maintained, each panel was marked out with a ground sheet of dark-blue paper stuck permanently to the wall. The ground sheet was a few inches bigger than the poster panel, big enough to frame the panel in a narrow band of dark blue. In between these panels came other, smaller panels for the Underground's own posters. They could be clearly distinguished by the fact that the unit size was slightly greater and the panel only one unit deep instead of two. The wall on the other side of the track was marked out in the same way, with a single row of tall vertical panels of sixteen units each. When he had fully developed this form of arrangement on the platforms he carried the treatment through along the subways up to the ticket hall and the entrance from the street.

Once he had got his new, orderly poster arrangements going, Pick was able to concentrate more and more on the task that posters were supremely fitted to perform – persuading people to make journeys it had not occurred to them to make. He started with a useful advantage of which not many people, and certainly not Stanley, could have been aware. For many years the North Eastern Railway had made more intelligent use of publicity than any other railway in Britain. In the north of England they still gratefully remembered how that company's activities in Scotland had brought a new prosperity to the Yorkshire seaside resorts; this was but one of many examples of the North Eastern's enterprise. But its enterprise had benefited that company also. Pick had learnt what the right kind of advertising could do for a railway. And he had also had opportunities of seeing how dangerous the wrong kind could turn out to be. Railways other than the North Eastern had started hopefully to use poster advertising to encourage travel for pleasure at weekends. They had followed their customary practice of concentrating on the great mass attractions, using a football match, an important exhibition for bait, as Blackpool or Skegness were being used elsewhere.

Pick knew he would have to do better than that. He must forget about the railways' practices and concentrate his mind on London and all that this great city meant, all that it had to offer. Not just the places and events that drew the great crowds but every kind of enjoyment, of education, the greenery of the open spaces, the pleasures of good architecture, the things that could make London an experience beyond the reach of all mankind, excepting only the lucky few who had the privilege of living there or of discovering it as visitors.

Half a century later the psychologists were to start questioning the belief still so tenaciously held in the advertising business that the impact of the message, its persistence in the individual memory, increases with the frequency of its repetition. They tell us that not only is repetition liable to blur the message, but it can set up an active resistance in the mind, a form of resistance similar to that which causes a person to shut ears and mind to some intrusive noise. If Pick had reached precisely the same conclusion as the psychologists, it was by a process altogether different from theirs. All through these years when he was concerned with advertising he was determined to avoid thinking of his public as a mass of formless, generalised humanity. He saw the person always, the individual passenger or would-be passenger. Just as there is no such thing as economic man so the average travelling man, too, was an impossibility, the only kind of passenger whose non-existence was certain. In a lecture he gave a few years later he said:

A poster must awaken a purpose in the mind, must stimulate a motive; and here we reach the most difficult part of our subject. It is almost impossible to define what will react to produce the object desired by the poster. Everyone is different and responds to different suggestions. And so the advertiser who is enabled to publish a whole series of posters has a far better prospect of success than the advertiser who must rely on one or two.

By changing your manner from one moment to another you could appear to every section of your audience in turn, and if you went on doing this for long enough the entire audience would end up on your side. Some people would be unable to respond to what you were doing at a particular moment but the audience would realise that, taking it all in all, nobody had been forgotten; there was something there for everybody.

32

Pick was, of course, exceptionally lucky in the nature of his general subject matter. It was not as though he were advertising a particular product such as a meat extract or a rubber tyre; he was telling people about the colourful and multifarious life of a great city, the most interesting city in the world. But all the time the individual person viewing the poster was as constantly present in his mind as was the subject on which he expatiated. A smiling landscape with trees and figures; a District Line train running along a great dark embankment by night; a pair of field mice outside their hole chanting: 'Live in wooded Ruislip'; London burning in the Great Fire ('Visit to the London Museum'); a sky-lark singing high over Hampstead Heath; Izaak Walton fishing in the river Colne.

The switching views and impressions flash by in quick, explosive sequence, like a film in which the tension is kept at full pitch by high-speed cutting. To heighten the feeling of contrast and surprise, he would use every kind of artist and every variety of style. 'There is room in posters for all styles', he once wrote. 'They are the most eclectic form of art. You can move from the most literal representation to the wildest impression, so long as the subject remains understandable to the man in the street. The subject may be treated historically or humorously, descriptively or allusively, so long, again, as the subject is not overlaid or lost.'

At the time when this was written he had produced a number of somewhat serious posters and there were people who at times would feel that he must be growing out of the childishness of those early cartoons. Was the Underground poster becoming re-spectable? They were soon proved wrong. 'Arrest the Flying Moment,' says the message, 'London's Underground Lends you Wings' – and a young man dressed like a bank clerk floats through space on a pair of outstretched wings labelled 'Underground' to hook a flying Cupid with the crook of his umbrella. At the entrance to Hendon airfield a German band is playing beside the parked cars to the accompaniment of howling dogs; a fat man collides with a waiter carrying refreshments; a passenger about to take flight in a biplane is being photographed with an outsize stand camera. In another design a procession of tar barrels preceded by rockets, catherine wheels and Bengal lights sets out on Guy Fawkes night to march to Hampstead Heath. A solar eclipse in April 1912 is announced in a poster in which the circular Under-ground device takes the place of the moon occluding the sun. A

33

portly gentleman wearing a bowler hat reclines on a cloud shaped like an armchair that is being pushed through the air by flying *amorini*. 'The Lap of Luxury: First Lap 5.0 am; last Lap 1.0 am', says the poster. A rabbit pops out of its hole to ask a pair of neat little Mabel Lucy Attwell children whether they, too, have come by Underground. In the month of December the Underground map becomes a Christmas tree: the railway lines fan out into roots, at each station a candle is burning and little dolls symbolise the neighbourhood of a station or its name.

Pick was not a man possessed of the common touch. What saved him from becoming coldly didactic was his keen sense of the incongruous. In this, as in other things that had helped to mould his character, he must have owed much to his early reading of Thomas Hood, to his experience of Hood's magical spontaneity, his appreciation of the perfect craftsmanship through which that spontaneity shone like the dancing flame of a candle through a piece of polished glass. If Austin and Bagehot and Maine had been examples of the way in which language should be used for the expression of serious thoughts, Hood had taught him how that same language could be employed to captivate and amuse. Reading Hood he had discovered and developed in himself the same love of the incongruous, the grotesque, as when in a schoolboy essay on poetry he singled out for special praise the caricature in which Wordsworth sees a daisy as 'A little Cyclops with one eye Staring to threaten and defy'. Moreover Hood, too, knew that the secret of successful entertainment is surprise. A great deal has been written about Hood's dual attitude to life, but all that this dual attitude really amounted to was that he knew how to surprise: reading the first line of one of his poems you have not the least idea whether it is going to go off in a rattle of verbal fireworks or bring a sudden lump to your throat. Pick's posters were a little like that. He was, without being aware of it, following Chaliapin's advice to actors: 'Never do that which the audience is expecting you to do.' A few years later he was suddenly seen to apply the precept in an altogether new direction that was to lead to London Transport's posters being held up as an example to the world.

34

2
DESIGN IN INDUSTRY: 1914-1930

The Poster in Peace and War

During the first four or five years Pick's Underground advertising had been both adventurous and highly entertaining. It had been conspicuously seen in all parts of London, but not much of it had been remarkable for aesthetic merit or interest. Most of the artists who had worked for him in those years had been routine commercial designers employed by firms of printers or working through agents, men who did what they were told like any good bookkeeper or rank-and-file railwayman. You explained to them what they were to do and if the work they produced was not what you wanted you would tear it up and they would go away and do it again. But now and then Pick would judge it necessary to have a serious discussion with an artist about some particular design problem. After he had been doing this for a little while the news got around, and presently designers taking the initiative would start to call on him with a letter of introduction. Among such artists was Walter Spradbery. His experience with the middleman had not been encouraging and about the year 1911 he became convinced that his best chance would be to bypass printer and agent. He would go to Pick, the client, and meet him face to face. His enterprise was well rewarded. He found that he and Pick were speaking the same language and it was not long before they became friends. One day Pick surprised him by dropping in at his studio in Buckhurst Hill in Essex. They would write to one another, about business at first but soon ranging over a great variety of subjects. 'How I had the nerve', said Spradbery many years afterwards, 'to write so fully, argumentatively and familiarly to such a busy man, and how he had the patience to consider it all and reply so understandingly, is just another aspect of my good fortune.' The truth is that nothing gave Pick more pleasure than a lively debate with someone who was master of his subject and let it be seen that he had a mind of his own.

Pick had always taken trouble over the appearance of his printed output, but now its appearance began to show character and quality, it was becoming remarkable not only for what it said but for its manner of saying it. He was learning to think about design. Many years later, answering a question from a friend about this period in his life, he wrote: 'After many fumbling experiments I arrived at some notion of what poster advertising ought to be. Everyone seemed to be quite pleased with what I did and I got a reputation that really sprang out of nothing.' No doubt what he really meant was that it had all been simply a matter of hard work and hard work was something he had always taken for granted. He went to great trouble to learn all he could about this part of his job and he was tireless in seeking out people who could advance his progress in self-education.

At this time, in 1912, Ernest Jackson was the acknowledged leader of the small group of English artists who were practising lithography as an authentic artistic medium; a good few of them had been taught by him and many more coaxed or stimulated to try their hand with the chalks. With Joseph Pennell he had started the Senefelder Club, a subscription society for the encouragement of autolithography, as it was called by its founders. Pick told him about his difficulties not only in persuading good artists to venture into the advertising field but also in getting printers to respond by trying to improve their standards of workmanship. He became very interested when Jackson talked to him about the Senefelder Club, and one day it was arranged that Jackson would act as a kind of editorial middleman for a series of lithographs with responsibility for the work of both artist and printer. As it happened there could have been no better moment for making this attempt to bring the print-maker and the commercial printer together, for the offset printing machine was just coming into use in the industry. Until then the lithographic artist or craftsman working on his stone or metal plate had had to draw a mirror image of the design; the mirror image was then reversed back in the printing. This awkward process was no longer necessary with the new machine which did the reversing for you: the printed copy was a straightforward impression of that which had been drawn on the plate. To the artist who was thinking of taking up lithography this simplification brought much encouragement.

The subjects of the series were chosen with care. Pick had no intention of turning the Underground into a picture gallery; he was never willing to do that at any time. It was necessary that each poster should earn its keep in a commercial sense; its job was to make people want to get around, to travel to places that were easy to get to by Underground, by bus, by tram. The thought occurred to him and Jackson that the four railway lines with which he was concerned had one common interest: the District was a riverside line that touched the north bank of the Thames at a number of points; the other three lines either led to the river or crossed it. And so London's river became one of the first of Jackson's subjects: Joseph Pennell drew the Thames at Charing Cross; Frank Brangwyn shipping at Wapping; Jackson himself did Chiswick Mall. In another set of posters the town was represented by Kerr Lawson's view of Trafalgar Square and the country by a large figure of a labourer with a scythe by Harry Becker. Then there were the amusements: a football match by Gerald Spencer Pryse, a theatre by A. R. Barker, a folk-dancing scene by A. S. Hartrick. The posters were powerful drawings in black chalk on white paper, drawings in which the lights and shadows and the depth of the modelling rose to a new kind of intensity, making them look more like the charcoal cartoons used by a mural painter or a designer in stained glass.

Early in 1914 a set of signed proofs was presented to the Victoria and Albert Museum, and presently Pick and Jackson found the fame of these lithographs travelling far beyond the streets of London. There is preserved among Jackson's papers a letter written in 1921 by an American collector, Dr Herman T. Radin of New York, who had one of Jackson's Underground posters in his collection of lithographic prints and was anxious to acquire more examples of his work. The posters had indeed travelled far by then.

To Pick the poster business still meant above all an opportunity of telling people about London, in truth not so much a city as a country, a country that somehow its inhabitants had never properly got to know. There was too much of it; it was hopelessly confusing. That is how London had struck him many years earlier when he had travelled up from York to get his first

37

sight of it and the mental picture he took back with him had never changed much on further acquaintance. In a letter written during the war he tried to communicate his impression to his friend Harry Peach:

> Another thing that seems to me so stupid is that here in London with unlimited opportunities one takes no advantage of them at all. When I lived in York or Newcastle I was much better able to know what was moving in things than I am now when I am in the middle of it. There a new book or a new idea or a new movement got into focus and one could know of it and see it, and now one can't.

Twenty years later he was lecturing one day on the growth of cities in history; he spoke about the fears expressed at various periods in the past that some great city was getting too big and about the steps that had been taken to discourage its further growth. His own personal reason for agreeing with these prophets of doom was somewhat different from theirs. The danger point, as he saw it, was the point at which a city had reached a size where it could no longer be 'comprehended and understood'. He had never lost the feeling that it was necessary for the health of London that London the living city should be comprehended and understood. And so the posters went on, telling about London.

The element of surprise that had caused his posters to be continually noticed must be maintained somehow, and if occasionally there had to be some repetition of subject matter a good interval of time must elapse before it came up again and the subject must be clothed in altogether fresh forms. A piece of eighteenth-century architecture might be followed by a circus clown, by jostling women at a sale, by a hugely magnified butterfly in full colour; the dignity and seriousness would be suddenly shattered by a healthy belly laugh, a riot of colour quenched in a harsh austerity of purest black and white. And then there was the timing. It was, for example, estimated by Pick that the effective use of the special sets of large designs by his Senefelder artists required an interval of two years. One or two single posters were indeed used – such as Spencer Pryse's workmen travelling to work which appeared late in 1913 – but it was not till the summer of 1915 that the second full set went up.

By this time Pick was becoming involved in the war and its

problems and presently thought he saw an opportunity for Underground posters to make a modest contribution to its conduct. The big official recruiting campaign that was started in the autumn of 1914 called for new, powerful forms of government propaganda. The Parliamentary Recruiting Committee from the first was a great believer in poster advertising; its belief however was not matched by its good taste or intelligence: most of the posters were on about the level of Kitchener's out-thrust finger and the little girl perched on father's knee who asks 'Daddy what did YOU do?' Pick watched the committee's activities with consternation. Martin Hardie and Arthur Sabin, in their book on the war posters of belligerent and neutral countries in World War I, have this to say about his experiments:

> While these early official posters perhaps served their purpose
> – and if they did, it was thanks to the good spirit of the British
> public and not to the artistic merit of the posters themselves –
> a series of recruiting posters was issued by the London Electric
> Railway Company. Even before the war, this company – or
> rather its business manager, Mr Frank Pick – was setting an
> example in poster work by securing the services of the best
> artists of the day. Its recruiting posters were a real contribution
> to modern art. They served their purpose, and at the same time
> were dignified in conception, design and draughtsmanship.
> Standing high among them in nobility of appeal and power of
> drawing were Brangwyn's 'Britain's Call to Arms' and Spencer
> Pryse's 'Only Road for an Englishman'.

A little later the Government Bureau of Information took up the production of official posters where Pick had left off; some admirable work was done under its direction with the indefatigable Ernest Jackson helping and advising. But the lithographic stone used for the first and most famous of Brangwyn's Underground recruiting posters, which was given to the Victoria and Albert Museum by the Lord Mayor of London and the artist jointly, is there to remind us of the railway company in London that first taught British war-time propaganda to use a language befitting the gravity of the subject matter.

In the middle of the war another very different designer made his appearance on Underground stations. If the constant variety of subject and presentation had accustomed the public to expect surprising things in Underground advertising they were nevertheless somewhat startled by the forcefulness of a set of landscapes boldly modelled in clean, flat colours, the natural forms smoothed and simplified into a record of broad and arresting legibility. The artist was a tall young American, 'a slim, russet eagle' Sir Colin Anderson once called him, with a great shock of auburn hair, twenty-five years of age. His name was Edward McKnight Kauffer. He was a native of Great Falls, Montana. In the previous year, 1914, he had been on his way back to the United States after spending a couple of years on the Continent. He had broken his journey in London, and presently he found that England did something for him that neither Munich nor Paris had succeeded in doing.

It did not take Pick long to make up his mind about Kauffer's stature as an artist. The lithographs by members of the Senefelder Club had been works of great quality but the modern poster was now becoming a recognised art form in its own right and not many of their lithographs had been true posters in this new sense. Pick saw that, of all the designers working in the main tradition of the twentieth-century colour poster, Kauffer was easily the most gifted, the most single-minded and assured. There was only one question in his mind: would Kauffer be able to produce the kind of posters that the Underground most needed? T. E. Griffits, the lithographic craftsman, remembered Kauffer telling him one day how Pick, having looked through the specimens of work that Kauffer had brought, said what a pity it was he couldn't do landscapes. Kauffer said he could, and Pick then challenged him to try a couple of sketches. Kauffer's first Underground posters, a set of four portraying different parts of the Surrey countryside, made their appearance in 1916.

After those first landscapes Pick went on to propose a succession of new subjects: the Fire of London, a piece of crystalline mineral, an occasional experiment in symbolic illustration like the mammoth silhouetted, in the words of a contemporary critic, 'against segments of a circle suggesting the movement of the earth through illimitable time'. The secret of Kauffer's outstanding merits as a designer lies in the fact that he was willing to give the whole of his mind to the art of the poster. To Pick the fact that an artist of his quality working in England should choose the poster as a vocation was proof that the English poster had truly come into its own. He spent a great deal of time talking with Kauffer and writing to him, prompting, encouraging, occasionally bullying, always with a sense of personal involvement such as he had never yet felt towards an artist. He was like an elder brother to him. ('Dürer overwhelms me', he wrote to a friend after the war. 'The sketches are quite close to Cézanne. The style is almost identical. I am going to show them to Kauffer.') It was a sign of their joint achievement that in 1924 two folio volumes should have been brought out by different publishers, both recording the emergence of a new school of British poster design. One of them appeared in the series of illustrated annuals published by the *Studio* magazine. The opening words of the introductory essay are: 'This is the day of the poster.' The author went on to pay tribute to Pick for having 'provided the mainspring for the modern British school which, but for London's Underground, might never have existed in its present form.' The other book, published by Cecil Palmer, was edited by Kauffer and dedicated by him to Pick.

A Typographical Event

When Pick had managed to keep his new, improved pictorial posters on a steady course for a year or so he began to feel able to give serious attention to all those other posters that consisted of type matter alone. There were not only the big standard-size posters for display at stations, there were also bills and notices of many kinds that appeared from time to time in railway carriages and buses and in other places; taken together all these items of printed information bulked considerably larger than the artists' posters whose quality he had worked so hard to improve. As the artists' designs became more and more interesting, so these plain typographical posters seemed by comparison to grow more drab and commonplace. At their worst they were just commercial rubbish hardly distinguishable from the advertisements of the second-hand furniture dealer and the dispenser of cough cures. Pick got some experiments on foot with the layout and arrangement of the lines of type but clearly it was not only the arrangement that was bad – the printer's types themselves were thoroughly unsatisfactory. And the artists who produced the pictorial posters were not helping; their more flamboyant letters could make his flesh creep. Then, one day, he found that by a fortunate coincidence the design of lettering and printing types was a subject in which Ernest Jackson had become deeply involved. He talked to one or two of his friends in the printing business and presently Pick was advised to approach one Edward Johnston, a man who was said to have dedicated his life to the study of the forgotten art of fine handwriting that Ruskin had rediscovered at about the time when Johnston was born. His book *Writing and Illumination and Lettering*, due for publication in 1902 but not in fact completed till four years later, soon became a classic. William Richard Lethaby had described it as 'astounding' and Sir Sydney Cockerell, in a moment of enthusiasm, had referred to it as 'the best handbook ever written on any subject', an opinion that many years afterwards he confessed might perhaps have contained some small element of exaggeration. By now, in the spring of 1913, this book, together with Johnston's executed work, had made his name known in many countries. He was the first modern craftsman to get down to the roots of the handwritten letter forms from which the historic European printing types originally derived. There was no one half so well qualified to give Pick what he was now eagerly looking for. Johnston, however, was, by conviction as well as by training, a craftsman, not a designer. Design to him was something you did with your tools. His own craft was penmanship; he had never worked with cutting tools, and he was not likely to welcome a suggestion that he should produce designs to be followed by a maker of printing types. He had on one or two occasions in the past consented to make designs for other craftsmen to carry out, but had bitterly regretted the lapses and had no wish to fall again into this same error. What kind of answer would Johnston give? In that slight, frail body, always tired, racked by a lifelong bronchial weakness, a rage for perfection combined with fierce loyalty to principle to form an inflammable mixture. It seemed a dismal prospect.

In June 1913 Johnston was finally persuaded to make the journey to London and to call on Pick. It was agreed between them that Johnston would design an alphabet for the Underground which would be based on the Victorian notion of an unseriffed or block letter, but whose forms would flow with the full and vigorous rhythms of the great Renaissance scribes. This was what Pick had been looking for. A few years later he told the students of the Leicester School of Art something about his ideas at the time. Great harm had been done to our letter forms by the self-conscious designers of the nineteenth century; the letters had become perverted; they had become 'the sport of artists'. The letters of the alphabet were the symbols that had held European civilisation together for more than two thousand years; you could not take too many liberties with that kind of symbol. He described to the students what other people were doing to restore the purity of letter forms, and he had a word of praise for the lettering that a young stonecarver called Eric Gill, a pupil and friend of Johnston's, had designed for the bookshops of W. H. Smith & Son. But though he thought highly of this lettering he did not feel that it was right for the purpose to which it was put. Gill's letters were modelled on those of the monumental masons of Ancient Rome, on letters designed as incised letters cut into a slab of stone; they were meant to be read with the bright Italian sunlight caught in the sharp groove of the strokes, set against a line of dark shadow. In the Smith shop fronts these letters were written out in paint on a flat surface and it was impossible that such an adaptation should be altogether satisfactory. Pick went on to explain to the students how the design of the Johnston letters had been approached. He had asked, he said, for an alphabet that would be clear and open, with a straightforward manliness of appearance that would prevent the management's communication being mistaken for a trader's advertisement by passengers in a hurry. And the letters must be specifically designed for printing on a flat surface; they must have 'the bold simplicity of the authentic lettering of the finest periods' and yet belong 'unmistakeably to the twentieth century'. P. M. Handover in his essay on the history of the un-seriffed printing types has described Pick's instructions as 'the first expression in England of a doctrine that was to become articulate in Germany and Switzerland, the doctrine that a letter form could be of "*unsere Zeit*".'

Priscilla Johnston, Edward's daughter and biographer, has told how it took her father a couple of years to get started. The outbreak of war may have been one of the causes of the delay but it seems likely that Johnston's own doubts and hesitations must bear part of the blame. 'I haven't done my best work yet,' he once said to his disciple Alfred Fairbank, and he added: 'I expect I never shall.' It was not an attitude conducive to prompt action. He spent a great deal of time making up his mind about the correct weight or thickness for the letter strokes. It is possible for a letter with thick and thin strokes to be spoilt by a wrong choice of weight but when the strokes are of equal weight throughout the result of such an error can be disastrous. It can seriously reduce legibility, it can destroy the steady rhythm of the patterns that give a line of type the continuity of the finest writing. When he had drawn the letters he spent much time working on the spacing between. The shape of the white spaces were as important to him as the letter forms themselves; your modern designer's way of squeezing letters together would have looked to him like a game played by a mentally backward child. The finished drawings with their detailed directions for spacing, now in the keeping of the Victoria and Albert Museum, were delivered in February 1916. The fact that they should have been completed within a few weeks of the first Kauffer posters is no doubt pure coincidence but it does help to mark the completion of what we can now recognise as a highly important stage in Pick's life and work. For some months Johnston's letters were used by the printers as a pattern for hand-drawn posters; the first of these posters were put up in October 1916 to advertise an exhibition of the Arts and Crafts Society at the Royal Academy and a series of lectures on the subject of design. In the summer of the following year the original sheets were transferred to lithographic plates so that copies might be printed off and circulated to different printers. It was not till some time after the war that arrangements were made to have types manufactured, wooden letters for the larger sizes, cast metal types for the smaller. Presently Johnston was asked to design two additional alphabets to be used for special purposes: a condensed letter for the destination panels on buses, and a bold version of the poster type, the drawings for which he finished at the end of 1929.

John Dreyfus, the distinguished typographer and historian of printing, has described the launching of the Underground lettering as 'a typographical event of unprecedented success and significance'; its adoption by Pick, he says, gave it 'a sanction, civic and commercial, such as has not been accorded to an alphabet since the time of Charlemagne'. But the real significance of the lettering lay not only in the use for which it was commissioned but to an even greater degree in the revolutionary character of the lettering itself. In the hundred years from 1816 – when the first unseriffed types appeared – to 1916 when Johnston's work was completed the design of this family of types had fallen more and more into the hands of draughtsmen working with set-squares

44

and compasses. It had become utterly lifeless. In all that crowding family of unseriffed letters, both British and foreign, Johnston's were the first to be designed by one who had studied the origin and development of European letter forms and was familiar with the work of the masters. Its far-spreading influence is not confined to unseriffed lettering alone, it is to be seen in the quality of all the lettering that appears today on buildings, on commercial vehicles, above all in every kind of printed matter. As Sir Nikolaus Pevsner said in an article written a generation later, 'Pick's vision changed the face of British printing.'

In 1909 when the new style name-plates had had a twelve-month run on station platforms the red disc design, now nick-named "bull's eye", suddenly made its appearance with the name 'UNDERGROUND' on it instead of a station name. As Pick went on using this bull's-eye device in poster after poster he began to feel that there was still something lacking in it. His assistant H. T. Carr remembered many years later how one day in 1916 Pick complained to him that the red disc, though it was striking enough not to be easily missed, somehow allowed your eye to glide over it. It did not sufficiently 'hold your eye'. And he went on to ask: 'How does the YMCA red triangle symbol manage to hold your eye?' He wondered whether it could be the white void inside the triangle that did it rather than the triangular form of the thing. He must also have had in mind at that moment the new pocket map of bus routes which he had produced in 1913. On the front of the folder he had put a simplified version of a familiar device that the London General Omnibus Company had placed on the body sides of its buses about the time when Pick first came to work in London, a spoked wheel crossed by a name-plate with the name 'GENERAL' on it. On the 1913 map he had turned this wheel into a plain ring shape about as thick as a ship's lifebuoy drawn in black outline. Suppose this outline ring were to be given a solid red infilling? When this idea occurred to Pick in 1916 he had no intention to indulge in any experiments of his own. Johnston, when he was approached, seemed a little taken aback to find that his lettering was to be used for a sign on which there was nothing except a line of capital letters. He had designed it for printing in a mixture of capitals and small letters and felt strong doubts about Pick's proposal. He was however sensible enough to see that Pick had made up his mind on the subject; it was better that the job should be carried out by himself than by some other person having little sympathy with his ideas. Priscilla Johnston in her book confirms Carr's statement that Pick 'had been struck by the YMCA triangle' and describes how her father got to work on the red ring, 'calculating its thickness and that of the label across it with his usual exactitude'. The use of his design necessarily had to be deferred till the war was over and the first known record of its appearance in print is dated April 1919. A few years later the design was enlarged for application to station name-plates. When a number of these had been put up in connection with minor improvement schemes there was general agreement that the Johnston emblem must be adopted for consistent use throughout the undertaking. Its first appearance out of doors took place in 1925 when a full-size plywood model was put up of a new kind of street entrance to be tried out at Clapham South station on the Morden Line.

It is sometimes said of Pick that he more than anyone is responsible for the obsession with ingenious 'house symbols' that has seized the businessman of our times. The corporate emblem, as it is occasionally called, has taken the place of that other evidence of good standing, the foundation date that goes back a hundred years or more. For nowadays, if a business wants to be accepted and looked up to, it must be not old and respectable but new and swinging and a house symbol is a convincing way of indicating that that is what you are. But the idea behind Pick's Underground symbol was altogether different. If later it became a proper symbol representative of the business, it was more by accident than by design. Its function at the time when it was created was quite simply to tell a traveller in an Underground train with the greatest possible efficiency that he had reached his destination. And few things about Pick are more characteristic than that he should have been content to leave this thing to grow and justify itself over the years, rather as a gardener might watch over the growth of a plant raised from some promising but not clearly identifiable seed.

Critics at Large

In the spring of 1915 there opened another stage in Pick's education, a stage which resulted in his finally becoming the man he was during his best years. His enlightenment was made possible by a body of people who called themselves the Design and Industries Association. They had not meant to try to educate him, they had looked upon him as one already among the converted whose example would help them to convert many others now living in darkness. But to Pick the discovery of this body meant a great opportunity. The Association could not unfairly be described as the last of the crusades of nineteenth-century England. It was one of the secrets of the greatness of that period that among all the countries in the world England was the one where the crusading fever was endemic. One of the longest and most arduous of these battles was that which was directed against the ugly and the meretricious in industrial design, and more especially in the design of what in the jargon of modern business is known as consumer durables. The founders of the Design and Industries Association were fond of recalling a lecture delivered by John Ruskin in 1859, in which he had urged on English manufacturers the necessity for making a grave and difficult choice. They could choose to make only that which is best; they could do as Josiah Wedgwood had done a century earlier, comparing themselves to authors writing books. 'As it is in the writer's power to publish what will educate as it amuses,' Ruskin told them, 'so it is in yours to publish what will educate as it adorns.' They could help to 'restrain the country's follies while they supplied its wants'. On the other hand, instead of restraining the country's follies they could choose to encourage and exacerbate them. They could 'catch at every humour of the populace as it shapes itself into momentary demand'. They could 'try to attract attention by singularities, novelties and gaudiness'. They could appeal to the the purchaser's vanity, they could 'foster in the consumer a habit of discontent'. If you pursue that path, your lives, he said, will have been spent in corrupting public taste, 'in retarding the arts, tarnishing the virtues, and confusing the manners of your country'. The choice was theirs. If they should choose the first way they could become something more than successful merchants pursuing their business in the States, they could become 'its guides, counsellors and rulers, wielding powers of subtle but gigantic beneficence'.

The Design and Industries Association was characteristically English in the mixture it contained of commercial good sense and hot apostolic zeal. But not many of the apostles in those days enjoyed the security of well-paid jobs or student grants; they were carried on a wave of deeply selfless idealism whose strength may be seen by recalling the personalities of some of the early members. One of these was Pick's friend Harold Curwen, who later was to turn his family printing business in Plaistow into one of the finest printing houses in the country. At the time when the association was formed he was in his thirtieth year; it was a bare two years since he had taken over the business from his father. He was now part of a movement whose main interest it was to strive after truth and purity in design, to tidy and scavenge and cleanse a world which had become, in the words of its chief spokesman, Lethaby, like a pawnshop full of old junk. Curwen himself had inherited a works that was full of 'junk'; the clever, fussy, pretentious Victorian typefaces spread about his composing room were an affront to all that the movement stood for. In 1915 there came an appeal from the government for printers' type metal to meet the shortage of lead which was needed for munitions. Curwen saw that a big challenge had come to him. He put aside his stock of Caslon Old Face and got his men to collect together the whole of the remaining types. There were more than two hundred different founts of type in all and every one of them was sent away leaving only that one fount, the type with which he had made up his mind to make the fresh start that his faith required of him. The months that followed must have been a terrible time. His workmen could not believe that a printing house so ruthlessly emptied of its equipment could long continue to exist. Herbert Simon has recorded how 'West Ham Corporation Tramways were furious to receive their noteheadings set in Caslon and abruptly closed their account with the Press.' The old manager, recently retired after thirty years with the firm, was moved by the prospect of impending ruin to offer his services in an attempt to save what could still be saved. For several years Curwen went on wearing the new discipline like a hair shirt; if the customers disapproved of his attempts to improve his work, so much the worse for them.

Such was the kind of movement in which Pick found himself welcomed and accepted as a founder member. Up to this moment his experience of the world had been like the experience of a traveller who moves from place to place meeting interesting people on the way, noting many instructive things, collecting novel and memorable apprehensions, but always conscious that he is walking like a curious spectator in an alien land. That is how he had felt as a schoolboy at St Peter's in York and now, working with the railway and bus people in London this same feeling was still with him. This was Austin's country; though Pick had learnt most of what he knew from his voyage through it, the place was one in which at no time had he felt truly at home. And then it was as if all at once he had arrived in another country that at first seemed very strange to him H. G. Wells gave a lecture at about this time in which he referred to the great gulf that separated the two: 'Things have been, says the legal mind, and so we are here. The creative mind says we are here because things have yet to be.' In this new country of the creative mind, Pick must have felt something of what we are told Ulysses felt when Athene drew away the mists that hung about him and looking up he saw with amazement that the place to which the Phaeacians had brought him was his own Ithaca, his native land.

Although the movement for better design had started in London it was not in London that the first active steps were taken in the achievements of its aims, it was in the manufacturing centres: the Midlands, the North. And among these centres the town of Leicester had gained an importance out of proportion to its size by the outstanding personalities of a small group of men of whom H. H. (Harry) Peach was a typical example. Peach had for some years been specialising in cane furniture designed and made by craftsmen to a standard of quality equal to that of the finest furniture made of wood. The business had prospered and at the time when the Design and Industries Association was formed two hundred workmen were employed in his shops. The friendship between Pick and Peach was made all the closer and more lively by the distance that separated them, for Peach was a formidable correspondent. In the long series of letters that passed between them from 1916 onwards, there are occasional words of mild complaint from Pick about the furious pace of the correspondence, but most of the time it was obvious that he found it highly enjoyable. Peach had some of the qualities he most liked. Fearlessly honest, provocative in argument, Peach would follow with keen interest the work of the Association's committees in London and in particular the work of the publicity committee of which Pick was chairman for a short period. B. J. Fletcher, the man who had inspired and encouraged Peach in his venture in furniture making, had been a source of inspiration also to many others. In the college of art of which he was principal he had done more than anyone in this country to narrow the great gap between art education and the manufacturing industries. It was largely owing to Fletcher that Leicester had become the strongest outpost of the Design and Industries Association. Peach was the self-appointed and highly effective spokesman of this lively Leicester branch; this was one more reason why Pick set special value on his friendship. Of only one of Pick's new friends could it be truly said that the relationship meant more to him than the one he kept up with Peach. The name of Harold Stabler was for many years connected with that of the Carter Pottery at Poole in Dorset which he had helped to found. His main business, however, was the design and production of silverware for ceremonial occasions, the battle of Jutland medal, the collar of the Royal Victorian Order, chairs and cups and caskets for presentation to eminent persons in many countries. He was the son of a Westmorland schoolmaster; his seven-year apprenticeship was served with a woodcarver in Kendal. In 1915 he was a broad, powerfully built man in his early forties, head of the art school at the Sir John Cass Institute in the City of London. Perhaps he was remarkable above all for being a craftsman who, while working in one of the most conservative of crafts, was yet able to accept unreservedly the role of machine production in the world of today. He was in many ways an ideal person to take Pick by the hand at that time, a master of several crafts who spoke with authority on highly technical matters, a clear-eyed critic who could be impatient and scornful but never ungenerous. The two of them soon became close friends. When Pick went to look at an exhibition, an old house, a new picture installed in a gallery, he was never happier than when accompanied by Stabler. The sort of arguments they had would delight and refresh him.

Having been caught up in a reforming movement, a movement concerned to spread a new gospel, Pick felt that his first duty was to reach a proper understanding of that gospel, to educate himself in its ideas, in the history of those ideas, in the social climate in which they had developed. For some years he was able to give most of his spare time to this study. In his patient, methodical way he would examine and sort such facts and arguments as he had been able to gather. Having set down the result on paper he felt the need to talk it over with friends. But the game of argument and counter-argument did not prove as helpful as he had hoped; better to compose his notes into a lecture and then when the lecture was over pay attention to what was said

50

by other speakers and let the old ideas and the new regroup themselves into a broader and stronger pattern. The first of these papers was delivered to the Art Workers' Guild in its building in Queen Square in February 1916. From the meeting there sprang a series of drafts for a lecture that Harry Peach arranged for him to give in Leicester during the summer; in October Pick was lecturing in the Royal Scottish Academy Galleries where the Edinburgh Branch of the Design and Industries Association had arranged an exhibition of printing. In this Edinburgh address Pick said:

> Everything is made for a use. The test of the goodness of a thing is its fitness for that use. So that boots eked out with canvas or paper, or fashioned of porous leather, are no good, for the essence of a boot is to keep the foot dry. So that flower-vases with narrow bottoms that topple over and make a mess are no good. So that a salt-pot in metal that corrodes with the natural dampness of the salt is no good. So that posters ornamented and confused until the words cannot be read at a glance (the main requirements of a poster) are no good. If you will keep an alert mind you can multiply examples from the common objects you meet with every day. The test of the goodness of a thing is its fitness for use. If it fails on this first test, no amount of ornamentation or finish will make it any better; it will only make it more expensive, more foolish.

On another occasion he turned to nature for examples; nature came out well by this 'first test'. In Hobhouse's *Morals in Evolution* Pick found one such example that he quoted once or twice in different lectures. In his first chapter Hobhouse illustrates his ideas about the relation between heredity and environment by describing the nest-building activities of birds. He tells how some birds will design special kinds of nests for special situations: 'the orchard oriole builds a shallow nest on stiff branches, but on the slender twigs of the weeping willow it builds deep so that the young will not be thrown out by the swaying of the nest.' If only the members of the Design and Industries Association could be made to live as faithfully by their great ruling principle as did the orchard oriole!

Certainly fitness for use must always be the first test. But it was not the only one. When Harry Peach first got into touch with Pick during the war he sent him a copy of a little pamphlet bound in blue paper, a reprint done in Leicester of an article written by Lethaby a couple of years before. There is a sentence which in the magazine version is printed in italics but in the pamphlet leaps out from the page in great capital letters: 'EVERY WORK OF ART SHOWS THAT IT WAS MADE BY A HUMAN BEING FOR A HUMAN BEING.' It is the sort of seminal statement whose meaning is caught only when the verb 'shows' has had time to print itself on the mind as the key word that carries the real message. In the language used by a great judge many years later we might say that it defines a work of art as a thing that is not just made by one human being for another but is 'manifestly seen' to have been so made. The question was how precisely was this special quality of humanity made manifest? Pick turned to his favourite device of comparative examples. He said: 'The gipsy caravan has its close-set ribs and frame, notched and carved and painted with gay lines and dabs of colour, red or green or blue, on its yellow surface; the farmer's wain away in the far country is the same; the little cabin in the stern in which the barge-dweller lives is still bright and joyous.' He contrasted these examples with the delivery van used by a big West-End store. The peculiar curve of its body is there

> not because the curve follows necessarily from structure, but because the curve has been consciously sought as being odd and distinctive. It shows no structure at all, but is encased in shiny sombre green and bears on its smooth finished surface the name of its proud possessor in precise and gilded letters. Such is the difference between the individual seeking the great adventure of self-expression heedless of the goal of distinctiveness and the individual seeking after the goal of distinctiveness heedless of the great adventure.

When he saw his friends in the Design and Industries Association studying the work of the latest German designers he warned them that the Germans had many good qualities but that this quality of humanity seemed somehow to be lacking in them. He reminded the Art Workers' Guild how Professor Naumann of the Deutsche Werkbund had urged the German architect 'to seize on the German house and create in it a German style . . . I remember reading once upon a time how the colour of the cat was included in the prescription for a German home. Alas, poor Thomas and Tabitha, you are to become outcasts, and strangers shall enter into your inheritance!' In his 1916 Edinburgh paper he pointed to the contrast between this display of cold rationality and the natural growth of the home as we in England have known it for centuries past, the home that is always changing

with the change of the years. It obeys the laws of growth: it decays and is renewed again. Maybe there are children and the scene shifts; our rooms find other uses . . . The activities and ardours of early life give place to the meditations of later days, and the scene shifts again . . . All these things become filled with a fragrance of loves and cares that is ever more sweet. Later, some things go to the new homes of our children, being endeared to them by youthful recollection. All the while the home grows it throws offshoots as it were – that is if it is really a home, a living home where a little circle of people related to one another carry on a common life.

It was a little matter that the old Greek philosophers in their writings about beauty would appear to have overlooked. He said:

A thing may be right and beautiful and true without being lovable, though a thing cannot be lovable without being also in itself right and beautiful and true. Love is the harmony which such a thing awakes in the emotions; it is the harmony of what it feels to be. It adds the heart, as we call it, to the conscience, the sense, and the mind, to make the four great organs of being. Probably it is the Christian contribution to this philosophy. It brings warmth and depth to it. It gives a passion for righteousness which is more than a calculated right.

Were Pick's thoughts at this time going back to the little draper's shop in York where he had first learnt from his father about the meaning of quality in man-made things? In September 1917 he said to an audience of art teachers:

A yard of cloth costs just so much to produce. It may cost just as much whether the cloth be good or bad. It cannot be sold below this cost, and truly it is worth more than this cost. It is worth so much more as an article of trade that the trader can make a profit on its sale as well as the manufacturer on its production; it may even be worth more than the price paid for it; it ought to be worth more if it is good cloth. It ought to have a colour, a texture, a pattern, which gives such pleasure to us that by our appreciation we enhance its value far beyond the fair price. It derives in this way a value which is not an economic value to be measured in terms of price, though to be sure it has a surplus value measured even in terms of price, for that is why most likely we bought it at all. It seemed of more avail, of more value, to us than the money we gave as its price. Now if any man would buy a yard of cloth he cannot be sold two yards, but he can be sold a yard of cloth and something which is in a sense a gift to him, a thing of beauty as well as a thing for clothing.

Art, too, is a gift. It is born of a surplus of aim, of thought, of desire, of care, put into work. Art cannot be bought; it can only be created out of love. The savage wove himself a mat, and because it was his mat and something of himself, and because he was glad in his mat he put into it some stripes or chequers by way of pattern, or mingled in it threads of a gay colour. This he did not because he must, but because he wished to do it out of love. Art can only be created from love; it can only be apprehended by love. Both in the making and in the enjoyment there must be a surplus, an overplus of energy, of desire, of vision, which bears us across the one mile of the tedious tract of labour into the further miles of the generous province of art. That a surplus exists is the only possible hope of a better life here. In the manner of application of that surplus lies our only chance of realising the republic of heaven here and now. All good things are bound up in this surplus; all the beauty and grace of life spring from such love.

Fitness for purpose meant usefulness, but usefulness only made an object complete and sufficient. To Pick this surplus of aim, this supervening perfection, was a giver of life. A thing is beautiful because its maker, an individual person, in the act of making it had made it come alive. He had talked about those older civilisations that had seen living divinities and spirits in nature, inhabiting the woods and the waters. Modern man had lost touch with those divinities and spirits and was left the poorer by this severance. But it was possible for a spirit to enter into man-made things also: it was man's business to see that his handiwork was filled with this living spirit. When he was speaking in Edinburgh he said:

The vital and miraculous result is this: if we seek efficiency in production, which is industry, and if we seek efficiency in the

54

product, which may be summed up in design, and if the efficiency that we seek leads up to a vast harmony of all things, then all things must become alive, part of the living world. Sometimes we say a picture or a statue seems to live. It does live, not in the narrow physical sense of being capable of movement, but in the broad spiritual sense that it enshrines life, the life that the man who made it had put into it of his own. The story of Pygmalion and Galatea is but a fable to express this truth. We think of ourselves as vessels of the spirit of God: so things, we may say, are the receptacles of the spirit of man. There may be as great a gulf set between God and man as between man and things; we can bridge it with our hopes and desires. When they are full of the spirit, things have souls – God's gift to us, man's gift to them. Thought of in this way things take on a great importance.

Man in his Habitat

In the spring of 1919 Pick accepted an invitation from Harry Peach to give another talk in Leicester. Moved by his special fondness for the Leicester branch he started to cast round for a subject worthy of the occasion. A little later he wrote back: 'I am taking man and woman as works of art in themselves or, as you might put it, this animal man in his habitat . . . I thought of taking a few slides from the masterpieces of classic art to show the human form at its best and by way of contrast with its actualities.' After a fortnight's interval came another letter: 'I shall edit the subject into two parts. Both can take cover under the same title, but the centre section of the one can be "This animal called man" and of the other "Architecture, old and new, as the expression of the good life." ' He called the lecture 'Man: A forgotten Factor in Reconstruction'. World War I and its sequel had enriched the English language with a number of new words and 'reconstruction' was one of those most often heard at that time. The lecture took the form of a commentary on a large and extraordinary collection of lantern slides: an advertisement for *Cassell's Popular Educator* ('the child – what will he become?'); middle-class children at play; swimming in the Serpentine; swimming in the sea; the water-cart wash; the park sand-pit ('a nursery for the agile flea rather than for the children'); boy scouts; views of slums (about Whitby: 'a slum is not the less a slum because it is an artistic slum'); a smoke pall over a factory area ('a testimonial to the medical profession'); the manufacture of match boxes ('the gospel of St Andrew Undershaft: the only crime is poverty'); workers in modern, well-designed workshops; a pavement artist ('the artist is often less beautiful than his works'); businessmen and gentlemen in top hats ('at some time and in some way their ancestors were successful'); the Savoy restaurant; sleeping out on the Embankment ('a new use for newspaper content bills: the paper controller has permitted a fresh issue of bed sheets'); Myron's Discobolus ('discipline of body and mind'); the Farnese Hercules ('the weary, bored look of one whose exhibitions of strength are a business'); the players and the crowd at a football match ('the modern animal is content to compete by deputy'); a May Day demonstration ('a pageant should be an inspiration'); the Venus Anadyomene ('a fine creature . . . sensible feet; just come up from a bath in the sea'); the Medici Venus ('she has only been to the municipal baths in Rome'); stage beauties; a funeral stele from the Athens museum representing a husband and wife and two children ('a DIA family'); a pretty village; a rural slum.

As his attention moved from things to people Pick was conscious of a close connection between the two. The people whose appearance he was scrutinising were the creators of things, and among the things they were capable of creating were their own physical selves. Seeing 'man and woman as works of art in themselves', that was the way he had put it to Peach. For the physical man and woman, the presence, the demeanour, these were the first, the most immediate ways in which it was given to human beings to express themselves. It seemed to him one of the most regrettable failures of our civilisation that, as he admitted in a paper called *This is the World that Man Made*, 'the capacity to express things through gesture and appearance is one of the gifts that have been largely lost.' In one of his letters to Peach he wrote about a walk in the City of London: 'I was in Threadneedle Street, or Throgmorton Street, I forget which, and certainly the City man is most unlovely. Or putting it another way, you have to take pains to be beautiful, beautiful in any sort of way; and taking pains takes time. A busy man cannot be beautiful.' But taking time and pains did not mean that there must be an act of volition, a conscious effort, beauty was not something about which you could make judgements and choices before you produced it; neither in the beauty of people nor in the beauty of things was there any room for preconceived ideas. Again and again in his papers he spoke about the irrelevance of our conventional ideas of the beautiful, and he would point now to the man and woman, now to the designed thing, to illustrate his warning. Many years later he was invited by the Imperial Industries Club to address an audience of businessmen on the subject of industrial design. It was in 1933, at a time when he was becoming known for his public activities in this field. He was concerned to bring out the limitations of our accepted ideas about beauty, to illustrate the ascending scale of values that is so imperfectly conveyed in that simple word. He could think of no better example than the human face. He described the conventional idea of beautiful features and went on to contrast it with those other sort of features that 'may carry such a light in the eyes, such a tenderness of love about the countenance, a tenderness born of the spirit that animates them, that we turn to them from the accepted beauties'. In those higher forms, he said, 'the spirit is conditioned by the experience through which it has passed, but that experience must be accepted by it, mastered, made its own.' That was the way beautiful things, too, came about.

The members of the Design and Industries Association had little difficulty in agreeing among themselves about the standards by which to judge the quality of design. Pick however was more ready than most to face the fact that a standard is not something that you just talk and argue about, a standard was only worth having provided you were continually using it, applying it, holding it up against your environment and making decisions about what you saw. It was good to carry a measuring rule in your pocket but far better to have it in your hand always ready for use. 'Let us all be critics all the time, at home, at business, at public gatherings, at play. Criticism is asking pertinent questions, not necessarily impertinent ones. Do not take anything for granted.' He went on to quote from the Gospel of St John: 'the truth shall make you free.' Pick had never been much impressed by experts and in paper after paper we find him insisting that the 'duty of criticism' is a matter for all citizens, regardless of any expertise they may happen to have. In an article published in the *Nineteenth Century and After* in 1922 he wrote:

There is plenty of thought about art when there should be none, for art ought to be a spontaneous expression. There is little or no thought about the object upon which the art is to

57

be spent, an occupation not for artists but for everyone. If there had been any thought by the common people about parks, should we have had the iron-railinged trees and grass plots framed with gravel and asphalt paths, and interspersed with uncouth statuary, that so frequently diversify our cities and towns? A good view is more important than a good picture and more worth maintaining. In so far as art means the accomplishment of a purpose, the satisfaction of a use, everyone is entitled to be a critic of the achievement.

True, there was a certain risk involved, criticism can often be mistaken, and anyone who accepts the duty of criticism must be prepared to find himself sometimes in the wrong. 'Even the most expert of critics', he warned, 'will make ludicrous mistakes and perpetrate extraordinary contradictions with a change in style or fashion.' But 'the fear of making mistakes is a deadly fear. The making of mistakes is an attribute of life: it is the human quality.' How many of those who listened to him were aware that he was giving them in a couple of short sentences the essence of a philosophy? To be able to be wrong was to be creative. If you had lost the capacity to make mistakes, you might as well give up. Pick had fought hard to conquer this fear in himself; some years later he said in a broadcast talk: 'I have ceased to be afraid to say what I think about things, even at the risk of sometimes saying something wrong, as you may soon find out; but this is a vast deal better than saying nothing at all for the fear of making a mistake.' But the important thing was not just to be prepared to be wrong, it was necessary to admit the error and to strive to extract from it the essential nutriment that made it worthwhile. He must really have believed that when he drew another person's attention to some mistake he was like one who points out to a card player that the card in his hand is a trump, or to a miner that one of the pebbles in his shovelful of rubbish is a nugget of priceless gold.

The war had not prevented Pick from continuing as an active member of the Design and Industries Association: he even managed to put in a little work on one or two of the association's committees. In 1921 he felt able to accept appointment as chairman. The first steps had been taken in the building up of this body formed under the stress of war upon a stable peace-time footing, yet most of the work still remained to be done. Office accommodation and staff had to be found and paid for; publications and exhibitions had to be got going; the membership must be worked up and the interest of the members must be stimulated and their keenness maintained at full pitch. In one of his letters to Peach he says: 'The secretary is a talk merchant and not given to careful, steady work. He boils over with enthusiasm but his enthusiasm is not matched by effort and perseverance.' Pick set himself to organise the careful, steady work of which the association was so badly in need. A larger set of offices was rented in Queen Square. Six standing committees were appointed to assist the council with its work and a number of trade groups were formed, each of which was to concentrate on developments in a particular industry. In the new offices a big room was turned into an exhibition room and a programme was drawn up for a series of exhibitions, one for each group, to be held monthly during the winter season. Each exhibition was to be opened with a lecture. Of all our industries at that time, the printing industry was to Pick the one most worthy to be held up as a model of steady design improvement and few members were surprised when it was chosen as the subject of the first exhibition due to be opened at the beginning of October 1921.

He was getting into his stride by now and in the following month there appeared the first issue of a journal called *Monthly News Sheet*; the journal lived up to its title by limiting itself to a mere four pages. A little later he was making an arrangement through his fellow-member H. P. Shapland of Benn Brothers for the production of the first of a series of *Year Books*, a big volume of folio size, handsomely illustrated. The Design and Industries Association, which so far had been concerned with the design of household goods and other manufactured products, is here seen to address itself to the wider human environment of town and countryside. It was a startling change. A few years later, when Pick had given up the chairmanship, the architect Clough Williams-Ellis became president and with impetuous energy drove the association forward along this same path into what is still remembered as the most powerful and effective of all its campaigns. In the summer of 1929 there appeared the *Cautionary Guide to St Albans*, the first of a series of publications that anticipated Ian Nairn's *Outrage* by twenty-five years. The DIA *Quarterly*, the association's new journal, came out at about the same time as the St Albans *Guide*; it carried a notice announcing the new publication which said: 'The *Guide* aims at making members follow Mr Pick's advice, which will be found later in this issue, to "go about with the quizzical air we wear abroad, making those contrasts and comparisons which will lead to the establishment of a better standard".' It was a reference to an article entitled 'Holiday Afterthoughts', in which Pick gave his impressions of some of the smaller cities he had visited on a Mediterranean holiday, of the excitement produced by the strength and freshness of their impact on his vision. The way to study the everyday world around you at home, he said, was to look at it as he had been looking then, as if you were in some far-away country seeing something new for the first time. In 1923 he spoke to the London Society about 'The Art of the Street'. He said: 'The everyday sights flit across the retina but the mind sees them not. We are used to them.' When you are travelling in new places something happens to you: 'Everything is strange. The mind wakes up and becomes active. The eyes are taught to see again.' The students at Leicester were told that 'After you have travelled either in time or space in your effort to escape, and have eventually come back to Leicester, your eyes should be open to the lack of harmony, the confusion, the conflict that goes on in this city, even if it is only for a few days, until you settle down again to your accustomed habits of life.'

'For a few days.' Nothing of that kind seems ever to have happened to Pick, for him there was no return to accustomed habits of life when all would be forgotten. His eyes once opened had a way of staying obstinately open. One day a friend sent him a snapshot of one of our historic buildings the exterior of which had been disfigured by advertising matter. Pick wrote a short letter to the managing director of the offending firm, a fellow-member of his club, and a few days later he was reporting back to his friend:

Sir Robert Waley-Cohen took the photograph that you lent me showing the two Shell signs on the wall at Kenilworth quite seriously, and the signs have been removed. Unfortunately, though he has removed the two in the photograph, it has not occurred to him there may be others all over the country which should be removed. It would rather look as though we had to send him a photograph of every advertisement sign that is bad to get him to take it down. This will make a good deal of work for you. I can assure you, however, that Sir Robert and the Shell people are most sympathetic.

At the time when Richard Coppock was chairman of the Parks Committee of the London County Council, Pick had been studying a plan for the improvement of Embankment Gardens which had just been published. His advice to Coppock was a curious mixture: Coppock, he said, should have a look at what had been done at places like the Mirabell Gardens in Salzburg, a model layout of its kind. And as for 'the horrible monuments' that the council intended should be left standing, 'if they cannot be destroyed they should be pushed into a corner with some shrubs planted round to hide them.' Horrible monuments were not the only things that cried out to be mercifully hidden; even in those moments when he hoped to find a state of happy relaxation the evil sights would intrude and cause pain. There was an evening many years later when he was present at a new production of *Prince Igor*; on the following morning he was still angry enough to send a letter to *The Times* newspaper. 'I go to the opera', he wrote, 'to see as well as to hear', and he went on to describe in detail some of the things he had had to sit and watch. And, finally, 'The time has come to protest against scenery and production which are an insult to the eye and to the intelligence, and which make the action of the opera ridiculous.'

It was bad enough that a considerable work of musical art should be made ridiculous, but at least in this sort of situation Pick was able to lay the blame firmly on shoulders other than his own. There were other offences with which he could not help feeling a sense of personal implication. Man's offences against the world of nature were to him the most grievous of all; the shadow of guilt fell not on particular people but on 'this animal man', on the whole of the society in which he lived and worked. The subject comes up again and again in his correspondence with friends: a typical letter is the one he wrote to Peach in the autumn of 1926 on his return from a trip to Devonshire. 'Coming back from Woolacombe', he wrote, 'makes the town look sordid. We make a horrid mess of our civilisation. It breaks out in little things at Woolacombe which you see magnified a hundred times in London. Dirt, corrugated iron, oil and grease, litter, ill-matched building, lack of plan – all kinds of dreadful things torment me.' In his 1916 Leicester paper he had talked about his impression of Portree in Skye, which he had revisted after an interval of many years. In the notes he prepared for this paper he said: 'Disorder has entered in there,' as though he were describing the work of some evil spirit. 'We have', he wrote, 'to invert the words of Isaiah, ashes for beauty, for the oil of joy mourning, a cloak of heaviness instead of a garment of praise.' He did not, however, use these notes in his address. His feelings ran too deep, he could not trust himself to speak about them at such length.

There had grown up with him from early manhood a strong awareness of the presence of evil in life, a presence first revealed in the form of cruelty. The vision of the hunted fox, the tortured fox leaping up at the wall, clawing desperately at the coping, leaping again to drop back shuddering into the jaws of the frenzied hounds, had bitten deep into his mind; and presently he had found himself recoiling in horror at the sight of man's inhumanity to man, and the collective inhumanity of nation to nation. There were occasions when he would find violence and cruelty freely displayed to the public by self-appointed teachers of history; some of our museums were typical examples of this misguided educational zeal. In a letter to Harry Peach he wrote about a visit to Nürnberg where, he said, 'a weary, ill-looking girl conducted the inquisitive stranger round the horrors of the torture chamber, and I wondered whether familiarity with them had blotted them out from her mind. Graphic illustrations adorned the walls and compensated for any deficiencies of a foreign tongue; I fear there was no escape for her from their blighting influence.' After a similar experience in London there came another letter:

On Saturday, by accident, I went into the Horniman Museum here in London, which belongs to the London County Council and is mainly visited by school children. It shows more grue-some exhibits than any other museum that I know of in London. Next time you are in London you ought to go and have a look at it, and somebody ought to write a nice, strong account of the way the London County Council provide museums for children. One of the exhibits of this museum is a torture chair from the Spanish Inquisition of the seventeenth century. A most beautiful piece of steelwork with gags, manacles, steel sliding seat, and every possible horror that you could desire, all carefully catalogued and set out for the instruc-tion of the young. Then there are some dissections made by some medical people showing the internal fittings of rabbits. Quite a number of devil masks used by native tribes of Africa;

62

particularly horrible pieces of Indian sculpture; a bad acquarium in which the poor fish and newts look as though they were at their last end.

'I must try to go and see the Horniman Museum', Peach wrote back. 'Am afraid children like really good shockers, like my recollection of a museum when I was a boy in Germany, where crowds used to go every Sunday when it was open to see details of folks' insides. I expect you were as bad when you were a child, only like the rest of us you are now trying to make amends.' He did not see that what had really upset Pick was not just a morbid interest in the internal fittings of rabbits, it was the manifestations of the evil of cruelty, a part of the greater cruelty that had caused the skies to be choked with man's poison clouds and beauty everywhere to be violated by the baseness of his handiwork. One day a friend asked Pick's opinion of a letter from a mutual acquaintance, a well known journalist who was looking forward to retiring at an early age in order to enjoy, as he hoped, many years of carefree leisure in the countryside; the letter was full of praise for the pleasures of simple rural pursuits, of the life of peaceful contemplation. It was also somewhat sharp in its disapproval of the people who prefer to spend their entire lives toiling in cities. Pick's comment on the letter was made with characteristic humility. He was far from being satisfied with the kind of city life he himself was leading. 'There are times', he wrote, 'when I realise the futility of it, and wonder whether it is worth going on.' The justification of his going on was put in a single short sentence: 'He must not condemn us', he said of his friend's correspondent, 'for standing by this ruined world which we have made.'

Among the various writings that came Pick's way there were a few that proved of help to him in giving depth and cohesion to his ideas about man and his world. One of the most influential appears to have been Sir Edwin Ray Lankester's 1905 Romanes lecture 'Nature's Insurgent Son'. Pick discovered it in 1919 in the volume *The Kingdom of Man* where it appears as the opening chapter. According to Lankester, civilised man was guilty of undue interference with the natural order of the universe; you could describe this interference as an act of defiance and rebellion, and this appears to have been the author's own view, or you could say that man was taking possession of 'a vast and magnificent kingdom' to which he had been made heir. Whichever way you looked at it, man had abrogated the laws of natural selection and other natural laws by which the world had been governed until then. But this usurpation of power, this interference, had put him in appalling peril. Modern man 'is threatened on every hand by dangers and disasters hitherto restrained. No retreat is possible; he must either go on and acquire firmer control, or perish miserably.' How was this firmer control to be acquired? The universities, said Lankester, must take the lead in establishing a synthesis between nature-knowledge, training in 'nature-searching', and a true love and understanding of literature and the arts. This new synthesis should become the master subject in our system of education; our political leaders should be chosen for their willingness to apply it to the tasks of government. Pick was deeply stirred by Lankester's picture of man as the new master of the world. He developed its details in many notes and presently he started to collect lantern slides to illustrate the notes. The address in which the whole was brought together into a consecutive argument was given the title *This is the World that Man Made, or The New Creation*; it was privately printed in 1922 in the printing class of the Bradford School of Arts and Crafts. Reading it one can see that though Pick had felt a deep sympathy with Lankester's ideas he was not altogether satisfied with the author's final conclusion. Lankester's message had been a clear warning of retribution to come. By failing to exercise firmer and wiser control over nature man would end by destroying himself; he would 'perish miserably'. But it was not the danger of man's physical destruction that Pick feared most. Whatever happened, there would be an end to man. He said: 'One day the ice will descend and blot out all traces of man's works. The earth will grow cold. Nature will return to her kingdom and spread her snowy pall over the last man, and there will be nothing but the barren rocks again.' The problem that filled Pick with a sense of anguish was not so much the physical vengeance that nature might one day take on man as the problem of the condition of man at the moment when the end came. 'Man will have disappeared from the face of the earth with the world that he had made. His day will be done. And the evening and the morning were the eighth day. Will man be able to say: "and, behold, it was very good?"'

64

3

LONDON TRANSPORT: 1912–1923

Steps to Integration

In January 1912, Pick, who had now served a little under three years in the post of traffic officer, found himself appointed the head of a new department, the department of the commercial manager. The change was one of a number made necessary by the Underground's take-over of the London General Omnibus Company. A railway company owning 200 route miles of local railways had now become the master of a route mileage of bus services more than six times as great. A year later a series of further deals brought into the Underground Group tubes of the Central London and City & South London Railway Companies with three tram undertakings that together accounted for the entire private sector of London's trams. The urgent need now was the setting-up of the common management for which a number of public bodies had long been pleading. Sir George Gibb went on working strenuously to bring the various transport systems together but his long experience as a management man proved of little avail. This was a job for the financial men. In the words used by Pick when describing his predicament many years later, he had 'got out of his depth'. Early in 1910 Gibb was approached by the President of the Board of Trade with a suggestion that he might perhaps be interested in the post of chairman of a new branch about to be set up. It had been given the name of Road Board and is remembered as the precursor of the Ministry of Transport. Was there any connection between the receipt and acceptance of this offer and the fact that Stanley's three-year agreement would be expiring at the end of March? There were plenty of rumours to that effect; when Gibb left to take up his new duties at the Board of Trade few of his colleagues showed any surprise to find Stanley, the general manager, taking over from him as managing director of the group and of each of the companies. Five years later the Underground Common Fund was established under the London Electric Railway Companies Facilities Act. The partners in the fund were the five companies that among them operated the railways and buses. Funds of this kind had long been a common feature of financial administration among the smaller railways of Britain; each of the member companies would undertake to contribute according to its ability and was to be assisted according to its need. The way was now opened for the Underground's common management to start action.

On taking up his new post in the great mixed undertaking Pick, who had already got well accustomed to carrying a heavy load of papers home with him at weekends, found it necessary to make an abrupt change in his weekend work. Not only did it become more than ever a very full two days' occupation, the greater part of the two days was spent out-of-doors going about exploring London. The London General Omnibus Company had just got rid of its last horse bus; there were only motor buses now. Yet the company's services, which had been built up in competition with the Underground, were still concentrated in much the same small horse-bus area and too many of them were carrying people to and from the same places as the trains. What Pick now had to do was to transform that pattern into a new kind of pattern in which the powerful new buses would strike out in all directions like branches springing from the central stems of the Underground lines. It was not a task to be performed sitting at a desk. Nowadays the same job would as a matter of course be done driving around in a car, but a car to Pick was never more than a means of getting from place to place; if you went out to see, to observe, to learn, there was only one way. You did it on foot. He must have walked many hundreds of miles in each of the two years he spent developing the bus services before the outbreak of the 1914 war. At the time when he started the London General Company was operating a total of thirty-three bus routes in an area extending over some sixteen miles from Ealing to East Ham, and about half that distance measured from north to south. The rate at which Pick went to work may be judged by the fact that already in the autumn of 1912 the number of routes had gone up by seventy and the area served was roundly five times as great. Pick could be bold in the making of plans, yet the meticulous forward estimating was never skimped. His qualifications for this demanding task were happily quite exceptional. He never forgot the debt he owed his two masters, Gibb and Ashfield, with their wonderfully contrasting personalities. In a paper he delivered to the Institute of Transport there is a reference to the lesson that each of the two had taught him:

> The first judged by statistics. I learnt from him how uncertain and inaccurate are guesses and estimates. I learnt to bring my actual observation to a proper proportion by the use of statistical measures, I learnt the interdependence of results, and the manner of seeking an answer not along one line of enquiry but along several so that one would correct another and the chances of proving right were improved. My second master carried my education a stage further. I learnt from him to take chances, not to await the last statistical proof before acting, to grasp tendencies and so to anticipate requirements. I learnt from him to plan largely and generously, knowing, as has indeed been confirmed again and again, that this in itself will bring success.

There are many capable mentors in this world, but there cannot have been many pairs of mentors having the same capacity to complement and correct each other as by a sort of polarisation of vision and thought.

After one or two experiments with Underground stations chosen at random Pick caused a careful assessment to be made of local demand over the entire Underground network and drew up a list of seventeen stations to be made interchange points for twenty-six bus routes. As he gradually moved outwards from the central area he began to study new housing projects and to make estimates of the passenger movement likely to be generated when building was completed. He also made it a regular practice to include the stations of the main-line railways in the planning of routes. The principle of the Underground extension still held good and the starting point of a bus route would as a rule be fixed at an Underground station, but there was nothing narrowly insular about his treatment of stations once the bus got under way. It was a sort of philosophy that the other railway managers had some difficulty in understanding; in their world of intense competitiveness it was just a little too good to be true. Their suspicions still come out very clearly in some remarks made by the general manager of the Southern Railway before the Joint Select Committee on the Railway (Road Transport) Bills of 1928. When the Underground was extended to Morden in south London a few years earlier the London General, he said, 'put on a large service of buses from Morden station right into our territory at cut fares; the result has been that what with the tube and the buses they have abstracted about four million passengers from our electrified system'. Sir Herbert Walker's statement was made in good faith; to him it was inconceivable that the Underground Group should have refrained from acting in this way. But when Pick came before the committee he was ready with his figures. The number of buses serving Morden Underground station on a weekday was 389, the Southern's Sutton Station was served by 630. To make doubly sure his bus people had undertaken a passenger count on a typical weekday; they had found that the number of passengers carried to and from Sutton Station by the buses was more than twice as great as the number for the Underground station at Morden. He gave the date of the passenger count and analysed his figures in some detail but no comment was added; the committee and Sir Herbert were able to draw their own conclusions.

All through the year 1912 Pick went on with his weekend explorations trying to find useful work for the buses to perform. Most of the time he had to feel his way gradually. In the more sparsely inhabited areas you could not just launch out with a full-blown service and hope for the best. On the Underground's railways he had made use of advertising to find employment for those 'wasteful margins' of unused vehicle capacity, and incidentally he had also kept down the cost of that advertising by putting to work those other 'wasteful margins' of unused poster space in the stations. This was going to be the same thing all over again. No doubt it would be possible to bring a few more buses into service but first he must try to get more work out of those that were already there. The question where to start was not a difficult one to answer. As he looked about him he found depressing examples of the under-employment of buses, but among these by far the most conspicuous was the sight of a garage full of idle buses that you would see on any Sunday of the year. The cause of this under-employment of buses had nothing to do with the private motor car which in those days had not yet taken over the

Englishman's Sunday. The management did indeed seem to have noticed the change that had come over the traditional English Sunday, but it was only too clear that it had greatly under-estimated the extent of the change. Pick's initial experiment started on the second Sunday in July 1912 with a fifteen-minute service from Hounslow station on the District Line out to Windsor by way of Slough. The announcement had promised a half-hourly service but as the appointed day came nearer public interest was such that the interval had to be cut by half; then, when the buses had been running for a fortnight, they were being so well patronised that the fifteen-minute interval had to be further shortened to a mere five. On the Sunday when that last change was made a second extension from Hounslow was tried with a ten-minute service to Staines. By late summer the number of Sunday services had almost doubled; they were being widely advertised on posters at the stations. But the Sunday bus was not allowed to become an end in itself and a careful watch would always be kept for any sign of a worthwhile seven-day demand.

In January 1912, when Pick was brought into the bus busi-ness, the longest of the routes reached only a distance of some eleven miles from the centre of London. The company had acquired power to operate over an area having a radius of fifteen miles measured from the General Post Office and Pick's immediate concern was to extend the services up to the limit of those powers. In the following summer the limit was abrogated by a decision of the High Court. Pick was now free to go for-ward into the 'outer ring' as it was called, a zone bounded by a circle with a radius of thirty miles. A number of smaller com-panies were already working in this outer ring and Pick had no intention of trying to compete with these companies on what he considered their own ground. Their main interest was to give a local service for a little community lying some distance away; Pick's on the other hand was to establish connections between these communities and London. At the year's end the General had negotiated upwards of forty agreements with other bus com-panies under which both parties accepted the fifteen-mile circle as a boundary line not to be crossed except by agreement with the other party. Yet Pick was conscious that he must not allow the boundary to become a wall; once a bus service had made its way into a local community then the general interests and needs of that community were a matter to which he was bound to give thought. When he was being examined by the select committee on the Railway (Road Transport) Bills he had found, he said, that 'in working our London business of projecting routes from London into the outlying country we were not giving attention to the requirements of these outlying districts.' He went on to describe the way he had tried to make good this omission. Arrangements had been made for two other bus companies 'to collaborate with us in the provision of local services within the London Traffic Area in conjunction with the through services of the London General'; the General had undertaken to provide these other companies with vehicles and garage space.

On weekdays in the office, the bus development business brought many new tasks. Pocket maps distributed on the buses explained where and how passengers could continue their journeys by train; posters at stations told them about the interesting places to which the buses would carry them. There was a new slogan now: 'Where the Railway ends', it said, 'the Motor Bus begins.' As he went on Pick would find more things to say about places; the soap and whisky advertisements on the General's bus maps disappeared to be replaced by an alphabetical index of places served and monthly lists of football matches, trade exhibitions and other exciting events. A leaflet for young people gave particulars of some sixty or seventy colleges and institutes offering evening courses in every branch of science and handicraft, it gave the days and the times, the buses by which to get there, the points at which to alight. But as was usual with Pick he could never be wholly serious and a new map issued at the end of 1912 featured among other attractions the weekly Votes for Women demonstrations at the London Pavilion theatre and newly born giraffe and elephant babies on view at the Zoo. By this time however Pick's attention had been suddenly diverted to a more serious matter. The citizens of London had showed themselves most appreciative of the new, improved motor buses that had now filled the place of the horse buses, but they were taking a little time to get used to them. In these latter days, when the regular daily massacre on the roads is cheerfully accepted as a small price to pay for the blessings of the private motor car, it is difficult to cast one's mind back to a time when a few motor buses, carefully driven by trained drivers, could cause such frantic alarm. It was in the 'silly season' of 1912 that the newspapers found the subject of street accidents a useful means of filling their columns.

A Public Safety League in Streets and Roads was formed by a barrister who had himself been injured in an accident. In October the Home Secretary convened a conference of bus undertakings. It was not only the buses that caused accidents; of all drivers prosecuted in the previous year for speeding or dangerous driving only one in five had been driving a bus or taxi. But the bus companies were organised road users; more than any others they had the means to do something effective to bring down the accident rate. The report of the Home Secretary's conference states that they 'showed an earnest desire to co-operate in every way in their power'.

The task of making the streets safer was tackled in at least three different ways. The acquisition of a number of bus undertakings and the making of arrangements with others made it possible for the General's management to sort out and rationalise the services in the busiest streets. And while congestion in the streets was thus being reduced a strong publicity campaign was launched by Pick in the early months of 1913. Passengers were told about the right way to board buses and alight from them, other advertisements were addresed to pedestrians, to cyclists, to passengers who set out to cross the road after getting off a bus. To each of these in turn Pick was like one who instructs a novice in the best way of doing a new and unaccustomed job. He illustrated the right way and the wrong way; the wrong way was seen as something ridiculous and slightly shameful. He never shouted or bullied or jeered; he was content to appeal to people to behave like sensible human beings, using words of calm reason, a voice that was quietly matter-of-fact. The campaign was backed up by the operating manager with a training scheme for drivers; his safety classes were made more effective by being linked with bonus payments which provided a powerful incentive towards greater care and better road manners. Once this two-pronged campaign got going the situation soon began to improve.

Early in 1917 Pick suddenly found himself diverted into a new occupation. In the previous winter many thousands of households in London had failed to get enough coal to keep themselves warm. Coal was the business of the Board of Trade and this had recently been given a new master. When Lloyd George brought into his administration of December 1916 a small group of experienced men of business like Cowdray, Rhondda and Devonport to help him put the conduct of the war on a more efficient footing Sir Albert Stanley had been one of the new men. A little later a new office was set up under a Controller of Coal-Mining with Pick in charge of a Household Fuel and Lighting Branch. Pick and his staff had to get to work with great speed; his rationing scheme was ready in August, in good time for the coming winter. But the effective rationing of coal meant a multiplication of small deliveries: the coal carts were kept busy taking hundredweights of coal to customers who formerly had ordered their supplies by the ton. Pick soon found this extra cartage work was making too great a demand on the country's manpower. The only answer was a system for co-ordinating and rationalising deliveries. Many thousands of cartage miles were saved by cutting out overlapping deliveries by different dealers in the same streets. Richard Redmayne, the official historian of coal mining in World War I, when writing about the work of the Household Fuel and Lighting Branch, explains that 'The management and direction of this Branch bristled with difficulties'; yet the result exceeded all expectations, for 'at no time has the very small consumer of household coal been better served than he was during the period of control'.

At the beginning of May 1919 Pick managed to take a ten-day holiday after which he went back to work part-time with the Underground. He was still struggling with his coal problems; in a letter he wrote to Harry Peach on 13 April giving him the news he said: 'The miners look like making the control of supplies necessary for another winter. The shortages have been acute lately, and the prospect of relief, except by reason of the summer weather, is remote. I have made up my mind to reorganise the coal business in the next months and finally to retire at the end of June.' The idea of retirement was not altogether unconnected with a similar move on the part of the President of the Board of Trade. The newspapers had just announced that Sir Albert Stanley had been taken ill. After a little while, when he knew that Pick was back in his Underground office, he wrote to Lloyd George asking him to accept his resignation. 'I must have a complete rest', he said. His reward came on New Year's Day 1920 in the form of a peerage. Now that he was about to take his place in the House of Lords Sir Albert felt that he would have to give rather more thought to his name than his father had given when he adopted the great territorial name of Stanley. The Knattriess family had its origin not in Sir Albert's native Derbyshire but in the neighbouring county of Nottinghamshire where his father Henry had been born in Sutton-in-Ashfield, and his grandfather Frederick, a baker, in the minster town of Southwell. And so Sir Albert Stanley now became Lord Ashfield of Southwell. Towards the end of the same year Lord George Hamilton, the Victorian statesman, having reached the age of seventy-five, announced his decision to retire from the chairmanship of the Underground Group. On 1 February 1921 the company gave effect to a new scheme of organisation. Lord Ashfield was appointed chairman while retaining his position of managing director. Pick became one of a pair of joint assistant managing directors, an arrangement that was brought to an end just three years later when his partner resigned and Pick took over his half of the job.

A New Greater London

In later years when he was doing a great deal of writing and lecturing on the subject of urban development Pick was once heard to describe public transport as 'the framework upon which the town is built'. His main business on his return to the Underground in the summer of 1919 was to produce a design for the framework for which the Common Fund was now to provide the means. The possible scope of the framework had been strikingly illustrated in the extension of the Bakerloo from Paddington to Watford, completed during the war, which had given London a local railway just five times the length of the original tube project as acquired by the Americans. This indeed was the sort of scale on which London's transport of the future must now be planned. But what exactly was this London for which he was required to design a framework? The Royal Commission in 1905 had said that for the purposes of traffic planning London should be assumed to be roughly a circle having a mean radius of some fifteen miles measured from Charing Cross. The boundary had been suggested by that of the Metropolitan Police District, to which it corresponded as closely as the outlines of the constituent local government areas would allow. That part of the circle which lay outside the county of London had later become known as Greater London. Was this the size of the area that should be treated as the London of the future? Nearly half a century later Parliament in its wisdom decided that this was in truth the correct size, and on 1 April 1965 the 1905 Commission's Greater

London of the transport planners was duly brought into being. In 1919 however the government had somewhat more advanced ideas. The branch of the Board of Trade responsible for London's traffic had given its official blessing to an area enlarged by the addition of a fifteen-mile band called the outer ring. This new circle having a radius of thirty miles was the real Greater London, the London of the 'framework'. A framework design, however, presupposes some sort of plan for the whole, and unfortunately the men who had been trying to make a plan for London had never yet got beyond the little Greater London of 1905. It was not till a year or two after the end of World War II that planners were required to adopt the Greater London of Pick's 1919 design as the basis for their work. There had been plenty of plans in the meanwhile, but they were the piecemeal plans of the 143 local authorities concerned; Sir Patrick Abercrombie, the author of the Greater London Plan of 1944, did not exaggerate when he complained that London had had less comprehensive planning than 'any other urban group in the Country'.

The area could not be said to be lacking in railway transport. If anything there was rather a superfluity of it – more than 750 stations in all served by several thousand route miles of local and main-line railway. Pick started by comparing this generous 'quantity of railway' with the quality of service produced by it. On his map he drew a series of concentric circles five miles apart; he marked the points to which the existing train services would carry you in a journey of forty-five minutes starting from Charing Cross. He found that it was only in the north-west and south-west that the ten-mile circle could be reached in that time. He went on to allow an extra ten minutes for the journey, but the area now covered still left a number of big gaps. Then, going outside the circle, he found that the fastest available trains would, in a journey of fifty-five minutes, take you to a score or so of isolated points of which only four lay as far as twenty miles from the centre. The commuter who could afford to spend so much time travelling was not well served by his transport system. The map showed the same sort of pattern of wild variations that was found in the incidence of workmen's trains. In trying to do something about the worst-off areas it was, however, necessary to distinguish between two quite separate problems: in some there were too many houses and not enough transport, in others too little use had been made of suitable building land because transport had not been forthcoming. The first problem was the more urgent since considerable hardship was often involved.

As soon as news got around of the Underground's work on their plans for the future of London's transport municipalities and other local bodies started to come forward to air their problems. In Pick's office the claims had now to be sorted and most carefully weighed. It was not altogether unexpected that the demand for more and better transport should have been loudest in the south-east and north-east. The only tube passing through the West End that was capable of being extended into south-east London was the Bakerloo. The southern end of the Bakerloo however pointed due south: its natural development would clearly be in a southerly direction and the population living between Camberwell and Croydon were most anxious that any extension should follow that natural course. But in Bermondsey, Deptford and Woolwich it was claimed that a tube connection with the centre was even more urgently needed than it was in the south; the municipalities here became insistent that an extension southwards would be seen as a grave injustice done to their hard-pressed populations. If only the Bakerloo could have been extended both ways! But that would have put too heavy a load on its middle portion. No doubt a way would have to be found of building a second tube one day to meet the demand in both areas; in the meanwhile, if they were to make a start by extending the Bakerloo, to which of the two should they give preference? It was an impossible choice. In north-east London, where the existing public transport services were causing even greater hardship, there was no dilemma of that kind. A vast industrial population had been sucked into the area by a record number of cheap workmen's trains, the price exacted by the government as a part of bargains made over certain Parliamentary Bills. Yet the Great Eastern Railway, having filled it with a dense population, had not only omitted to make plans for improving the transport services on which the people depended, it had ruthlessly obstructed the efforts of others to bring such improvement about. People still remembered the sad case of North Tottenham in North London. In 1901 a Bill authorising a new tube which was to link this part of London with the City had come before Parliament. The builders had got busy putting up houses, the London County Council, acting with commendable promptness, had made use of powers recently conferred on local authorities to purchase 140 acres of land lying some distance outside its boundary. But it was not till 1905 that the railway Bill was finally passed and by that time the interest of investors had cooled off. In 1910 the promoters had been compelled to go back to Parliament with another Bill which would give them an extension of the time allowed them in the original Act. And then the Great Eastern Railway, which had its own little station in White Hart Lane, had snatched at this new opportunity of killing a scheme it had always disliked; and not being satisfied with killing the Bill it had decided also to sue for costs on the grounds that the company had been unreasonably and vexatiously put to expense in opposing it. In July 1910 a select committee of the House of Lords had thrown out the Bill and awarded costs to the Great Eastern.

Pick in 1919 had also considered this area in his plan and his proposal for extending the Central London Line along the main-line railway tracks to Chingford and Ongar was now being studied. Nothing could be done in this neighbourhood without the co-operation of the Great Eastern. Unfortunately its board of directors had many other problems on their minds. The Great Eastern was an important main-line railway. The lines round Walthamstow were only an infinitesimal fragment of that railway; the people of Walthamstow might be deserving of relief but they would have to wait their turn. Another part of the programme for north-east London was the projection of the Piccadilly Line northwards over the lines of the Great Northern to New Barnet and Enfield. Between Finsbury Park and Wood Green there had developed a shortage of public transport that was now as acute as any in London. Finsbury Park was the terminal station of two Underground railways: the Piccadilly tube coming from the West End and the Great Northern & City Line from the City. It was also a station into which the steam trains of the Great Northern and North London Railways discharged passengers from Kings Cross and Broad Street, and many more coming from the Hertfordshire country in the north. The place had become a busy interchange point for the buses and trams which ran out in different directions. A number of things had happened to make the overcrowding here grow rapidly worse. The London County Council housing estate in Tottenham had set off a wave of development. The Great Northern steam trains were slow and unreliable and the high-lying station platforms were known as the coldest and wettest in London; one of them, Bowes Park, went by the local nickname of Pneumonia Junction. Thousands of passengers had deserted this unpopular railway and were now travelling to work by tram and bus, paying less in fares for a less uncomfortable journey. But the passengers arriving at Finsbury Park by Underground had also to use these trams and buses to take them home, and so there occurred this dreadful congestion.

Pick's plan provided for an electrified track to carry tube trains a distance of some seven miles along each of the two Great Northern's lines north of Finsbury Park, reaching High Barnet on the main line and Enfield on the Hertfordshire branch. The directors of the Great Northern were invited to consider this scheme. There might, they said, be something to be said in its favour; the truth was that at this moment they, like the Great Eastern, had other, more important things to think about. The people of Finsbury Park would just have to wait. But there was another way in which the Great Northern might be able to help. On more than one occasion the Underground Group had been reminded by local authorities and associations of ratepayers that the authorised plan for the Piccadilly Line had never been carried out in its entirety. One of the two railways that together formed the Piccadilly Line had originally been promoted as a line running out as far as Wood Green. If the Piccadilly tube could now be extended it would do much to relieve the hardship suffered in this neighbourhood. And so, when in the early months of 1920 the Underground Group considered again the various lesser extension plans that did not involve the use of suburban lines owned by other railways, they felt that this short extension to Wood Green though it had not been found worthy of a place in Pick's development plan, might yet have to be considered. The claims of this unhappy population were strong.

The Piccadilly tube had been built under an arrangement with the Great Northern. Its stations from Kings Cross northwards stood on land leased from the Great Northern and the company had itself carried out some of the constructional work. In return for this help the Great Northern, Piccadilly & Brompton Railway Co which built the tube had had to sign an agreement formally renouncing the scheme for the extension from Finsbury Park to Wood Green, and moreover to give an undertaking never to build a railway line north of Finsbury Park. The same prohibition was included in the leases for the station sites which were granted later. Pick and his colleagues knew that it would be difficult to

77

get the Underground released from the terms of these agreements. But the situation at Finsbury Park was such that they decided the attempt must be made. They went to plead their case. The date of the agreement was 1901 and already at that time the shortage of transport had been felt; in 1905 one witness after another had come before the Royal Commission to describe the plight of those who lived in this area. Now, in 1921, things were worse than anyone could have imagined at the beginning of the century. Though the short extension to Wood Green authorised by Parliament years before would not give north-east London all it needed, it would be better to do a little than to do nothing at all. But the Great Northern had secured this prohibitive agreement and it was not to be thought of that this should now be torn up. As for north-east London, the Great Northern had its own ideas of what might be done to improve local transport services; it would tell the public about them in its own good time.

While the various ways of moving forward into London's outer ring were being thus painfully explored there suddenly came some good news about that other great impediment, the problem created by the weakness of the bus undertaking which was to have provided the financial support for the railway plan. The year 1921 had been a disastrous one for British industry; at the opening of the autumn session of Parliament the Chancellor of the Exchequer, Austen Chamberlain, was driven to move a resolution that the whole of Parliament time be taken for bills dealing with what he described as 'the worst unemployment for a hundred years'. Just a week later there followed the second reading of the Trades Facilities Bill, the purpose of which was to provide help for essential industries in the raising of capital. High priority was to be given to electricity supply and to the improvement of public transport by railway and inland waterway; Pick's design for London would undoubtedly be among the enterprises most likely to qualify for help. But the giving of help under this Trades Facilities Act was strictly limited to a period of twelve months. There would not be much time. The Underground Group had tried its best in those parts of London where new and better services were most urgently needed. In the north-east it had been brought up sharp against the railways that another generation had built to bring to London a new freedom of movement and that now, by some mysterious process of change, had turned into an impenetrable barrier. Pick had no choice but to go through the remain-

78

ing parts of his plan in an attempt to find somewhere a point where it would be possible within the limited time to make a breach in the closely knit circle. Would they have to fall back on the old City & South London? The City of London & Southwark Subway, as it was originally called, was the father and mother of all tube railways. It was also the first railway to be worked with electric trains. The little stretch of line of the first promotion had been planned as a cable railway, but then the electric locomotive was invented and the company was quick to make the change. Having started life as a railway a mere mile and a half in length the tube soon began to grow; at the outbreak of World War I additions made to it from time to time had increased its length to some eight miles. There was just a small engineering problem to be overcome before this old tube could be made to play its part in London's developing Underground system. The tubes that came later had all been built with a wider tunnel; the difference was not very great, only a matter of eighteen inches or so, but it was great enough to make the old tube unsuitable for the rolling stock now in general use on the other lines. The plan for linking up what was now called the City & South London Railway, which included the widening of the old tunnel, had been authorised by Parliament shortly before the war under a Bill that provided also for the Euston terminus to be connected to the Hampstead Line at Camden Town; this work was put in hand in the summer of 1922. At Golders Green the excavators were turning up the fields for the extension of the Hampstead Line; they had started there a couple of months before.

Pick had always had it in mind that the City & South London must one day be extended towards the south. The City was not quite the direction in which south London's need for better transport was greatest but the problem now was to find any point on the Underground's periphery where a breakthrough would be possible. Clapham undoubtedly was the most likely place. In his 1919 plan Pick had described Clapham Common as 'an artificial terminus'; once the City & South London had been modernised the line, he said, should be carried through to the fringe of the built-up area. His idea then was to run the line through Balham and Tooting and on to Mitcham by way of Tooting Junction. It was four and a half miles from Clapham Common to the proposed terminal point at Mitcham. As this plan was now examined again it was seen that the proposal to turn

79

the line eastwards to Mitcham could prove a dangerous one. The tube would short-circuit the lines of the main-line railways that met at Mitcham Junction; the plan would provoke these railways to bitter opposition. In his discouragement Pick turned to another railway project which had the advantage of having already been authorised by Parliament in 1910. The Wimbledon & Sutton Railway Company, its owners, was now a part of the Underground Group; though it had never been able to build its railway, the engineering plans had been completed and the estimates got out. Pick until now had given no high priority to this line but he had been careful to cover the cost of building in his report. Would the rights conferred under the Wimbledon & Sutton Railway Act provide the opening for which they had been searching? The trouble was the District Line, of whose Wimbledon branch this new railway would become an appendage. There was no hope of the District, whose middle portion was already so seriously over-loaded, being able to take this additional traffic flow. And then there was also the agreement entered into a couple of years before the war under which the Metropolitan District Company undertook to make no attempt to extend beyond Wimbledon without the consent of the London & South Western, the owner of tracks used by its Wimbledon trains. Though the particular problem that had led to the signing of this agreement had now ceased to exist the agreement unhappily still stood. The likelihood of the South Western giving its consent was slim indeed. Yet the Underground possessed those powers to build a railway as far as Sutton; perhaps Parliament might yet be disposed to allow them to run out to Sutton by another route, a route that would serve a more useful purpose in some really hard-pressed area? Rather more than half of the projected line lay between Sutton and the point in Morden where the line would cross the main road to Epsom. That southern end, two and a half miles of it, could very conveniently be connected to the City & South London. The remainder of the Wimbledon & Sutton Railway could wait. The Underground must get going with something: they had powers for running a railway to Sutton, and Sutton it would have to be.

Pick took out his plans and started again to study the new line of the City & South London Railway, which was now being connected to the Hampstead Line on the north side. This link at Camden Town would join the two railways together so that people living between Camden Town and Edgware would be provided with through trains not only to the West End but to the City also. But the people living in south London would not have any such access to the West End; their trains would take them to the City only. If the tubes were to be united was it not better that they should be united properly, bringing the same double service to both north and south? The Hampstead Line had its southern terminal at Charing Cross; Pick had made no provision in his plan for carrying this railway south of the river. But as he looked again at the scheme for gathering the two railways together he found that another link on the south side could double the usefulness of the new railway from Clapham Common to Sutton. There would no longer be a railway from the north dividing into two branches but a long line from the extreme north to the extreme south with a centre portion split between east and west that straddled the middle of London. He saw the emerging pattern of the line that is known today as the Northern Line.

The prospect of having to work a double train service starting on a single joint line to diverge on to a pair of lines, and then re-uniting on the other side of London to run on a single line again, was not received with much enthusiasm by the operating men. It would not perhaps prove too difficult with trains working to a half-hourly interval, but with only two minutes or less between one train and the next the weaving in and out would be a tricky operation. It was true that there was already a great weaving in and out of trains on the District Line, but each of the branches of this Line had its separate ending point, and even then the District was quite troublesome to work. This new double line would have a common finishing point at either end. The trains running through the City were estimated to take ninety seconds longer to reach Camden Town than those that went by way of the West End; a small delay or irregularity on one side of the middle portion might effect the whole line for hours afterwards. But Pick was determined to go forward. The new Bonar Law government which came into power at the end of October, fired with an unaccustomed enthusiasm for its predecessor's Trades Facilities Act, had brought in a new Bill extending the period of financial aid for a further twelve months. More than that, the Prime Minister had invited the Railway chairmen to meet him to discuss their problems, and had informed them that the amount made available was to be lifted to double the maximum allocated under the original Act. Was there truly a chance of Pick's plan going through by the last day of November 1923? He would have to get moving quickly with the necessary Parliamentary Bill: a second Bill would be needed to authorise the extension of the Hampstead Line southwards to the junction with the City & South London at Kennington. The new tube would run midway between the lines of the London & South Western and the London, Brighton & South Coast Railways, separated from them by about one mile on either side. The general managers of the two companies were invited to discuss the plans; they were reminded that an Underground line to Sutton by another route had already been authorised and a hope was expressed that they would feel themselves able to give their support to the new Bill. The reply, which came a few weeks later, took the form of a joint letter bearing three signatures; the third was that of the general manager of the South Eastern Railway whose company was about to be amalgamated with the other two under the Railways Act of 1921. The letter said: 'Our directors feel that they would have no alternative but to oppose any such scheme if presented to Parliament.'

When the Underground's City & South London Railway Bill came before a select committee of the Commons in April 1923 the Southern Railway, as it had now become, started by attacking it on grounds of redundancy. The proposed line could do no more than milk traffic from the Southern's lines; it would perform no useful work, its effect would be merely destructive. This was a theory that Pick had little difficulty in demolishing. He was able to point to the experience gained elsewhere as, for example, with the Bakerloo after its extension to Watford. Notwithstanding the heavy traffic carried on this line from the day it was opened, the number of suburban passengers arriving at Euston station by main-line trains and continuing by Underground had gone up. It was still going up. The London & North Western knew that the Bakerloo extension into Hertfordshire had resulted not in a loss to the main-line railway but in substantial gain. The select committee having digested the facts did not feel that the case made by the opposition had been very convincing. Presently the Bill went to the Lords, and now the Southern Railway decided to try another line of attack. It had assured the Commons committee that the proposed tube extension would ruin the Southern; it now expressed its conviction that it was not the Southern that would be ruined, it was the Underground. Pick had told the story of

Golders Green but it was no good citing Golders Green as a precedent. Counsel for the Southern, Hugh Macmillan, made great play with the differences between the two areas:

Golders Green was promoted at the time the Garden City boom was on, at the time when building was cheap, when houses could be readily put up, and a large population of the particular class that favours the type of house at Golders Green was ready and willing to go there. There was a considerable class to be catered for, the overflow of the intelligentsia of Hampstead were ready and willing to take those houses. How different is the situation with which we are confronted in the south! Even the most enthusiastic of the promoters' witnesses did not suggest that the country in the Morden neighbourhood is comparable with Golders Green.

As his speech wore on there crept into these words of disapproval a note of stern moral indignation. He felt the Lords were being put upon; he must resent the affront that had been made to their dignity:

My Lords, it is suggested in some mysterious fashion if the tubes are permitted to emerge from their underground burrows and become surface railways, where the cost of construction is less, they will then by going into rural districts at present not populated, but which they believe will be populated in consequence of their advent, they will hope in some mysterious way, out of that project and speculation, to rehabilitate the finances of the companies generally. I should have thought, my Lords, that the proposition was a highly speculative proposition at the best, and that a policy founded upon such a proposition was little better really than a gambler's throw.

A gambler's throw! The accusation might have carried little weight with the committee of the House of Commons but on the audience to which those words were now spoken they had a startling effect. It was an occupational interest of many members of that audience to watch over the commercial rectitude of the companies whose boards they adorned. What was now being asked of them was that they should give their approval to a 'gambler's throw'. A few hours later their chairman, Lord Beauchamp, announced that the Lords' committee had rejected the Bill.

At this point it became clear that there was only one possible way out. The Underground must compromise. Unfortunately there was no time left now for manoeuvre: the extended period of financial support under the Trades Facilities Acts was due to close finally in the following November. And the Southern Railway was still most fiercely opposed to the idea of an Underground line running out to Sutton to connect with its own suburban lines. The company however had let it be known that it would offer no objection to a line going as far as Tooting. Perhaps that was the best that could be done. But to Pick a line stopping short at Tooting did not make any sort of sense. No point short of Morden, he told his board, could be seriously considered. A terminus at Tooting would be bad business; what was even more serious, it would be bad for the Underground's reputation and would make a dangerous precedent for the future. He said:

> The question has passed beyond the stage at which it can be looked upon as open for settlement as a private matter between two companies. It has become a public question with political repercussions. On this account it is important that any proposal for curtailing the present scheme should be seen to have been forced upon the City & South London Co. The Underground Group could only accept it as a decision of the House of Lords committee.

But the scheme as it turned out was not destined to be curtailed. When the select committee met again at the end of July 1923 it reported that the Bill was to be amended by agreement. The City & South London would run to Morden; the Underground Company would drop the idea of forming a connection with the Southern. It would also make the Southern a present of the Wimbledon & Sutton Railway Company. On this understanding the Southern was willing to withdraw its opposition to the Bill. These difficult final negotiations had given the Underground only an additional three miles or so of railway from Tooting to Morden. But the Southern Railway had started by opposing any kind of extension south of Clapham Common; the Southern had been strong and determined in its opposition and yet it had been made to give way. The City & South London Bill had been the occasion of a trial of strength which was the first of its kind, and though the Underground had got less than it had hoped for it was yet an undoubted fact that the obstruction had been overcome.

The moral advantage thus gained was likely to prove a substantial asset in any future contest of this kind.

Piccadilly Line

When the engineers moved into Moorgate station in August 1922 to start work on the City & South London Railway the news brought much satisfaction to the people of south London. But there were other parts where it was received with somewhat different feelings. A few months later the Minister received a deputation, the first of a series, from the area round Finsbury Park, the finishing point of the Piccadilly and City & South London Lines. Next came a Press campaign that ran in the *Daily Mirror* for some weeks; it told of men and women fighting like rugby footballers every evening to get a place on the buses and trams, of the pickpockets that infested the struggling queues outside Finsbury Park station. Witnesses were interviewed on the subject of the hardships suffered by women and girls; the nervous breakdowns, the diseases of the chest, were described by local doctors. In June 1923 another and more high-powered deputation came up with a petition bearing the signatures of 30,000 local residents. It had become known that the Underground Group had abandoned the Finsbury Park scheme and gone to south London because of the obstruction put up by the London & North Eastern Company, the new group into which the Great Northern had now been merged. The deputation had been timed to reach the Minister on the day on which the Commons were due to debate one of that company's private bills. Some very angry speeches were made. 'The conditions', said Lord Ednam, 'are such as exist in no other civilised city in the world', and later the Minister of Transport was driven to admit to the House that the transport services were 'deplorable' and 'a danger to life and limb'. As a gesture of protest local Members induced seventy-five of their fellow-Members to vote against the Bill. The speeches and articles continued; deputation followed deputation. In February 1924 a Member told how on three occasions he had been knocked down by the crowds while attempting to board a tram. Then, early in the following year, the government had an idea that may not have seemed at the time to be altogether an inspired idea but that nevertheless turned out to be productive of far-reaching consequences. The idea was that they would look into the matter. They would institute a public enquiry.

85

In November 1925 Pick was called as a witness. It was true, he said, that the Underground Group had intended to give priority to the extension of the tube further into north and north-east London, and that circumstances had forced it to abandon this plan and go to work in other parts. But its hands had since then been freed by the abrogation of the restrictive agreement and the Underground would make the extension of the Piccadilly Line its next job. This would now be carried as far as Southgate, a distance of about ten miles from Piccadilly Circus. There would be no competition with any main-line railway whose trains ran into a terminal station like Broad Street or King's Cross; a railway such as that had the great advantage of higher speeds and its real business was to provide for people travelling to and from the areas further out. The Great Central Railway had set an example by placing its first suburban station nearly seven miles from its Marylebone terminus. If the London & North Eastern were to be driven by the construction of the Southgate tube to follow that example, and to devote its attention to the people living north of Southgate, it would do that company no harm. The report when it came out on 17 March 1926 asserted with some firmness that what north and north-east London needed was a service of trains running through into the heart of the West End. To provide such a service the Piccadilly Line should be extended to Manor House where arrangements should be made for quick and easy interchange with the trams; after that the line should be carried on to Wood Green and, if possible, to Southgate. The improvement of the London & North Eastern suburban services was a more complicated matter which the committee proposed to examine in a separate report.

While Pick was busy coping with the enquiries he had managed to get his plan for the Piccadilly Line extension worked out in considerable detail. His experience with the amalgamation of the Hampstead Line with the City & South London Railway had confirmed his view that it was no good making piecemeal improvements to an existing line; you must study the line as a whole and make a healthy enterprise of the full extent of it from one end to the other. The Piccadilly Line ran from Finsbury Park to Hammersmith on the west side where it connected with the District Line. For many years past the District had been unable to provide an adequate service on its western branches, and more particularly on those lying west of Hammersmith. These branches had been built in the early days to feed traffic into the middle portion of the Line; the branches, however, had been too success-ful and the once under-utilised middle portion had gradually become a bottleneck. A number of schemes had been considered for relieving the District of this excessive load; the most recent was the pre-war plan for extending the Piccadilly Line westwards along the District's tracks. In 1925 the line was carrying no more than twenty-four trains an hour at the busiest times; it could easily manage another six and with a new signalling installation there would be no difficulty in boosting the number up to forty. But even this great improvement in the train service would not justify the extensions being carried over all four of the District's branches and Pick had to rest content with using only two of them, the ones running to South Harrow and Hounslow. He had put the plans aside again early in 1924; in the autumn of 1925 there seemed a good chance of their being able to go forward with this work.

The capital for the City & South London enterprise had been raised with the help of government aid supplied under the Trades Facilities Act of 1921. In 1927 it looked as though the Piccadilly Line project might be similarly dependent on government aid in one form or another. Would the government again be compelled to act? The state of chronic unemployment that had been the cause of the earlier arrangement still continued. If there was any hope in that direction Pick must lose no time in getting down to another spell of work. Government assistance if granted would be conditional on the approval of two vital estimates. First, there was the forecast of the total road and rail revenues over an initial period when the main support would still be coming from the Underground's Common Fund. Then there was required a fore-cast of the ultimate earnings of the new line after an interval that the railways were accustomed to fix at fifteen years, the time required for the capital investment to yield its full expected return – to 'fructify' as their phrase went. Pick started by studying the results for the Morden Line. The year 1925 was the first year in which the new tube trains had run for the full twelve months from Hendon in the north through the reconstructed tube of the City & South London to Clapham Common in the south. In that year this line and the old Hampstead Line together had carried 79 million passengers. In the following September the Hampstead had been connected to the City & South London at Kennington, and trains had run through to Morden on both these lines for the last three and a half months of the year. In 1926 the lines had carried 104 million passengers. It was already clear that the year 1927 would be a good deal better than that; the total number of passengers might well rise to 120 million or even higher. The Morden enterprise had not been a failure. Its results augured well for the Piccadilly Line project. He looked again at his population statistics for the areas to be served. At the northern end the average density had gone from $7\frac{1}{2}$ persons to the acre in 1891 to 17 in 1927; he estimated that it was likely to rise to 30 persons by the time the new line was working. He drew up his estimates of traffic, of the expected average fare per passenger, of the receipts per car mile of train service, of the cost of operation per car mile. He found that when the line had reached its full earning power it would yield a little under 5 per cent on the capital expended. The prospects for the western extension looked a little brighter, and it was also to be noted that the point of full earning power would be reached sooner at this end than it would at Southgate. The northern extension might perhaps be something of a hazard but the one on the west side would save the line. The complete line would stand a good chance of becoming economically viable.

In April 1929 there came a piece of interesting news. The source of the news however was not the government in power, it was the Labour Party speaking with the voice of Ramsay MacDonald at a great meeting in the Albert Hall. And then only a couple of months later the unexpected happened and MacDonald's government took over. It was only a matter of a few weeks before the Development (Loan Guarantees and Grants) Bill was drafted and in print. Once the Bill had been rushed through the government were able to arrange that the Underground Group should raise the whole of the money in the form of loan capital and to undertake to meet rather more than one-half of the interest charges on that capital for the normal period of fifteen years. The complete programme qualifying for this aid included not only the extensions of the Piccadilly Line at either end but also the rebuilding of fifteen tube stations with new escalators to take the place of the old lifts. Six of these were on the Piccadilly Line: King's Cross, Russell Square, Leicester Square, Dover Street, Hyde Park Corner and Knightsbridge. Holborn Station was to be remodelled at platform level to make a joint station with the Central Line whose British Museum Station would become redundant. Negotiations had, most disappointingly, broken down over Euston Station because the London, Midland & Scottish Railway said it intended to rebuild its main-line station there and could enter into no discussions until their own plans had been finally settled.

The extension of the Piccadilly Line to Southgate was the biggest single job in the programme; its cost was nearly one-half of the cost of the whole. It was also the only part of the programme about which there was some possibility of public controversy. So great had been the outcry over transport services in north London, so complete the disclaimer of the London & North Eastern Railway of any further responsibility for their improvement, that neither Pick nor Ashfield expected any serious opposition from that quarter. But early in February 1930 Ashfield had a conversation with Lord Farringdon, one of the directors. The London & North Eastern had announced in 1926 that it would offer no opposition to a Bill for an extension of the line as far as Manor House. Lord Farringdon said his board would stand by this undertaking. But since it was now proposed to continue the Piccadilly Line as far as Cockfosters they had decided that they would have to fight the Bill and they intended to oppose it with all their strength. Three months later a select committee of the House of Commons spent six days on the Bill. Thirty-nine petitions had been lodged against it, but the only one involving a serious conflict was that of the London & North Eastern. The general manager, Sir Ralph Wedgwood, the first witness for the company, explained how many years ago the Underground companies had come to the Great Northern with their scheme for a new combined station at Finsbury Park which would enable passengers arriving by the steam trains from Hertford and Hatfield to change direct to Underground trains. It was perfectly true, he said, that if the Underground were now to be extended to the northern boundary of Southgate it would prove a blessing to many thousands of passengers who now travelled by bus and tram and changed to the Underground at Finsbury Park under conditions of great discomfort. But the Underground trains were bound also to draw many passengers away from the steam train services that ran on either side of the proposed new line. The steam services into Finsbury Park were bringing in gross earnings of over £250,000 a year; it was estimated that if the Bill went through the loss of business suffered by the London & North Eastern would be equal to two-fifths of that sum. It was hoped the Underground's Bill would be thrown out, and as an inducement to the House he had been authorised to make an offer. His company had been anxious for some time to electrify its main lines as far as Welwyn, with branches to Hertford, High Barnet and Edgware. It now proposed to make an immediate start with this work. When pressed, Wedgwood had to admit that his scheme depended on his board getting good terms in the City for their capital issue, and that they would only hope to do this with the aid of a government grant. He then, being pressed further, said that they had put in their application to the government and that it had been rejected.

Presently Pick was called. He was full of praise for Wedgwood's plan. There was no overlapping between that plan and his own; the two were complementary and he hoped that both would be carried out together. He said: 'We designed our railway to go as near as possible midway between the two lines of the London & North Eastern so as to avoid, so far as we could, this allegation that we are competing with them.' He showed how the proposed Underground Line would open up new areas for housing improvements which were badly needed. 'The moment you get past Wood Green there is an almost entire absence of development. The population of East Barnet is at the rate of half a person to the acre.' All through a long cross-examination he kept firmly to his contention that the tube extension would cause these empty spaces to be utilised and that instead of robbing the other trains of passengers it would bring them many more passengers than they now carried. The cross-examination continued on the following day. It was now being urged that even if the London & North Eastern should be unable to finance its scheme the steam trains were still there; would it not be more sensible to see if more use could be made of these trains? Pick pointed out that though the steam trains were indeed there, the services were so poor that the buses and trams had perforce to carry most of the traffic in that area. The Piccadilly tube was delivering passengers at Finsbury Park in trains which in peak hours carried six hundred people each. He said: 'It is extraordinary how small a proportion of this traffic changes to the main-line railway. Of every hundred passengers arriving by the tube seventy-eight continue their journey by road transport. These large blocks of passengers have to be picked up and carried along to complete their journeys in buses with fifty seats and trams with only a few more. You are ladling out traffic from a bucket and picking it up in a teacup.' The buses were overloaded; the steam trains seemed unable to help. What was wanted was a new train service with a different kind of capacity altogether: 'You have a railway to New Barnet with fifty-three trains a day in one direction and fifty-seven in the other, and another railway to Enfield with sixty-eight trains in one direction and sixty-seven in the other. At Tooting Broadway we have 459 trains in each direction. That is what we mean by service.'

When counsel for the London & North Eastern followed Pick he did not pretend that the Underground would not give a far better service to north London than his client could hope to provide. But the company was worried about the heavy fall in revenue which the new line was bound to cause. The loss would fall, he said, not on London alone, it would fall even more heavily on the industrial north. What Pick was asking was that the factories of Yorkshire and Durham and the great northern coalfields, by bearing the loss inflicted on London's suburban steam trains, should in effect be made to subsidise passengers on the new tube extension. He said: 'That is the point of view from which I want to ask this committee to consider this case. I want to ask you, sir, that you will not be quick or anxious to do anything which depletes the revenues of this great trunk line in order to provide one less change on the Underground for a man or woman going to work in the West End.' The committee however, was not greatly impressed with counsel's argument. The Bill was read and agreed in the first week of April.

Having failed to convince the select committee of the Commons that the extension to Cockfosters would impoverish their own railway the London & North Eastern decided that in the Lords they would take a leaf out of the Southern's book. When the Southern Railway had opposed the Underground Bill for the extension to Sutton in 1923 it had told the Commons that the Sutton enterprise would ruin the Southern Railway and it had lost its case. It had then warned the Lords that the Sutton enterprise would ruin the Underground; it was no more than a mad speculation, a 'gambler's throw'. And it had won its case, or at least it had won it so far as the Underground had had to accept a compromise solution. This was the argument that counsel for the London & North Eastern now presented to the select committee of the Lords in the last week in May 1930. Unfortunately for him, seven years had elapsed since that other committee had listened to the same argument; in those seven years the Underground had had much practical experience of extensions of this kind. Pick told the story of the new lines to Edgware and Morden and of the great housing estates that had grown up along those lines. He produced his maps and charts, his tables of statistics. He explained how the Underground and the London County Council were now working together, and how the council had made it their policy to plan their new housing estates round the new Underground stations. The scheme for the Sutton line had been an act of faith; the scheme for the extension to Southgate was founded on cold calculation. Before the month of May was out Pick learnt that the Bill for the Piccadilly Line was safely home. It was the last hurdle.

The Piccadilly Line was only nine miles long but it had been for some time the liveliest member of the Underground's family of railways. It was the first tube line to speed up its ordinary train service by making some of them run through a few stations without stopping. On this line Londoners were first introduced to lifts with press-button doors and automatic landing controls, to high-speed lifts, to escalators, to cars with mechanically operated doors. Then had come the reconstructed Piccadilly Circus station, accepted everywhere as the most advanced underground railway station in the world. And now the new extension project was to lengthen the line from the original nine miles to nearly nineteen. Pick had estimated that in its first year the extended Piccadilly Line would attract an additional fifty million passengers to the Underground railway system; the total number of passengers using this system and the Metropolitan Railway which thirty years before had been 245 million would then have risen to 700 million. Of this total the Piccadilly Line would be carrying one-sixth. It would be the busiest single traffic line in London. There would be more trains than ever, running at shorter intervals: a normal service outside the rush hours of twenty-two trains an hour was planned for the stretch from Wood Green to Hammersmith, but the whole line from end to end was to have a signalling system designed for forty trains an hour, a train every one and a half minutes. And the trains were to be speeded up. A saving of $3\frac{1}{2}$ minutes would be made by trains passing through four District Line stations between Hammersmith and Acton Town without stopping. And then it would be possible to make some savings of time at other points also. Between Piccadilly and Hammersmith the stations lay close together; it had been the policy of the original builders of the tube to place their stations as nearly as possible half a mile apart. New, better trains with improved acceleration and more powerful brakes were all very well, but a half-mile run was too short for a driver, however efficient his equipment, to work up a good speed before starting to apply his brakes. All Pick's plans were based on average speeds from one end of the line to the other of 25mph. To achieve this speed, tracks on the surface portion were being re-laid so that curves would be widened and eased and gradients flattened out, but these technical improvements would be of little avail unless some tube stations could be closed down to make longer runs possible. And so the plan provided for the closing down of seven stations. As it turned out the plan proved too ambitious, the public could be persuaded to accept the closing of only three – Brompton Road, Down Street and York Road. But even the elimination of this small number of stops proved useful; the closing of the two on the west side enabled 7½ minutes to be saved on the journey from Northfields to Piccadilly.

It was, however, not just the trains that had to be speeded up: the whole journey had to be made to consume less of the traveller's time. A new station recently built had taught a useful lesson. When the tunnels for Kennington Station on the Morden Line were being designed it had been found convenient to separate the two new tunnels for the branch running through the West End and to place one or either side of the old City & South London tunnels which were left to lie close together in the middle. It now became possible for passengers to change trains simply by crossing from one side to the other of a shared platform. This might not perhaps be of great consequence at a station like Kennington, where only a small number of passengers had to change, but at those stations where the fast Piccadilly Line trains were to run alongside the stopping trains of the District it could be very important indeed. And so from this fortuitous arrangement at Kennington there followed a series of stations designed on a new principle – platform interchange; stations in which each of the two island platforms lay between a pair of tracks on which trains ran in the same direction. To make this possible, costly track reconstruction work at Hammersmith and Acton Town stations had to be undertaken carrying one track across over the other to fit into the new arrangement. Elsewhere the same island platform device would make it possible to run the escalators right down to platform level so that down at the bottom there would be no steps for the passenger to climb up or down. Some of the other improvements were more technical: a big step forward in the ventilation of the tunnel, air exhaust plants at four tube stations and many powerful plants at other points would extract foul air and, what was even more important, the excess heat generated by passengers, moving machinery, the application of brakes; to prevent heat from the escalator machine rooms escaping into the stations a separate air extraction plant would be installed for each of these rooms. Lighting, too, was to be improved; not only would station lighting be stronger but the emergency lighting installed against possible electricity failures would give half the light output of normal lighting instead of only a quarter.

At the northern end, where the new tracks were being built, the wider spacing of the new stations was severely criticised by local interests. A particular cause of complaint was the distance of nearly 1½ miles between Manor House and Turnpike Lane. Pick was obstinate in his refusal to put an intermediate station between these two. A railway line with stations spaced half, or even three-quarters of a mile, apart was bound to be inefficient. And moreover this Line was going to be a perfect model of the functional unification of the various forms of transport. At every stopping point between Cockfosters and Manor House existing bus and tram routes converged on the station from different directions. But between Manor House and Turnpike Lane there were no such points of confluence, the railway trains ran parallel to the road services: if a station were to be built on this stretch it would be of no help in connecting rail and road services together. That was the great object, to make the services feed each other, to make each play its part in a single design. This single design would be most clearly expressed at the main point of intersection, Manor House. Access to this station would be by nine stairways, the most elaborate approach system yet attempted; one of the approaches would be from new street islands in the Seven Sisters Road where for the first time in London there would be realised an old dream of a station where passengers could make a quick change under cover from the trams and buses to the Underground trains, a process that under normal conditions should here take just about a minute to accomplish. After a couple of years' work the Piccadilly Line was opened as far as Arnos Grove in the third week of September 1932. A month or so later Pick got a letter from the president of the Federation of Ratepayers' and Kindred Associations of Middlesex, an influential group formed by forty-three local associations whose long fight for better transport had at last been crowned with success. Nearly half of the foolscap sheet was taken up by a list of these associations and the names and addresses of the eleven offices of the federation. The letter said: 'Your new venture has now been in operation for its first month and naturally I shall be especially interested to know if the returns so far are to your satisfaction. Blessings have been showered upon your undertaking by thousands daily during the past month.'

4

DESIGN AND
LONDON TRANSPORT:
1923-1933

An Architectural Idiom

In the summer of 1923, with the passing of the Underground's
City & South London Bill, Pick was able to start giving serious
attention to the problem of station design. His approach to the
problem was a simple one. The station was a shop in which you
received the customer, and there was a lot to be done to this shop;
the manner in which existing stations received you was far from
satisfactory. The customer would make his way through a narrow
doorway into a passage full of draughts where he awaited his
turn to address the ticket clerk hidden behind the bars of his little
window. A recent improvement scheme carried out at Kilburn
Station had shown how the narrow passage could be got rid of:
the entire ground floor space had been opened up to form a sort
of entrance hall where the clerk worked in a glass booth in the
middle of the floor. But the new stations would need something
more spacious than that Kilburn lobby. And the entrance, too,
must be broader, broad enough to make the new interior visible
to the passer-by in the street.

Among the old stations marked down for modernisation was
the old District Railway station at Westminster. It had been built
in 1868 and looked it. The station was just the place for a bold
experiment. It occupied an important position facing the Houses
of Parliament; the cost of substantial improvement would be
money well spent. When the first stage was completed in the early
part of 1924 it was seen that the bottom part of the facade had
gone; there was left only a great opening twenty feet wide carved
out of the fussy Italianate stonework of the St Stephen's Club

Throughout his career Pick was concerned with good communication and the clear presentation of information. Here and on the following pages are shown some of the innovations which London owes to him. *Above left:* bus stop post; *above right:* destination blind on bus; *below:* map and timetables on bus shelter.

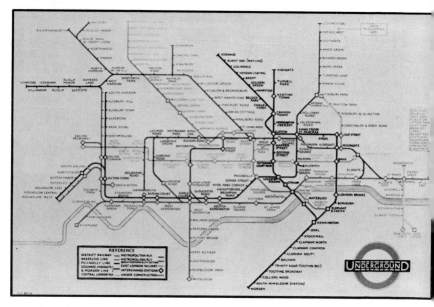

A pocket railway map of 1935.

The alphabet designed for the Underground by Edward Johnston in 1916.

ABCDEFGHIJKL
MNOPQRSTUV
WXYZ abcdefgh
ijklmnopqrstuvw
xyz (&£.,:;'!?-*"")
1234567890

Signs on and about a station building.

Left: a bifurcation sign as found at the foot of stairs to platforms.

Right: an information stand in a station ticket hall.

Left: the station sign on a platform wall.

Below: a free-standing station sign.

A poster of 1909. All posters illustrated measure approximately 40 in ×
25 in (102 cm × 64 cm), unless indicated otherwise.

FLEET upon fleet; argosy upon argosy. Masts to the right, masts to the left, masts in front, masts yonder above the warehouses; masts in among the streets as steeples appear amid roofs; masts across the river hung with drooping half-furled sails; masts afar down thin and attenuated, mere dark straight lines in the distance. They await in stillness the rising of the tide." Richard Jefferies in "Nature near London."

UNDERGROUND

THE WAY OF BUSINESS

LONDON DOCKS AT WAPPING OR ROTHERHITHE STATIONS

'London Docks', by Sir Frank Brangwyn, 1913.

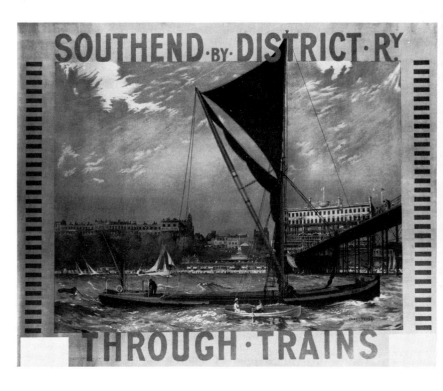

Above: 'Southend', by Charles Pears, 1915; *below:* 'The Workers' Way', by Spenser Pryce, 1913. Each 40 in × 50 in (102 cm × 127 cm).

'At War: The Women Take Over', by A. S. Hartrick. Four designs from a set printed for private circulation.

where tides of grass break into foam of flowers Swinburne

'Where Tides of Grass', by John Farleigh, 1937.

'Into the Country', by Graham Sutherland, 1938.

MODEL OF A CUBIC SURFACE XYZ-K3(X-Y-Z-I)³
SCIENCE MUSEUM

Victoria & Albert Museum
Geological Museum
Natural History Museum
Open free—Weekdays 10-6 : Sun. 2.30-6

SOUTH KENSINGTON

'South Kensington', by Edward Wadsworth, 1936.

'Uxbridge', by Edward McKnight Kauffer, 1920.

GIANT PANDA

Stations for the Zoo
Camden Town · Chalk Farm · St. Johns Wood

Two rail-car draught-screen panels of the 1930s, each measuring
10 in × 12½ in (25.4 cm. × 31.8 cm).

BOAT RACE
APRIL 4

BUSES: To Chiswick Baths-55·155
To Hammersmith-9·11·27·33·72·73·91·93
To Putney Bridge-14·22·30·74·85·93·96

Four bus-body panels, each 10 in (25.4 cm) deep.

Because he likes to have plenty of money for his leisure occupations, he is always ready to save if no sacrifice is entailed. His Season Ticket gives him a nice little saving on his business journeys between Pinner and Aldersgate. It pleases him, too, that this same Underground Season Ticket lets him travel free to many of his evening amusements. For 33/9 a month he obtains swift, reliable travelling and still keeps a credit balance.

LONDON TRANSPORT

EIN.662

A press advertisement designed by Feliks Topolski.

building. The opening was clear of any obstruction – the jambs on each side quite concealed the wide collapsible gates that were drawn forward when the station closed for the night. This new transport shop was a shop without a front, the forerunner of many hundreds of similar shops and supermarkets that were to invade our High Streets a quarter of a century later. The inside of the shop, too, was different. The tickets now were issued from a line of little glass booths standing in the middle of the floor. These were the booths that had been given a trial at Kilburn Park Station at the end of 1921. 'A new device called a passimeter' Ashfield had called them when reporting to his board meeting. Another time-saver was the provision of a separate path by which season-ticket holders could go through without being delayed by passengers buying ordinary tickets. Extra stairs had been put in so that people coming out were no longer jostled by those hurrying in to catch their trains. Londoners were quick to take note of these changes and the station soon began to attract new custom; in the first twelve months after the opening of the new entrance and ticket hall the number of passengers using the station went up by more than a quarter of a million.

The designers of the old Underground stations in central London had developed a type of station front made up of a row of big arches which could either be left open or filled in with walling. The station as a rule occupies a site with a long street frontage; there are seldom fewer than four arches and sometimes up to ten. The arches are tall enough to contain a low upper storey providing space for the lift machinery. Their architecture today seems singularly unattractive; they are pompous in manner; their colour, the colour of ox liver – about the most unattractive ever used in the streets of London – looks almost black when lit up by the street lamps at night. Then, after the war, came the stations on the northern extensions of the Hampstead Line: Brent and Hendon Central, completed at the end of 1923, and Colindale, Burnt Oak and Edgware which were opened in the following summer. The railway here ran on the surface; this was unlike any of the earlier Underground lines, for it was the first appearance of the Underground trains in the new suburbia of the 1920s. For it Stanley Heaps, the staff architect of the Underground Group, developed a series of simple, unassuming designs having an air of cosy domesticity. The stations were to be good neighbours to the homes of the commuters for whose daily travel they were built;

their tiled roofs are distinguishable from the roofs of the detached brick houses only by the absence of chimney stacks.

While engineers were busy with the reconstruction of the City & South London tunnels Pick was trying to make up his mind about the design of the new stations for south London. He did not know what he wanted but he knew he would have to produce something better than the Georgian domestic manner of the new stations in the Edgware area. After a while he came to the conclusion that he must bring in an outside architect to work with his own architect, Heaps. He talked over his problem with a number of friends who had been in one way or another associated with good modern buildings and was interested to find that among the names of architects mentioned with special respect was that of Charles Holden. It was a name that Pick himself had already had in mind for some time. He had first got to know Holden during the war when both men were involved in the beginnings of the Design and Industries Association. He had been following Holden's work with interest. He liked him for his energy in pursuing the simple, honest, functional approach to design for which the association had made itself the advocate. Of all the people that Pick had been considering Holden seemed the most likely. The thing to do now was to make arrangements with Holden's firm, Adams Holden & Pearson, for a small trial, preferably with something less than a complete building, a minor commission that would be accepted by the Underground architect's department without question or demur. Holden at that time was forty-eight years of age. He was a man of short stature with a calm, earnest face enlivened by reflections from the round-rimmed gold spectacles which he was never seen without. From each side of a lofty forehead, the forehead of a great chemist or mathematician, the hair hung down almost vertically; the little beard, meticulously trimmed, suggested an unimpressive chin. Somehow when you had got to know him a little you were not surprised to discover that he was a Quaker; that he was a craftsman who knew how to use his hands; that he neither smoked nor drank; or that his home was in Welwyn Garden City. He spoke little, in a soft colourless voice; it was as though he distrusted speech and used only the barest necessary. He was an unusual architect in many ways. At the evening class at the Manchester Grammar School which he attended as a young man he had made friends with painters like Francis Dodd and Henry Lamb; no

architect of his generation was closer to his contemporaries practising painting or sculpture; no one since the eighteenth century
had known how to employ artists to such advantage on the
enrichment of his buildings. This special gift had caused him to
be much talked about in London when he brought in Jacob
Epstein to add lustre to Agar House, the British Medical Association's new headquarters building in the Strand.

When the work on Westminster Station was in the planning
stage, great importance was placed on the need to keep the
station open to traffic without any interruption. To make this
possible a temporary entrance had been contrived at the rear of
the ticket hall area which was being rebuilt. This back entrance
lay between the corner of Norman Shaw's New Scotland Yard
buildings and the adjoining office block. It did its work well, so
well that Pick felt it would be worthwhile to keep it as a permanent second entrance. The space available was only a few feet
wide, just enough for a portal of quite modest dimensions. As a
project for Holden it seemed almost too insignificant but if
Holden would accept the job it would make a most suitable introduction for him.

Many years later Holden recalled how Pick had explained to
him that he was looking for someone to join him in a search for
'a new architectural idiom' suitable for his new stations. It was
the sort of brief that made a strong appeal to Holden and he set
to work at once. His portal became redundant when the street
level entrance from the Embankment was later replaced by a subway giving direct access to Westminster Bridge, but it still stands
there as Holden built it, a simple arrangement of flat surfaces,
defined only by a series of shallow set-backs but proportioned
with thoughtful care. As a specimen of 'a new idiom' it is hardly
what one would call impressive, but it was only meant to be a
first step: what mattered to Pick was that the step, such as it was,
had been taken in the right direction.

The experiment accomplished a number of things. It
furnished what Pick a few years later described as 'the model of
the latter-day Underground ticket hall'. It encouraged him to
press forward with his employment of Holden, and it set on foot
the kind of collaboration with the staff architect without which
that employment could never have become fully effective. Its
importance, however, lay not only in the satisfactory solution of
some key problems but more especially in the one problem it

115

failed to solve. As you walked down the broad flight of steps from the street you saw in front of you the ticket hall. A little trickle of daylight came from a couple of awkwardly placed skylights at the bottom of deep, chimney-like light wells in the middle of the building blocks that rose high above the station. But this dim light was only barely visible from the street. The abolition of the entire street wall of the ticket hall did indeed give passers-by a clear view of the interior but as you walked past on a sunny day that interior, which should have looked bright and inviting, was just a blank void in which electric lights fought a losing battle with the darkness. This must have been where Pick had fully brought home to him how fortunate had been his choice of Holden as architect. The problem of daylighting was very familiar to Holden; it had indeed featured more than any other part of his professional experience in determining his approach to design. With his partner Percy Adams, a specialist in hospital design, he had been concerned in the building of many hospitals and, in working out a treatment for his exteriors, he had found in the large windows of operating theatres an intractable difficulty. It was a difficulty that had troubled other architects before him: the painters' studios on the top floor of the Glasgow School of Art, for example, had presented Charles Rennie Mackintosh with precisely this problem. How could a glazed opening of such vast dimensions be combined with ordinary windows in a conventional facade? It was plainly an impossibility. 'I came to the point', Holden is reported as saying, 'when I had to consider laying down the old and taking up the new.' A writer or a painter when he decides to take up the new is able to do it single-handed; for an architect it is necessary that there should be a client prepared to join him in the enterprise. As Pick spoke to him about his ideas, Holden realised that he had found the client for whom he had been looking. In the Underground stations there would be no hopeless struggling with incompatible window shapes, and, moreover, although his firm would be nominally responsible, he would in fact be working on his own, with a sense of independence he had but seldom enjoyed in the past. When he confessed that 'from that time onwards design became a fascinating problem' he was no doubt referring to the opportunities opened up by this convergence of two minds struggling with the same problem, the invention of an architecture able to bring full daylighting into big interior spaces, but he was also at the same time paying to Pick the most graceful compliment that it is possible for an architect to pay to a client.

Holden's starting point was a pair of old stations on the existing City & South London tube that were to be modernised – Clapham Common, which was then the terminus, and Stockwell. He knew his real chance would come only with the new stations on the extension to Morden and these two reconstruction jobs were no doubt of no more interest to him than they are to us today. Yet in some ways they managed to give an indication of what was to come. The new Stockwell Station was to stand at street level like the old one, with new escalators going down from an escalator hall at the rear of the ticket hall, and so we find most of the ceiling area of this escalator hall taken up by a big skylight some 25ft or more in length. Clapham Common, on the other hand, was planned as a basement-level station lying under the road with access stairs on either side. One of these stairway entrances is an open one placed in the middle of the pavement like so many others that were later to be built in various parts of central London; the stairs were protected from the rain by a glazed canopy which was removed many years later. The other stairway lies in a low single-storey building which is no more than a circular stairwell covered by a glass dome spanning from wall to wall. In both stations the presence of all available daylight is strikingly noticeable. Each of the ticket halls is a straight carry-over from the Westminster experiment: the big open floor; the light-coloured teak used for all finishes and items of equipment that could be made of wood; the centrally placed ticket booths with their press-button printing machines that put all the required printed matter on a blank ticket in a quarter of a second precisely. The new type of escalator was another conspicuous amenity; instead of jumping off sideways from steps that disappeared under a partition placed at an angle, you stepped forward over a steel comb that fitted into the wooden cleats on the steps. These improved escalators had just been tried out at Bank Station, where they took the place of five antiquated lifts. They were thought a little alarming at first but passengers soon got used to them and before long these Bank Station escalators were moving a record number of 30,000 passengers an hour in the peak hours. The same type of escalator was later used in all the new stations on the extended line.

With Westminster, Stockwell and Clapham out of the way,

Pick and Holden were free to devote themselves to the further development of the 'new architectural idiom'. Just as at Stockwell and Clapham Common the structures standing at street level were dominated by great skylights, so in the designs on which Holden was now working the exterior is dominated by a great window. Then, coupled with this main requirement of lighting, there was another requirement arising from the position and shape of the sites. Most of the new stations on the Morden extension were going to be built on corner sites; the corners however were not rectangular, they were set at all sorts of angles; no two of them were alike. If there was going to be something like a recognisable standard station front it must be so designed that it could be adjusted to these various angles. The sketches Holden produced for the first of the new series of stations, Clapham South, were based on the principle of a three-leaf folding screen. In the summer of 1925, when his ideas had been fully considered and discussed, a model of the entrance front and ticket hall was set up in one of the engineering workshops at Earls Court. It was what architects call a mock-up, built of scaffold poles and sheets of building board to a rough and only partly developed design, but it was a full-size model that you could walk into and study from every point of view. Pick and Holden worked diligently upon this mock-up in the following months, trying out a number of different ceiling arrangements, making experiments with the artificial lighting installed in the canopy over the entrance. About this time Pick was writing to Peach and at the end of his letter he told about his plans. He said:

By way of an exciting finish, I may say that we are going to build our stations upon the Morden extension railway to the most modern pattern. We are going to discard entirely all ornament. We are going to build in reinforced concrete. The station will be simply a hole in the wall, everything being sacrificed to the doorway and some notice above to tell you to what the doorway leads. We are going to represent the DIA gone mad, and in order that I may go mad in good company I have got Holden to see that we do it properly.

It will be gathered from the last sentence that his ideas had not gone through without some hard words from members of his board. At the end of the year he knew that the debate must be closed down; time was running short. He wrote to Holden:

I have again been to Earls Court to see the model. I think it is much improved. In so far as the architecture of the station is concerned I have no more comments to make upon the exterior. I am still critical of the roof of the interior, and I think it needs further consideration. Some slight modification in the lighting is also necessary on the outside to ensure that the bull's-eye signs fixed on the canopy are illuminated over the whole extent of their surface, but our signal engineer will attend to this. There is one matter which, one day, will come up for solution, the exhibition of posters upon the outside, and while it is not the intention to put posters upon the outside of this station at this time we should have in mind that some day they will appear. It seems to me that there is space for posters upon the piers, and it will be wise that you should consider this problem now rather than that it should be patched later.

He was never able to forget his advertising though for the moment architecture was the thing.

Clapham South Station stands on a site overlooking a corner of the Common. The high block which is the station proper is flanked on either side by a low wing containing small shops; it is faced not with faience slabs as had been originally contemplated but with Portland stone. Its special character is emphasised by a broad frame of plain masonry that gives the building something of the formality of a stage proscenium or a great portal. The treatment is one that was afterwards to become perhaps a little too popular with designers of shops, factories and cinemas; there was just a touch of pseudo-Egyptian grandeur about it that seemed to make the entrance look more impressive than inviting. Under the projecting entrance canopy there is not the one 'hole in the wall' that had at first been contemplated but the set of three 'holes' demanded by the shape of the site. The idea of a folding screen is clearly expressed in the round columns that like a sort of hinge divide the great window into its three parts. How versatile this articulated window turned out to be is shown in some of the other stations that followed after Clapham South; the angles of the fronts range from the flat front of Morden to the acute angle of one of the two corner entrances to Tooting Bec Station, where the breadth of the apex is so small that the entrance openings had to be moved back towards the rear of the building. Over all these entrances runs the same projecting concrete canopy with its blue fascia bearing the station name in white letters. The canopy serves three purposes: it keeps the rain out of the entrance; it enables the station name to be boldly displayed; it contains the fittings that throw light both upwards over the face of the building and downwards over the entrance. The Underground bull's eye device finds a place in the middle of the main window; two others, mounted on the little masts that have since appeared in so many other places, are bracketed out from the wall on either side. At Clapham South the fact that the angle of the corner site is almost exactly 60° brought a temptation to form an hexagonal ticket hall that Holden was not able to resist. The ticket hall is full of daylight coming in through the big window but the light from this source cannot reach back to the escalator landing at the rear, and so a set of three polygonal skylights are introduced at this point; the same shape of skylight is used again in some of the other stations on the line.

When the extension was opened in the autumn of 1926 the event was recorded in a handsome brochure, most of the text of which bears every sign of being Pick's own work. There are two dozen illustrations in all and it is interesting to find that only a couple of them are of the new stations – Pick had not let his personal involvement in the architecture distract him from the main job of paying tribute to the engineers who had built the tube. The caption he wrote for the photograph of Clapham South starts by asking 'What is a station?' and goes on to give the answer: 'An inviting doorway in an architectural setting that cannot be missed by the casual pedestrian.' In later years his aim in station design was to grow rather more complex but the 'inviting doorway' always remained one of the essential requirements. The only other illustration in this brochure is a sectional diagram of Tooting Broadway. The site conditions at Clapham South had made it necessary to turn the escalator shaft at right angles to the tracks. This most unusual arrangement involved design complications which could most easily be got round by putting the bottom escalator landing just above the level of the running tunnels and connecting it with the platforms by means of flights of stairs. Pick, however, was anxious wherever possible to keep to the typical City & South London arrangement in which the landing and the platforms were grouped together between the tracks all on the same level. In the end the engineers managed to find a way by swinging the tunnels wide apart, far enough to allow the lengthened escalator shaft to squeeze in over the top of the nearest tunnel down to the level of the platforms. Yet though the need for stairs had thus been avoided another design fault had not been avoided – passengers making for the southbound platform would have to turn round at the bottom and continue in a reverse direction to that in which they had come down the escalator. Pick's efforts to make up for this unavoidable fault led to an interesting design improvement. The escalator landing was extended right and left to give two-way access to each of the two platforms. The extensions had the effect of turning the landing into a long hall or concourse lying between the platforms. It was something quite new in the Underground's subterranean architecture, a new idea that in later years was to be further explored.

Another invaluable lesson learnt from the operation of the Morden extension stations was the ease with which the basement-level station idea would lend itself to the design of stations of different size and capacity. If this sort of station was going to be built in central London a new Piccadilly Circus Station would be the obvious choice. In the space of less than twenty years the number of passengers using this station had gone up from $1\frac{1}{4}$ million in the first year to 25 million, and it looked as if the figures would for some time continue to rise. A more spacious station was needed. The existing building would not allow any sort of enlargement, and moreover its position directly over the point of intersection of the two tubes, while very suitable for lifts, would prove extremely awkward for an escalator installation. What was this new station going to look like? Bank Station, the prototype basement-level station, had little amenity value – it was a formless void about as interesting as a warehouse floor. Pick had made up his mind that the new Piccadilly Circus Station must above all have form. And now that Nash's lovely Circus had been destroyed, leaving only a name that meant nothing, why not make the station into a circus and give the name back its meaning? As soon as Holden had finished his first sketch-plans the problem was again taken to the engineering shop at Earls Court where a full-size mock-up was built, tested, taken to pieces and re-arranged. What finally emerged was a big round chamber, more distorted circle than ellipse, with its 50yd long axis lying roughly north and south. Radiating out from the ticket hall are five subway passages giving access from no less than eight entrance stairways of a width that Pick and Holden would undoubtedly have made a little greater if the Westminster City Council had allowed them to do so. Half of the middle area of the ticket hall is a big escalator landing, the other half a structure containing bookstalls and shops. Round this middle portion there runs what Holden described as an 'ambulatory': a double row of fifty columns serves both to help carry the roof and to lend an exciting sense of movement to the interior design. The concourse today gives little indication of its appearance when it was finished at the end of 1928. Holden's aim had been to reproduce in miniature the effect of an arcade of shops or pedestrian shopping street at night. There were no ceiling lights then – the only light sources round the ambulatory apart from the brightly lit window displays set into the outer wall were the lantern-shaped fittings suspended in pairs at the top of each column. The lighting enabled the carefully chosen finishing materials to look their best: the Travertine marble wall panels, the polygonal columns of red scagliola framed in narrow bronze fillets with their capitals and bases of solid bronze. It was a novel experience to see materials of this quality used in a railway station in this country.

The impression created by the Piccadilly Circus interior owed a great deal to the use of an ingenious new ticket machine. Experiments had been going on for some time with the object of simplifying the business of buying tickets. The first do-it-yourself passenger-operated machine had been introduced in 1904; eight years later this was superseded by an electric model which saved the passenger having to stop to pull a handle. The next big development was the introduction in the new Morden Line stations of the automatic ticket printing machine for the use of the ticket clerks. And now, almost but not quite in time for the opening of Piccadilly Circus station, the same manufacturer delivered a batch of a couple of dozen machines that did all these things but were designed to be operated by passengers merely inserting a coin or coins. They would also give you change when you used a sixpence or a shilling for buying a lower price ticket. When tests were made of passenger movement from street to platform an average saving was found of $2\frac{1}{2}$ minutes on the time taken in the old station at the corner of the Haymarket. This may not be a great deal of time but it made a most useful addition to all the other little savings that were helping to speed the traveller on his way. And these machines had another advantage which was to prove a boon to the station designer. The older kind being designed to hold a big stock of printed tickets were necessarily quite tall, mostly well over 6ft in height, but the new machines at Piccadilly Circus, with their rolls of blank paper, stood no higher than a man's shoulder. As you looked around the ticket hall you could see over the top of them, the view of the interior unobstructed by the usual clutter. Coming between the first big programme for tube extensions and the next, Piccadilly Circus marks the end of a chapter of Underground design and fore-shadows the opening of another. Pick was using the station as something that was part stocktaking exercise and part spring-board. Down below, the neat recessed head-wall panel in which the signal lights were combined with the train interval clock, the fire-fighting gear, the built-in automatic machines, sand bins, refuse bins, all told the same tale. Nor were the new standards of design confined to the spaces used by the public: the ticket booth interiors, signal cabins, permanent way tool rooms and other staff quarters, were all treated with the same concentrated care. Everywhere Pick was searching for new ways of doing things, and particularly ways of tightening design discipline and bringing a great wholeness of order into the completed work.

The results of his constant preoccupation with the passenger and passenger amenity are seen not only in the design of the stations. When the trains started to run again on the old City & South London line to Clapham Common at the end of 1924 the public found that the most antiquated tube rolling stock in London had been replaced with cars of startling modernity. Batches of new cars had been built for the Underground from time to time since the first tube trains of the early years of the century, but improvements in design had been mostly a matter of engineering materials and techniques, like the substitution of pressed steel for cast iron in certain parts; as far as the passenger was concerned there had been little noticeable change. In these new cars there were more cross-seats than in any of the earlier ones. There were arm-rests between every longitudinal seat and the comfort of the seats was something quite new. So indeed were the light fittings with their opal glass diffuser shades; the lighting was more power-ful but because no naked light bulbs were visible it was free from dazzle. And noise, too, though not abolished, was much reduced. Pick may not have been the first to discover the fact that tube trains were noisy but he certainly was the first to call in an expert in acoustics to study the problem of noise as it affected the rolling stock and give assistance to the engineers. A number of experiments included the fixing of sound-absorbing material round the bogies; this gave disappointing results and was later abandoned. When it got round to the transmission of noise through the car windows, however, the research team scored a real success. It was said of the new standard window, which was about half the size of the old types, that it had brought about 'the virtual elimination of rattle'. A more directly useful improvement was the arrangement and design of the doors. Press-button doors worked by compressed air had first been adopted just after the war but they were a labour-saving device rather than a passenger amenity, and when a little later all the doors on the train were worked by one guard from a single button the saving in labour was indeed substantial. Pick, too, was interested in saving labour but he was much more interested in saving passengers time and trouble. Any avoidable delay in getting passengers in and out of the train would prolong the waiting time of the train in the station and this in turn would increase the total journey time. Were the old doors really doing their job of unloading and loading as efficiently as they should? The doors were power-operated but they were the same as those earlier doors, opened and shut by hand, doors in which you could still see the likeness of the original ancestor, the single-leaf horse-carriage door just wide enough for one person at a time; the only difference was that they were more awkward and time-wasting than the horse-carriage door because they all opened by being swung inwards. In the new cars there were no single doors. Four pairs of double doors, two pairs in each side, were so positioned, well away from the ends, as to be equally accessible from every seat in the car. And the old idea of a door hung on hinges, too, had gone for good. Each pair of sliding doors as it rolled open left a clear opening 4ft 6in wide unobstructed by a middle pillar. For the first time in our railway history passengers about to board a train did not have to stand on the platform waiting for the ones who were getting out – the two streams could start moving together. To say that a new piece of equipment is in advance of its time is to use a meaningless phrase, but in these tube cars designed in the early 1920s the functional requirements had been defined with a thoroughness that left no dark areas for a later generation to explore.

Honest Building

In the autumn of 1926, when the trains were running on the tube line to Morden and preliminary work was going forward on the new Piccadilly Circus Station, Pick and Holden turned to their next job – the new headquarters office building. The existing building put up by the old Metropolitan District Company lay straddled over the railway tracks with a long frontage facing due north in the direction of St James's Park, after which the station took its name. At ground level the frontage was split into two parts by the central station entrance and ticket hall. Just before the war the company had been ready to start rebuilding the long block in sections, one section at a time; then the war had come. When the plans were taken up again it was decided to make a start with the half that lies between the station and the block of flats known as York Mansions in Petty France. They pulled down this portion and built a new six-storey block on the site. It is a dull-looking building with a front of glazed brick, white above a workhouse-brown lower part. In 1926 the board decided that the rebuilding of the other half should go forward. Their intention at first was to do no more than replace the old office block standing in the shallow space between the railway tracks and the street, and this was the site originally proposed to Holden. Pick however was never happy about the idea. The site was in truth a most awkward one, a sort of unbalanced rhomboid with a piece chopped out of it where the old offices stood. In an article written a little later Holden explained his disappointment at finding that it 'offered little opportunity for satisfactory development round its periphery'. In a private note he went further and told how 'many rough plans were prepared and all abandoned without a second thought'. Pick for his part was anxious to avoid having a new building that would perpetuate the awkward access to St James's Park Station. The great majority of passengers using the station came from the direction of Victoria Street; to reach the station entrance they had to make a long circuit in the street round to the far side of the building. Would it not be possible to give these passengers a direct means of access from Victoria Street through the back of the station? The company owned all the land at the rear. He asked Holden to produce a plan for a building occupying the whole of the site and containing a passage that would lead from the corner on the Victoria Street side straight into the station. But when he saw Holden's sketches he could not but agree that there was no satisfactory way of inserting such a passage into a building designed to fit neatly into the boundaries of the difficult site. Presently, as Holden worked on the layout of the passage which would cut the ground plan into two unequal halves, he suddenly saw how the passage formed the base of an isosceles triangle which was the north-eastern half pointing down Tothill Street. A line bisecting the triangle would cut across the passage at right angles. From this discovery it was but a natural step to imagine the entire length and breadth of the site occupied by a building of cruciform shape sitting diagonally athwart it. It was a kind of building first made familiar by Alfred Waterhouse's University College Hospital; Holden and his partners had later adopted a similar plan for the new Belgrave Hospital in Kennington. The idea made a strong appeal to Pick. There was just one difficulty – the board of directors had intended to proceed at this stage only with the replacement of the existing buildings and to leave the development of the rear part of the site till a later stage. This plan of Holden's was quite unsuitable for carrying out in stages; if the plan was to be accepted the whole site must be cleared; the new building must go up in one piece. Pick never lost much time in making decisions, but on this occasion he acted with more than his customary speed. On the morning of his board meeting he sent for Holden; they had a final talk just after luncheon. Later that same afternoon, after the meeting, he sent Holden a message telling him that the board had agreed to go ahead with his entire scheme.

Pick at this stage had no clear idea of the kind of building he wanted but his idea of the kind he did not want was very clear. In the previous ten years or so he had watched new buildings going up in the City and West End and in his own City of Westminster. The more he saw of them the less he liked them. As usual, he set himself to rationalise his feelings, and as he put those feelings into words there grew in him a new perception of the part that buildings should play in the architecture of a great city. He talked about it in the address he gave to the Art Workers' Guild in February 1917. The subject of the address was 'Art in Household Things', but there were some matters not concerned with household things that he had to get off his chest and this was one of them. He said:

126

The elevations are in perfect symmetry on all sides. Tower balances tower; pilaster, pilaster; window, window; flourish of carving, flourish of carving. Nothing is left to chance. See a bit and you can guess the rest. The stonework throughout is mechanically perfect. All the corner stones of its angles are rusticated – but rusticated to a pattern. All the carving on capitals and keystones is alike. Now who shall dare analyse the significance of this? It is the servile State with a brainless master.

In the article he wrote in 1922 for the *Nineteenth Century and After* he said of the new Port of London Authority building that 'if it expresses anything at all it is a bureaucratic pride'. The same vulgar pride in newly acquired social power, or what was imagined to be social power, appeared in all of these buildings, in the hugeness of their scale, in the height, the rotundity, of their fluted, garlanded columns. This is not 'following a tradition. It is rather some weird metamorphosis of intelligence demanding the attention of a mental specialist. It is making a folly of the achievement of the age.'

In the event Pick's belief in Holden's ability to produce an important office block free from the extravagance of stock symbolism was to prove well justified. The critics writing about the finished office building were struck by its sincere acceptance of the conditions of its time, sincere but not ostentatiously so. The best contemporary architecture is animated by a high regard for honesty and truth and the Underground building was immediately recognised as a very honest building. When Robert Byron published his *Appreciation of Architecture* five years later it was still the only London building to which he could refer in words of unqualified praise. In order to explain what he means by good architecture, Byron invites the reader to compare it with buildings like Baker's new Bank of England and the ICI headquarters in Millbank, 'an agglomeration of borrowed themes, cheap symbolism, and tea-shop elegance'. The Underground building for all its faults shows 'consideration for the capacities of the human eye'; it is clear that its designer knows what has constituted architecture through the ages.

The comments quoted above represented expert views. What did the general public have to say? It has to be admitted that to the general public the building was known less for itself than as a setting for a display of the most unusual kind; it was, said *The*

Times, 'the first example of an important building decorated by a group of well-known artists commissioned for the purpose'. It was 'a great achievement'. The only pity was that eight of the ten pieces of sculpture were placed so high above street level. At the point where the wings are set back, just above the sixth floor windows, a broad band of Portland stone runs continuously round the four wings to form parapets to the flat roofs. On this band eight flying figures carved in bold relief symbolise the four winds, three by Eric Gill and one each by five other sculptors. Each figure occupies a space in the wall design which, though clearly defined, is not in anyway accented; the sculptures seem to grow out of the wall almost casually like the carved brackets in a medieval church. Their quality is unequal; the most interesting is undoubtedly Henry Moore's 'West Wind', a strong, plain figure unencumbered with the wings and draperies that are used with varying effect in the others. Unfortunately, being placed upon the north wall of the west wing, it cannot be seen from either of the adjoining streets.

Lower down the building, at a height of 15ft above the Broadway pavement, there had been working in that spring of 1929 another artist whose daily arrivals and departures excited much curiosity; already the critics and the letter writers to *The Times* who had gathered to attack Epstein's memorial to W. H. Hudson in Hyde Park were sharpening their pencils in anticipation. In the third week of March the *Daily Mirror* had a spicy piece about the artist's working dress which included 'an astonishing red jersey'; three weeks later the *Daily Graphic* came out with a picture of 'Mr Epstein, muffled and mysterious, entering the locked hut on the new Underground building where he is working in extreme secrecy'. At the end of May the Press were invited to a private view of 'Night', the first of the groups to be completed. It was a group strongly carved in a kind of boldly projecting flat relief, about 9ft high. A male form lies extended in the lap of a brooding maternal figure, it is the traditional Pietà arrangement but instead of mourning there is peace and rest: the mother is drawing her great hand over the recumbent body, her own eyes are closed while with a gesture of incantation she seems to be stilling her son to sleep. Epstein's work had always aroused controversy; the entry of the Hudson 'Rima' into the wooded grove had incited the critics to anger, but never to such anger as this; James Bone writing in the *Manchester Guardian* spoke about

128

'storms of criticism rising at times into terms of full-blooded abuse that are rarely heard in art controversy in England'. Then the scaffolding came down and the Press photographers arrived for shots of the curious crowds. 'New Epstein enigma': said the *Daily Herald,* 'What nationality is the woman?' A reader of the *Daily Express* wrote describing her as a 'prehistoric blood-sodden cannibal intoning a horrid ritual over a dead victim'. Among the few lonely voices raised in defence was that of Edgar Wallace, the novelist.

When 'Day' was revealed to the public gaze on the last day of June the fat really was in the fire. 'Even worse than "Night"' seemed to be the general verdict. 'Aesthetically meaningless', said the *Telegraph*; the *Daily News* confessed itself 'staggered'. In the *Manchester Guardian*, whose cautious editor had felt obliged to have the photograph bowdlerised, James Bone described it with unusual understanding:

A large father figure with a fierce face, flat and hard and round like the sun at noon, holds and presents a male child standing between his knees, while the child stretches up his arms towards the neck of the father, his face turning upwards in a gesture of reluctance to face his task. The main pattern of the group is made of the two pairs of arms, the small ones within the larger, and the four legs forming the base. It is one of the most inventive Mr Epstein has evolved. The power to imagine and deliver his idea with its uncanny fire are tremendously there . . . Do we know that Epstein is bringing new beauty to our generation?

The answer, clearly, was no. 'They are neither Christian nor pagan,' cried Percy Gardner in a letter to *The Times,* 'but only bad dreams.' Sir Reginald Blomfield, the architect, joined the mob that gathered in the pages of the *Manchester Guardian* to protest against Bone's suggestion that Mr Epstein's work, although perhaps a little different from that of Madame Tussaud, was not the less deserving of serious attention. 'Bestiality still lurks below the surface of our civilisation', he wrote, 'but why grope about for it in the mud, why parade it in the open, why not leave it to wallow in its own primeval slime?' As if in answer to Sir Reginald's question a squad of intrepid hooligans driving past bombarded 'Night' with glass containers full of liquid tar. No doubt it was only by its inaccessible position that it was spared the painted swastikas with which our native Jew-baiters had decorated the Hudson memorial a few years earlier.

On 4 July 1929 a meeting of the Underground boards was held. There had been some angry letters from shareholders and everything pointed to a somewhat stormy debate. Among the directors present was Sir Ernest Clark; many years later he was still able to give a lively account of it. The board felt, he stated,

> that the Underground Group had become involved in a scandal; Epstein had brought disgrace upon them and it looked as though something would have to be done to remove that disgrace. A proposal came up that the sculptures should be erased from the building. It could easily be done; the wall could be cut back to a plain surface and then the trouble would soon blow over and everything would be forgotten. But the shareholders' money had been spent and if the sculptures were destroyed then that money would be wasted. Yet was it not better that their money should be wasted than that they should suffer such ignominy as this? The shaking of heads was finally interrupted by another director, Lord Colwyn, the septuagenarian cotton and rubber magnate. The sculptures should come down and some other sculptor should be asked to replace them with works more acceptable to the people of London. Lord Colwyn personally would foot the bill, the new sculptures were to be regarded as a gift. It was a generous offer and the board received it with suitable expressions of gratitude. Pick, however, asked for and obtained a few days reprieve.

The minute of the meeting records that he was to 'consult with the architect upon the matter with a view to ascertaining whether any modification could be made to meet the criticism'. Clark ended his account by telling how Pick on that same evening handed Ashfield a letter offering his resignation. Stanley Heaps, the Underground's staff architect, recalled what happened next. At Pick's urgent request Holden agreed to speak to the sculptor. There is a passage in Epstein's autobiography which suggests that at one point a compromise solution was proposed by James Bone's artist brother Muirhead, whose intercession with the First Commissioner of Works in 1925 had prevented the Hudson memorial being thrown out of Hyde Park. A little later the scaffolding was again set up in front of 'Day' and Epstein mounted to the top. After he had worked for an hour or two it was seen that the little boy's member had been reduced to somewhat more

130

infantile dimensions: it was now shorter by 1½in. The operation was doubly successful. True, it did not prevent Holden, at the time when he was appointed architect to the new London University buildings, being told that it was a condition of his employment that Epstein must never be allowed near them. But it did save Epstein's 'Night' and 'Day' from the fate that befell his row of high-relief figures on the headquarters of the British Medical Association, when that building was acquired by the pure-minded government of Southern Rhodesia. It also removed any danger, if such did in fact exist, that Pick might be finding himself out of a job.

Presently there came another letter from Stabler, who was anxious to see Pick and asked him to suggest a date. But Pick was able to offer no such suggestion. Though the Epstein storm had started to subside by then he was 'still struggling with the critics and with my own judgement'. Was his own judgement perhaps the main difficulty? He had never been an admirer of Epstein's work. He had seen a good deal of it for some years past, at the Leicester Galleries' exhibition of 1924, in Hyde Park where 'Rima' was unveiled in the following year. At Christmas time in 1925 he had been to the Royal Academy winter exhibition of international art; he had been somewhat depressed by the quality of the English contribution which he told Harry Peach was 'very poor'. And, he added, 'I am thoroughly tired of Epstein's ugly women.' Some ten years later when he got to know Nikolaus Pevsner he talked to him about Holden's headquarters building one day. There were a number of things about it that he did not much care for, he said, and among them were the sculptures. He had been compelled to put up a fight for them but it was really for Holden that he had done the fighting. He had given Holden the job; how could he possibly have failed to back him up?

The Idiom Perfected

The new headquarters building had been in occupation for some twelve months when the next stage in the Underground's architecture was opened by the passing of the Act authorising the two-way extension of the Piccadilly Line. The siting of the stations here would offer the designer greater scope than had any of the new stations built so far. These earlier stations lay in built-up areas so that their exteriors had of necessity to be treated as an

131

integral part of a street; in no place had it been possible to design a complete building 'in the round'. In the Piccadilly Line stations this interesting possibility would certainly arise. Pick was in no way dissatisfied with the architectural idiom that Holden had developed for the Morden Line stations but it would be out of the question that they should carry on with it as it stood. The procedure with Clapham South Station had shown how valuable a full-size prototype could be in getting the minds of all those concerned focused on an architectural problem. It looked as if Sudbury Town would be the most suitable place for another such experiment and this station was at once put on the short list of priority rebuilding jobs. The railway general manager sketched out his first layout plans and within forty-eight hours of their arrival on Pick's desk the plans had been thoroughly discussed in full committee and sent to Holden for development. After that came a period of anxious discussions. Holden's first sketches for the station building were examined at the end of May 1930; a number of comments and suggestions were made but no clear conclusions emerged. Pick had to make up his mind quickly what should be the next step.

When Holden was working on the Morden tube stations he had been employed as a consultant alongside Stanley Heaps, the Underground's staff architect, supplying him with so-called 'finished roughs' to be used by Heaps in the preparation of full working drawings. But in 1930 Heaps and his office staff were heavily loaded with other work and it was arranged that Holden's firm should act as the fully responsible architects as for the headquarters building, with Heaps advising on practical railway matters. It now occurred to Pick that since Holden was to give the company so much more of his time it might be useful if some of that extra time could be given to a little further exploration. And better still perhaps if the exploring could be done by the two of them together. Towards the end of July he set off with Holden on a journey round northern Europe. In the space of two and a half weeks they travelled to Berlin, Hamburg, Düsseldorf and Cologne; they also visited towns in Denmark, Sweden and Holland. They looked with some excitement, not unmixed with envy, at the splendid collection of stadiums, arenas, swimming baths, playgrounds for the youth of the new Germany, that remain the principal legacy of American aid to Europe after World War I. The buildings were simple, unpretentious, expressive only of a new kind of concern for the physical health of the people. But the new architecture of the cities was different. On the one hand there was the traditional sort, 'massive, grandiose, unpleasant . . . Perhaps it is fortunate for Germany that her architects have concentrated on the new rather than the old.' Yet, on the other hand, in the 'new' the revolt against tradition was too extreme, too violently iconoclastic. 'German architecture has gone farther than that of any other country in its break with the past and the results cannot be said to be particularly satisfactory.' Having noted with dismay the sharp division between ponderous orthodoxy and exacerbated rebellion which they found in Germany they moved on to the adventurous romanticism of Gunnar Asplund and other Swedish eclectics – 'a grand hotch-potch of all that has ever been done before.' Here, too, came disappointment. In a letter to Stabler Pick wrote:

> Everywhere in Sweden you see experiment taking place, but experiment which is not wholly successful. It almost always reflects something else which can be seen to better advantage in some other city of the world. For example, the Stockholm town hall is frankly based upon the Palace of the Doges at Venice, only it is not as fine a job. The Skandia theatre is based upon a medieval tilt yard. The Stockholm concert hall borrows the Palladian tradition. The elements of failure appear in all sorts of places. It is no doubt extraordinary that there should be so much experiment taking place in a relatively small place like Stockholm, but the accomplishment is not such as to warrant Stockholm being held up to us as an example.

On the final stage of their journey the travellers met with a more rewarding experience. As had happened to English architects many years before, in the reigns of Queen Mary II and her sister Anne, their eyes were opened to the virtues of an architecture as practised by the Dutch. Pick, when he wrote to Harold Stabler, had nothing but praise for the simple brick architecture of Hilversum and Bussum. What was it that made these Dutch buildings so satisfactory? 'There is a restraint and sanity', says the printed report on the tour, 'which contrasts favourably with the extravagant revolt of the new architecture in Germany. Some of the most interesting examples were seen in Hilversum. The general impression is one of orderly planning which, however, has nowhere been permitted to become mechanical or dehumanised.' The town hall at Hilversum was the reverse of Stockholm – practical, down-to-earth, prose that was not ashamed of being just good prose. And indeed the architecture of Holland in the period between the wars made an impression on Pick that he was to carry with him till the end of his life. In a short book *Britain Must Rebuild*, which he wrote ten years later, he came back to the subject. 'Functionalism, based on the necessities of construction and plan, fulfilled its task of eliminating all that was superfluous and extraneous, but it has not yet organised itself as a style.' In Willem Dudok's town hall there is 'an outstanding example of how, without departing from fulfilment of purpose, an asymmetrical assembly of cubical elements can be piled up in a dynamic manner to interest the eye and stir the mind. Imagination has played around it.' He concluded:

> Where imagination is scarce, as in sober fact it is, some touch of the baroque seems to be the garnish with which functionalism should be served: it should prove as natural an association as the scent that goes with rose and lily, or as the dapple of stripes or spots on zebra and giraffe. Before functionalism can take its place fully and gratefully as the current style of building it must learn what it is that it lacks to make it cultured. Its vitamin content is too low.

At the time when Pick wrote those words most people had forgotten all about the Hilversum town hall; the only style for which the new forward-looking architects had any use was the international concrete style. It was not till the late 1940s that people started to rediscover the modest virtues of Dudok's building. 'A declaration of love and admiration', was what Mumford called it then, 'for the higher purposes men hold in common.' Little wonder that the report of the Pick–Holden tour tells us that among the various countries visited Holland was the only one in which the travellers wished they had been able to spend more time. Here, in this clean, homely, straightforward architecture of the Dutch, they felt they had found the right idiom for the experiment at Sudbury Town. It had all the right qualities. It was 'controlled by use and purpose'. It was producing buildings that you could not only 'walk round' but that seemed to grow better as you walked round them. To Pick perhaps its greatest quality lay in its relationship to the traditional. The main concern of the Germans seemed to be to demonstrate their execration of the past; in Sweden the architects were quite fond of the past, but they were fond in the wrong way – they would dress up their buildings in a random mixture of old styles as little girls will show themselves off in their mothers' old party dresses. To the Dutch architects the past was a subject neither of hate nor of playful affection; it was soberly accepted and used as a starting point for present design. Their new architecture, says the report, carried on 'the spirit if not the letter' of the old. It had grown out of the past, their own past. It 'connected'.

No doubt the Dutch architect owed a great deal to his material. 'He has one enormous advantage', the report points out, 'over his colleagues in other countries. The problems of the most suitable material with which to cover his building have been solved for him, for he has to hand that beautiful Dutch brick which is at once so delicate and so flexible, and which does not seem materially to have changed its character since the days when Pieter de Hooch began to portray it in his pictures.' And this material most fortunately was to be found also in England; it was not rare in this country though it was most rare among mankind at large since it existed on only a small part of the earth's surface. It was a material that more than any other circumstance of geography or population had bestowed its peculiar character on the level regions stretching from the Baltic across the Channel, up the Humber, up the Thames Valley as far as Reading and beyond. It was a friendly material and a beautiful one. Countries not endowed with the right sort of clay would make pathetic attempts to emulate its qualities; when Pick was in Stockholm he could sympathise with Ivar Tengbom whose Högalid Church, he pointed out, 'suffers from the use of the same ugly brick with which all Swedish architects have to contend'.

The report on the trip was duly circulated and Pick spent a week or two discussing it with his colleagues; after that he settled down to work with Holden. The prototype station at Sudbury Town was ready in the third week of July 1931. The old Metropolitan District station, whose place it took, was one of those long, dim bungalow structures held down by a gabled roof of the shiny slate so beloved by the builders of our minor suburban stations of the last century; the roof sprang forward over the middle portion to form a canopy adorned with the traditional scalloped valance; the windows and doors were openings cut out at random having no relationship to one another; posters of every

135

size and shape were squeezed into the intervening spaces. To crown the edifice a pair of ponderous chimney stacks, heavily corniced, stood high above the roof. Such was the building that had now been swept away to make room for the Holden station. If the general dimensions and shape of this new station are not very different from those of Morden, its character is utterly dissimilar. Instead of the masonry treatment with its spare mouldings we find great masses of plain brick walling, meticulously bonded, left to spread unencumbered by any architectural accretion or embellishment. Instead of the canopy protruding over the entrance that divides the typical Morden structure into two parts of unequal size we see a pair of tall openings, run up the full height of the building, in which the glazed window areas come to a stop over the entrances casually, without fuss; the windows might be only rolling shutters made of glass drawn up to let the passengers in. The whole building is so neutral, so devoid of emphasis, that as we see it today and compare it with its successors it looks less like a prototype than an unfinished study in massing, proportion, basic form – a head roughly blocked out by a sculptor in preparation for the features which when they have been worked into it will make it an individual creation of the human mind. Nevertheless it was no doubt true at the time that it was this very quality of self-denying austerity that appealed most strongly to the architecturally minded public. When Morton Shand was reviewing the Royal Academy 1932 summer exhibition he wrote of the architect's perspective drawing: 'Though it is hung low and almost in a corner, Adams, Holden & Pearson's Sudbury Town Station projects itself stereoscopically, by virtue of its actuality, from the potpourri of lavender-scented memories from all our faded yesterdays which virtually monopolise these walls. Every other untraditional building in the room is subordinate to it in interest.' 'A landmark', Sir Nikolaus Pevsner called it when he was writing about it some years later. 'Its completion marks the opening of the "classic" phase of Underground architecture; 1930–1935 can be considered the "classic" years.'

Pevsner's statement that Sudbury Town Station may be regarded a 'landmark' in the history of Pick's work is true in more senses than one. For it was to Pick not just a new and better sort of building. Ever since the completion of the Piccadilly Circus job, he had been determined to tighten up the arrangements for station furniture and equipment. The example of

Charles Rennie Mackintosh had left him feeling that it just was not good enough that a new station building should be handed over to the management as the empty shell of a house is presented to its owner. The jobs that managed to bring out the best in Mackintosh were those where he had an opportunity of producing a house with its principal rooms completely fitted out – decoration, fixtures and furniture, everything treated as a part of a single comprehensive design. It was not, however, till 1930, when Pick and Holden went on their tour of the north European countries, that Pick suddenly saw the possibility of putting Mackintosh's example to practical use. The Danes did not at that time hold any position of international leadership in design; what had impressed Pick in their country was not the sort of high quality that causes individual products to win international fame, but the consistent use of qualified designers regardless of the size or importance of the job. The printed report of that European trip has a revealing paragraph on this subject:

In the østergade there was a small shop going by the name of Tedds' Teashop in which not only the interior decoration but even the paper wrappers for the tea had been designed by Helweg Møller. This characteristic of using the architect for the design of things quite other than buildings appears common in Copenhagen. At the time of our visit, several new buses and two new trams were running about the streets of the city which had been designed by the city architect. It is, indeed, this extension of the principles of architectural design to things like buses and trams, and to quite small objects like tea wrappers or match boxes, which is perhaps one of Denmark's most interesting contributions to contemporary design.

In the summer of 1930 Pick sent a memorandum addressed to the general manager and the chief civil engineer instructing them to supply Holden with a complete specification of all the equipment required for each of the stations along the Line. 'Nothing shall be built', he said, 'which has not been specially designed to conform with the general architectural scheme.' It was something never before attempted in the history of the railways. After that Pick kept away from Sudbury Town Station till the Saturday following the day the trains started to run. What he saw made him furious. 'Too many afterthoughts' was his comment to the general manager. 'For example, as you enter the station I was not aware that we were going to have two illuminated tombstones upon which to display formal notices. The size is wrong for the purpose of the notices, but in any event the tombstones are merely obstructive of the clear space of the hall. The manner in which they are fixed is what I would call jerry-built, and you will note the gas piping, once more, for carrying the wiring cable. I think the whole performance unsatisfactory.' Fire extinguishers had arrived but no place had been provided to accommodate them.

On the platforms I found that some seven or eight automatic machines have been dumped down and are now going to spoil the cleanness and clearness of the platforms. Somehow there seems to be a desire on the part of everyone to break up and destroy the tidiness and spaciousness of this station. The only way in which, in my opinion, the spaciousness can be filled properly is by passengers, and not by a lot of impediments . . . Going over the bridge I note that the whole of the lighting of the bridge is an afterthought. The bulkhead lights are now being screwed on to the concrete instead of being sunk into the concrete as would have been done if the lighting had been designed properly and at the proper time. There is an entire lack of design and orderly workmanship.

Wherever he looked Pick could see evidence of the same lack of thought. He concluded: 'Our effort to provide a model station at Sudbury Town appears to have failed. The criticisms which I raise upon Sudbury Town have application to all our other stations which are now in course of building. Now that we know we have failed we had better review the plans of all the other stations, to make sure that all items of equipment are properly dealt with once more.'

After that, as he went on inspecting station after station, he came to the conclusion that his general manager's station committee was not the right organ on which to fix the responsibility for co-ordinating all the contents of the buildings. He must take on the job himself, at his weekly engineering meetings. Towards the end of August 1931 he wrote to the chief engineer about his idea for the new procedure:

Unless some special effort is made, there is every prospect that the stations and works will have to be botched, just as Sudbury

Town station had to be botched, by a failure to have a clear plan of what is required before the work is carried out. I think, therefore, we should have placed before us, at once, plans showing the lighting scheme for all stations, and the whole of the miscellaneous equipment required; also plans showing the location and form of all signs and notices at stations, and a plan showing the water supply and any further arrangements that may be necessary for cleaning. We cannot regard a station as being approved for execution until all these various plans are agreed.

He was tough in his criticism but he knew how to praise when appreciation was called for. In May 1933 he found himself studying Turnpike Lane Station, which was only just fully finished though it had been open for traffic for the previous eight months. He wrote to the chief engineer: 'I am pleased with Turnpike Lane station now that it is completed. The subways are an improvement upon subways previously built. I also think the lavatories are very good; and the canteen sets a new standard. Altogether the group of buildings that we have here are a credit to our undertaking.'

The next big stations at the western end of the line were Sudbury Hill, Alperton and Acton Town. Sudbury Hill has three windows, one each on three sides of the building, instead of the pair on the front only. The strong horizontal accent of the canopy is used again both in this station and in Acton Town, but it is used with discretion, to serve a clearly seen purpose; at Alperton smaller ancillary structures add emphasis so that further reinforcement by a canopy over the entrance becomes unnecessary. At the northern end of the line the shape of the Bounds Green site demands that a corner should be splayed off and so the ticket hall becomes an octagonal block, a reminder of the Clapham South hexagon; the four tall windows fill the whole of the narrower sides that form the four corners. Turnpike Lane offers a problem not unlike that at Sudbury Hill and the solution here is a very similar one. Then, all at once, a new conception appears. In his memorandum of instructions about station furnishing and equipment Pick had inserted a paragraph which said that wherever there was a chance of acquiring extra land over and above the station site proper this should be done so that the station might be made part of a larger architectural layout. At Southgate the estate agent's department had been fortunate. The big site forms a corner where two roads meet at an angle of about 60°; it is big enough for the tip of the corner to be cut off by a short length of private roadway. The tip is left as an elliptical island and on this island the station building stands with a crescent of shops as a background. Its shape is that of a low circular drum; its height can be kept down because the building is given the necessary substance by its central position in an extended unit. The combination of a station block of less than average height with a broad architectural setting was never again achieved on the same scale as at Southgate. The lack of height does, however, cause this station block to compare somewhat unfavourably with the circular ticket halls of Chiswick Park and Arnos Grove that rise in a splendid sweep above a lower rectangular structure. At Chiswick Park a small tower is introduced, intended no doubt to make the building more visible from the main Chiswick High Road which runs a couple of hundred yards away. It serves the practical purpose of a signpost. This Chiswick Park tower was not felt to be a success. At Bounds Green and Turnpike Lane the engineers need high-level air intakes for the tube ventilation plant; the practical utility of these towers, expressed in heavily louvred openings, proves a help to the designer in his task of conjugating them with the building below.

There was still no satisfactory solution to the tower problem; these last two station towers are very different from the Chiswick Park one but they are no better – they are bulky, they sit too heavily on the ground. Presently at Boston Manor and Osterley we find fresh experiments with a slim decorative column standing on a tower block of less height as on a pedestal. It is a device that had attracted the attention of Pick and Holden on their visit to Holland. They had found the Dutch architects to be most soberminded people not given to extravagance or playfulness in their buildings, but there was one amusing exception, a fondness for a sort of single obelisk-like column, or 'thin tower' as it is called in the report of their tour, introduced for no discernible purpose except that of announcing the presence of a building. Two of these towers which they came across in Amsterdam had struck them as of particular interest: the one that marked the main entrance to Jan Wils' city stadium, and the one placed on top of the *Telegraaf* newspaper building designed by J. F. Staal, a polygonal column with a heavily sculptured surface standing on a square tower attached to the main building. This was the type of outsize finial that Pick and Holden thought might be appropriate for Osterley. The station here would stand on a slight elevation heavily screened by houses and trees and with no main approach road to show it off. It needed some crowning feature that would allow it to be seen. In these days, when we have become accustomed to see the nakedness of new buildings relieved by abstract sculptural forms, Osterley Station would very likely be considered an experiment of considerable merit; indeed, if it had not been a product of the Pick–Holden partnership its merit might well have been recognised at the time. The fact that it was so badly received is no doubt to be seen as a tribute to the solid quality of the best of Holden's work – the flawless integrity of buildings like Southgate and Arnos Grove. A few years after the completion of these last two stations Hugh Casson described them as 'perfect examples of functionalism; a complete synthesis of the modern and the traditional, and an effective answer to those who object that modern architecture is characterless by reason of its internationalism.' It will be seen that Casson's judgement uses almost the same words that Pick and Holden used when they were defining their aims at the start of the Piccadilly Line adventure. Not only does it show considerable perspicuity on Casson's part, it also confirms that the two men did in fact succeed in doing that which they set out to do. 'The most perfect examples in London of the style of today, serviceable, uncompromisingly modern, and yet in keeping with the quiet distinction of the Georgian brick house.' Arnos Grove is the subject chosen for the illustration which appears on the page facing those words, the words of Sir Nikolaus Pevsner in his *Outline of European Architecture* published in 1943. Ian Nairn, a critic of the following generation, still finds Arnos Grove 'as fresh as ever after thirty years'. The little group of stations to which it belonged were, he says, 'the first modern buildings in England which did not throw their style in the public's face, and they are now reaping their reward for it, whilst the slick cubist theorems are already stone-dead.' They are likely to be remembered by future generations for another reason, too: in them we see the last flowering of that most endearing of all architectural materials, the genuine English brick, moulded or cut from the wet clay, now long since supplanted by a painted substitute.

5

LONDON TRANSPORT:
1923-1939

Public Board

In the summer of 1922, when work was under way on the first two sections of the extended Hampstead tube, Pick and his colleagues were faced with an ominous development. Large numbers of the General's buses had been called up for war service abroad; at the time of the armistice London was having to manage with only a little more than half of the company's fleet and now, nearly four years later, the buses were still far below strength. The situation was one of which the small independent operator could hardly have failed to take advantage. Once the first few had got going it was not long before they were joined by many others, often encouraged by offers of financial support from the commercial vehicle industry whose productive capacity had been stepped up during the war. 'They are the forerunners of a large army', warned *The Times*. 'They are a law unto themselves, their own traffic authority. Every week there are cases before the police against drivers of rival omnibuses for obstructing, racing or "blanketing" each other.' In a paper printed by the Underground Group at this time Pick described some of their ingenious tactics. He told how a bus would 'from hour to hour make sorties into every part of London, carefully choosing those streets where the pickings were likely to be fattest at a particular time. He gave the itineraries of individual buses that in one day had made between fifteen and twenty journeys to and from ten different terminal points. One bus had followed a trip from Charing Cross to Shepherds Bush and back with three trips between Victoria and the City. Having twice run out to Hendon during the afternoon it had finished the day by travelling from

Shepherds Bush to Walham Green. 'One of the proprietors', he wrote, 'in the course of one month changed the routes of his six buses 499 times. The buses appeared spasmodically at East Ham, Westbourne Grove, Dulwich, Stratford, South Croydon, Shepherds Bush, Camden Town, Putney, Barnet, Richmond, Ilford and other places.' During that month those six buses managed to disorganise twenty of the General's regular routes. No less than sixty-three routes in all had, he claimed, been gravely interfered with. Since they concentrated on skimming off traffic from the busiest routes the independents managed to keep their buses well filled. This meant that they could usually afford to undercut the General's services; in places like the area north of Finsbury Park where the demand was especially brisk their fares were on average about a third less.

Early in 1923 Ashfield made up his mind. His plan was disclosed to the public at a Press conference held at the Underground's headquarters. In the statement prepared for the meeting Pick explained how the Underground Group had been compelled to take firm measures against this reckless competition. 'In the long run', it said, 'wasteful provision of transport means inefficient service, with higher fares for the public and a more precarious employment and lower wages for the employees. The evils attaching to needless competition in transport are recognised everywhere. In New York, Paris, Berlin and other larger cities an authority deals with the problems of co-ordination.' The statement went on:

> The Underground Group of Companies represents the greatest measure of co-ordination yet attained in London transport. The services which it provides include many unremunerative routes and extensions of routes. If other undertakings operate services on the best routes only, and do not take their share of the lighter routes, the Underground Group cannot continue this policy and both the public and its own employees will suffer.

The Group therefore was compelled to fight back. The massive injection of independents into its regular routes was a shocking waste of precious resources but unfortunately the only way of combating this waste was to arrange to add still more to it. Buses would be taken out of bus-starved regular routes and poured into the swirling forays along the sixty-odd threatened routes, together with the new buses which were now being delivered at the rate of twenty-five a week.

At the Ministry of Transport, a new ministry set up at the end of 1919, they were still working on a Parliamentary Bill designed to put an end to the invasion. The London Traffic Bill, as it was called, would give the Minister powers to introduce a kind of rationing. Bus routes as well as the number of buses per hour on each route would require the Minister's approval and, moreover, a list of 'restricted streets' would be drawn up to which only a specified total number would have access. But the Bill made provision for a development of a more long-term significance than the cleaning-up of the bus trouble. Back in the summer of 1920 Ashfield had persuaded the Minister of Transport to invite the Leader of the London County Council to call at the Ministry for a talk with the Minister and himself. Among various points on which agreement had been reached was 'the necessity for the unified operation of local passenger transport services in London and adjacent districts'. The Bill had been drafted accordingly to empower the Underground Group and London's municipal tram undertakings to enter into financial agreements similar to those that had brought together the members of the present Underground Common Fund. But when the Bill came up in the House it was seen that this part had been jettisoned. The proposal was too controversial, it was bound to get the Bill into trouble. What the Bill finally did do when passed was to give the Minister powers to appoint a London and Home Counties Traffic Advisory Committee. Just twelve months after the passing of the Bill the committee started on the first of its enquiries – the enquiry for north and north-east London. In November 1925 Pick was called as a witness and members spent the better part of three days listening to him as with great thoroughness he expounded to them his plan for putting London's transport services on a satisfactory footing. When the committee's report came out, the members were found to have put themselves solidly behind Pick's arguments. There could be no improvement in the situation, said the report, so long as the destructive competition between one form of transport and another continued unchecked. And it went on: 'The proposals submitted by Mr Frank Pick, on behalf of the Underground Group, for the establishment of a common management and a Common Fund appear to present a possible solution of the whole problem of London's passenger transport, and these

144

proposals should be carefully examined without delay.' And so in its final report, published at the end of July 1927, the committee goes on to examine Pick's proposals in some detail. The Fund should include all local transport; while the suburban portions of the main-line railways would not at first be brought in there should be freedom to make any special pooling and clearing arrangements with railway companies that might be found expedient. The main partners in the Fund would be the LCC, the Underground Group, and the Metropolitan Railway Company. It took a couple more years of sordid Parliamentary manoeuvring before it suddenly looked as though something might start to happen. Pick had now taken over Ashfield's duties as managing director. At the beginning of June 1929 the second MacDonald Government came into power and Herbert Morrison was appointed Minister of Transport. A few days later Pick wrote Harry Peach a letter which ended with a few words on the subject of the new political scene. He said: 'I cannot say that I was very perturbed at the prospect of a Labour Government. I think it will be a very respectable Government for a while and then break down. But for the next year we shall have a progressive administration and that will be all to the good. We may get a few things done.' 'We may get a few things done.' That was what mattered. On the first Monday in December Morrison rose in the Commons to read a statement. The government, he said, accepted the analysis of the general problem on which the Ministry's committee had founded its scheme, and they agreed that a common management must be established for London's passenger transport. But they had decided that common ownership must come first. His government's policy was to start with 'the substitution of a single and simple form of public ownership for the complicated network of separate interests, private and municipal, which now add so greatly to the difficulties of the situation.'

On 1 August 1931 the Bank of England was forced to apply for credits to the Bank of France and the Federal Bank of the United States. There followed ominous speeches from the leaders of the Conservative and Liberal parties, the Prime Minister's hurried return from Lossiemouth and, on 24 August, his resignation. With the majority of junior ministers Morrison refused office in the National Government which MacDonald was commissioned to form. At Christmas time Harold Stabler and his wife Phoebe sent Pick a piece of bright blue pottery in the shape of a fish. 'The blue bird stands for happiness,' said Pick in his letter of thanks, 'but what of the blue fish that swims into my study? It has so many tails upon which to hang things; it may have as many significances as it has tails . . . But it is blue. I am blue. Things are blue. The world is blue. The rosy tinge has faded somehow. Still, yours is homeopathic treatment. All shall come well.' And in truth Morrison's Bill was still very much alive. MacDonald had brought in a Liberal, Percy John Pybus, as his Minister of Transport. Pybus worked steadily on the Bill through the winter and the spring of 1932. With the assistance of the main-line railways he induced the Metropolitan Railway Company to agree terms for the take-over of its undertaking; it was one of those problems that the original Bill had left for the future board to work out for itself. Another elaboration which was later to prove of great value was the proposal for a still bigger financial pool which was to take in the passenger earnings of the main-line railways' local services as well as those of the new board. Meanwhile the ten-year stretch of furious activity had left its mark on Pick. Early in 1932 he went down with acute bronchitis and congestion of the lungs. After a month's illness he was strong enough to sit up and write a few letters. 'I have been wanting to write you all this last week,' said his note to Stabler, 'but they would not let me. I have gone a nasty crash and will be some time pulling myself together again.' He spent the first half of June convalescing in the country; after that went away on a sea cruise the effect of which proved disappointing. When he returned to work in July his friends reproached him for coming back too soon. Towards the end of the year he was confessing to Stabler that 1932 had been 'an unlucky year all ways. I feel quite depressed . . . The weariness of the world and of age begins to beset me.' Presently, after a few more weeks, the London Passenger Transport Bill started again on a laborious journey through both Houses.

As soon as it became known that the London Passenger Bill was likely to proceed through Parliament in the session 1932–3 Pick and his railway colleagues went back to their study of the next stage in Underground railway development. The Bill made provision for two changes of immense significance. The first was the acceptance of the principle of an enlarged Common Fund. The main-line railway companies had refused to have anything to do with the idea of a common management but they had been persuaded to agree to the plan for a revenue pooling scheme.

The details were left to be worked out after the passing of the Bill but it was accepted by all the five parties that the state of competition between the Underground Group and the railways would cease; on the 'appointed day' the five of them would start to work together as partners. It was quite an event. When Forshaw and Abercombie referred to it in their 1943 *County of London Plan* they described it as 'an heroic endeavour to harmonise and rationalise the system' and they added that 'it has achieved a large measure of success'. Even before the setting up of the pool something had already been achieved: the way had been opened to agreement between the Underground Group and the London & North Eastern over the bitterly contested scheme for carrying the Underground out into the hard-pressed Essex area. The second big change now impending was the so-called 'transfer' of that other unaccommodating neighbour, the Metropolitan Railway Company. These two changes taken together would make possible a great leap forward in the development of the Underground's railway system. But the programme would be a costly one. Would this new board be in a position to do what the Underground had never yet succeeded in doing in the past twenty years – earn enough money to pay out of its own resources the cost of the capital to be raised? And then came another stroke of almost incredible good luck. It was two years now since the May Committee of bankers and insurance experts had presented the notorious report that led MacDonald's first National Government to prune public expenditure with an unheard of severity, and during those two years the critics of the report had been gathering their forces. Just as the London Passenger Transport Bill was coming up for its third reading they went into battle.

The government was going in the wrong direction: what the country really needed was not further curbs on spending but a programme of massive capital investment that would put the unemployed back to work. It was a situation that had occurred twice before in this present century; on both occasions it had brought financial aid towards the improvement of the Underground railways, first for the Northern Line and later for the Piccadilly Line. And now, in June 1933, the government announced its decision that the same medicine should again be tried – another plan in aid of important public works was in preparation. At the time when the Chancellor made his statement, the London Passenger Transport Board, which was expected to be one of the principal beneficiaries under his plan, was just three weeks old.

In his 1919 design Pick had made the Central Line one of his first priorities. It had however been treated as a somewhat special case. All his main proposals, excepting only this one, had been put forward for the purpose of equipping the railways to cope with a rising pressure of demand. The trouble with the Central Line was a surplus of capacity rather than a lack. It was the least busy of all the tube railways; his figures suggested that it was under-employed to the extent of some 50 per cent. The scheme for carrying it forward from Wood Lane, as White City Station was then called, was well under way at the time. But if the line were to be put to work to its full capacity it would be necessary to extend it a considerable distance both in the east and in the west. Then, in the 1920s, circumstances had made it possible to extend those other tube railways, but the Central Line had had to mark time. The westward extension, while it would have helped to fill some empty seats, was not treated as a matter of urgency; the one to the east, the pressure of demand for which increased at a greater rate even than Pick had foreseen, was held up by the determined opposition of the London & North Eastern Railway. But in 1933 London Transport and the London & North Eastern were working together as partners and that opposition was no longer to be feared. And yet there were still difficulties to be overcome. The North Eastern had been hopelessly backward in modernising its suburban lines and was now working hard to catch up on its arrears with a great programme of electrification. When Pick produced his design for the eastward extension of the Central Line it became necessary that the two undertakings should reach agreement on the allocation of areas to be served. The problem was finally taken to the general manager of the Southern Railway, who had agreed to act as mediator, and it was settled that the London & North Eastern would tackle its line from Liverpool Street to Shenfield including a couple of branches; London Transport for its part would proceed with its plan for carrying the Central Line out to Epping and Ongar.

The Metropolitan Railway was sadly handicapped in several ways and not the least by the fact that it was not altogether master in its own house. Its main line north of Harrow was held on lease by an operating body called the Metropolitan & Great

Central Joint Committee; the Metropolitan and the London & North Eastern (which had absorbed the Great Central) took it in turn to manage the line for a period of five years. The joint committee lines were notoriously the backward children of the British railway family. If the Metropolitan services were to be modernised there must be continuity of tenure and management. The right way would be to share out the line between London Transport and the London & North Eastern leaving each undertaking permanently in charge of its portion. The London Transport area as defined in the Act stopped short a mile or so beyond Amersham. The London & North Eastern must be invited to make itself responsible for all services beyond Amersham, leaving London Transport the inner portion. But the introduction of the London Transport type of standard interval service over this inner portion would still be full of complications. The worst problem was that of the twenty-three express trains of the London & North Eastern that used the line each day. Because of the difference in the speeds these trains at one point required a clear headway of thirteen minutes in front of them; the limitation was made more severe by the fact that their timekeeping was somewhat unpredictable. Pick went through the statistics; there was a useful set of figures for the two weeks before and after the Christmas of 1933. On these fourteen days the late running of the London & North Eastern's trains had added up to an average of seventy minutes delay on each day. This was not perhaps a serious matter for the long-distance trains, but the lateness of these trains had been the cause of the lateness in the Metropolitan trains amounting to a total that averaged nearly 400 minutes on each of those days. The figures had been available only a week when Pick wrote to his friend Sir Ralph Wedgwood, the general manager of the London & North Eastern, who readily agreed to go into the matter in person.

A first instalment of the improvement work had been started some time ago by agreement with the Metropolitan. This was the extension of the Piccadilly Line along the Metropolitan's tracks from Rayners Lane Station to the station which that company had built at Uxbridge in 1904. The extension completed Pick's design for the lengthened Piccadilly Line, now $37\frac{3}{4}$ miles long from end to end. It was opened on 23 October 1933, twelve weeks after the opening of the last stretch to Cockfosters at the other end of the line. The Metropolitan station in Belmont Road,

Uxbridge, was not well situated; the work was hardly finished when plans were being made for carrying the tracks further into the town and building a new terminal station in the High Street. It was not, however, the Piccadilly Line but the Bakerloo that now appeared the most effective instrument for drawing the Metropolitan into the main Underground network and blending its services with those of the Underground. North of Baker Street the Metropolitan tracks as far as Finchley Road had become badly overloaded with traffic since the opening of the Stanmore branch at the end of 1932. To get round this congestion problem the Metropolitan had planned a new relief line north of Baker Street, but it would have been necessary for the greater part of this relief line to be built in the form of an underground tunnel and unfortunately the Ministry of Transport had refused to give its consent to such a tunnel being used by trains made up of non-corridor compartment carriages, the only kind the Metropolitan possessed. As Pick went over his plans he thought he could see a simple way out. The relief tube railway would be made part of the Bakerloo. The new branch of the Bakerloo would then take over the Stanmore trains that were choking up the surface tracks of the Metropolitan; the main tracks to Finchley Road would revert to their original job of carrying the Amersham and Uxbridge trains. To balance these two new tracks in the tube at the Baker Street end, an additional pair of tracks would be built beyond Harrow-on-the-Hill; this would give the equivalent of a full four-track way the whole distance from Baker Street to Rickmansworth. The Bakerloo branch would enable the Metropolitan to work more efficiently, but it would be a healthy thing for the Bakerloo also. The Bakerloo had been one of the first tubes to be carried outside the inner area of London; the long extension to Watford was now nearly twenty years old. Nothing had been added to the line since then. Its southern terminal had remained at the Elephant and Castle for nearly thirty years – one of the two Underground terminal stations still left in the central area of London. The Bakerloo was still a single route from end to end, without branches. The most useful Underground lines at this time branched off at one end, sometimes at both, running out into a two-pronged fork; it was the business of the branches to load the middle portion with traffic to its full capacity. And the middle portion of the Bakerloo was not now properly utilised by the trains that came from Queen's Park and Watford. The

Stanmore trains were just the thing to make it to pull its weight in the Underground system.

At the other end of the Metropolitan Line arrangements had been made for some of the line's trains to run on over the District Line's tracks from Whitechapel as far as Barking. The trains did in truth help to relieve congestion in east London, but the gain was limited: the tracks could be used only for six-car trains coming from Hammersmith; the longer trains from Uxbridge were prevented from entering them. The trouble was the shortness of the little connecting curve over which the eastbound Metropolitan trains swung away from those of the Inner Circle just outside Liverpool Street station; a train of more than six cars could not stand waiting its turn without fouling one of the junctions. The difficulty was overcome by the building of a new Aldgate East Station further east, between the old station and the new one, St Mary's, which lay a mere fifth of a mile away. In this way the curve was made long enough for the eight-car trains and at the same time a little redundant station was disposed of without giving cause for public complaint. A number of lesser works at this point included the lengthening of the old Whitechapel Station where little platform extensions 2ft wide had been squeezed into the tunnels to enable the station to cope with the District Line's eight-car trains. Finally the accession of the Metropolitan to the Underground family also made possible an important improvement in the King's Cross Station area. Here there were found, within a distance of only two or three hundred yards, five different railway stations connected by long and awkward subway passages, two main-line stations – King's Cross and St Pancras – and the three stations of the Northern, Piccadilly and Metropolitan. The two subways linking the Metropolitan station with the main King's Cross Station were dark and unpleasant tunnels several hundred feet long. The old Underground station on the Piccadilly Line stood in front of the great twin arches of the old Great Northern terminus on a site which, in the course of time, had become littered with a collection of mean little buildings. The Underground Group had already secured Parliamentary powers to pull down this Piccadilly Line station and build a new, combined station for the two tubes, but there had been difficulties and the work had never been carried out. Pick had to admit that this frustration had not been altogether unfortunate: it would now be possible to bring in the Metropolitan

Line also and to substitute a new and better triple station for the double station originally planned.

The last of a series of Parliamentary Bills needed to put the plan into operation was passed in the session of 1935–6. There was more paper work in the City: a new company was formed for the purpose of raising the money and lending it to London Transport and the other parties. In the meanwhile a little group of officers of London Transport and the London & North Eastern were busy on the detailed planning of the first big instalment of the work – the extension of the Central Line into Essex over the London & North Eastern's lines. For Pick this work involved an awkward personal problem. When the new Piccadilly Line stations were completed in the autumn of 1933 the Pick–Holden partnership was just ten years old. It had been an extraordinary alliance. In those ten years, after a modest start in south London, a sequence of stations had gone up in widely scattered parts of London, each one different, each thoughtfully adapted to the conditions of its particular site, yet all moving steadily towards a consistent family style of splendid quality. But in the latter part of the ten-year period there had come a change. Holden was appointed architect for the new university buildings in Bloomsbury; as so often happens this somewhat spectacular commission brought other important work into his office and not always of the kind most welcome to him. No doubt many of his friends would see the change as a great advance to the pinnacle of professional success; to Holden it merely meant that he was being increasingly diverted from doing that which he would have most wished to do. Pick knew only one way of dealing with designers. He had got used to it while working with graphic designers in his early days; when he became involved in the design of buildings, though he was punctilious in having the chief engineer present at all the meetings with architects, he had insisted on keeping up this person-to-person intercourse. In the latter part of 1931, when talks were going on about the eight stations for the northern extension to Cockfosters, Holden had arranged to bring in one or two associate architects able to give the work that portion of extra time which he himself was now prevented from giving. He had been lucky in his first choice: C. H. James's work on Bounds Green and Oakwood stations, which were completed in March 1933, had given much satisfaction. At the Uxbridge end of the line Holden had not done so well; some of the stations, such as Rayners Lane and Eastcote, had left Pick with a deep sense of disappointment. But now, in the spring of 1937, when the Central Line stations came up for discussion, Pick felt there was a chance of going back to the old ways. The Central Line works were big indeed, the architecture part of them, however, was in no way comparable in extent to that of the Piccadilly Line. London Transport would be building only three new stations: the ones serving the short length of tube that was to branch out from the London & North Eastern line just outside Leytonstone Station to run beneath Eastern Avenue on a course broadly parallel with the Colchester main line, a mile or so away to the north. It was agreed that these three stations, together with St John's Wood, on the Bakerloo – four stations in all – should be well within Holden's capacity. A draft of the paper about his employment was sent to Pick who crossed out the words 'personal attention' and in the margin wrote one word: responsibility.

When these four stations were completed they were seen to include a couple of architectural experiments of a kind never before tried on London's Underground. The experiments had an amusing history. In the spring of 1935 a small party of Underground engineers travelled to Russia to attend the formal opening of the first ten-mile section of the Moscow Underground or 'Metro'. They had been there before to work with the Russians at the design stage; this was their first chance to see something of the result of their joint labours. The party brought back glowing accounts of things it had been shown, and more especially of a new kind of sub-surface station with a great concourse – something like a cross between a cathedral and a palace ballroom – lying between the tracks. Over the vaulted ceilings that covered the 'nave' part ran a wealth of moulded enrichment and in some of them a line of crystal chandeliers would hang down the middle. The Russians had learnt a great deal from their visits to London's Underground, and indeed their debt was handsomely acknowledged when Pick received the award of an Honorary Badge of Merit from Stalin, but nothing like this was to be seen in any of the new works they had come over to study. If these Moscow concourses owe something to English precedent the inspiration could only have come from the earliest of all our Underground stations, those of the North Metropolitan Railway built by the Great Western a few years after the completion of Paddington to connect that station with the City of London. The tracks and platforms in these stations are spanned by great vaulted roofs, some constructed in solid brick and built over, others of timber-framed glazing carried on slim iron arches. In the cast-iron corbels supporting these arches we can perceive little echoes of the only major Victorian station with ornament successfully employed in the iron roof, Brunel's Paddington which was designed in collaboration with Matthew Digby Wyatt, a close friend of Owen Jones, the leading authority on the Islamic architecture and decoration of the Mediterranean countries.

So keen was the interest aroused by the descriptions and photographs brought back by the travellers to Moscow that Pick could not but agree that they must find some places on the Underground where a concourse of the Russian sort could be tried out. There was indeed an obvious place for a first trial, the new King's Cross St Pancras station that was to link the two main-line terminals with three Underground lines. Now that the Underground's Northern Line was about to be extended out to Mill Hill and Barnet the job had had to be given high priority. The reconstruction was to bring the upper and lower parts of the station closer together, which meant scrapping the old North Metropolitan station, now more than seventy years old, and building a new set of platforms near the escalators that were to replace the ancient tube lifts. It would be a fairly simple matter to put a Moscow-type concourse between the resited tracks. When the station was opened in the early spring of 1941, passengers discovered a great hall of something like Moscow dimensions but a little dull in appearance. Pick had never so far brought in an architect to deal with interiors lying below the level of the ticket hall and here, too, the engineers had been left a free hand. The only features showing a touch of imagination are the lighting fittings: the old stations on this line were lit by big gas lanterns spherical in shape; the engineers had discarded the bottom half and re-used the upper part as a shade. The fittings have a certain theatrical charm quite unspoilt by their incongruity.

After that came Holden's turn. The concourse idea was to be adopted for St John's Wood and for Gants Hill, the last of the three stations on the little Eastern Avenue tube. Unlike King's Cross both of these were deep-level stations; the concourses therefore would have to be built in the form of tunnels, something the Russians had not yet attempted at this time though they were to do so a few years later with conspicuous success. Holden's drawings were ready for Pick to see in June 1936, a little over a year after the engineers' visit to Moscow. The designs were approved with only one modification: Pick, following his familiar practice of going forward one step at a time, decided that the length of the first concourse to be put in hand, the one at St John's Wood, must be reduced by more than half. The engineers found this understandable because the ticket hall here was contained in a handsome little building at ground level; the second station, Gants Hill, would be visible on the surface only as a cluster of widely scattered holes in the pavement. The St John's Wood concourse, when it was completed a couple of months after the outbreak of war, turned out to be only a trifle bigger than some of the older escalator landing halls but it had something more important than size – it had architectural quality. Gants Hill, work on which was held up during the war, was something different. The concourse here is 140ft long and 50ft wide, measured between the platform edges. Modest enough compared with its Russian prototypes (its height is a mere 20ft) it still seems a little overambitious for this very minor suburban station. When it was finished in December 1947 it certainly more than made up for the lack of public attention accorded to St John's Wood; a Canadian critic went so far as to call it an 'architectural triumph'. For us today it is difficult not to see it as a dashing finale for Pick's contribution to the 1933 statutory London Passenger Transport Board which was abolished by the Labour government a couple of weeks after Gants Hill Station was opened and brought into use.

A Risk of Torpor

On the last day of June 1933 Pick was writing to an old friend: 'At midnight to-night we all pass into the control of the London Passenger Transport Board.' 'It is a new start in life,' he said in answer to a letter of congratulation, 'all that I have done in the past may be forgotten; I write upon a clean slate. I hope I may have wisdom enough to write better upon the clean slate.' In another letter of acknowledgement he said something about the nature of his task: 'Now begins the tussle to show that the Board of public character can conduct its business on strictly commercial lines.' Why this reference to commercial business? At the head of the board of seven Members there were still the

155

twin heads of the Underground Group: Ashfield, the chairman, and Pick, now re-named vice-chairman. But working alongside them were five part-time members chosen to represent the special experience of local government, organised labour, the Ministry of Transport and the world of finance. The 'character' of the board was in truth made plain for all to see. Pick spoke at some length about the opening stage of his 'tussle' in a lecture he gave in the following year: he was required, he said, to negotiate the take-over of 'five railway companies, fourteen municipally owned tramway undertakings, three company-owned tramway undertakings, sixty-six omnibus and coach companies, and the whole or part of not less than sixty-nine other omnibus and coach companies which have been refused consent to operate under the terms of the Act.' Frederick Menzler, the board's actuary, writing to an old colleague in the summer of 1934, told how Pick and his assistants had been working till ten o'clock at night and later for six weeks on end. Certainly counsel briefed by London Transport, one of whom was Walter Monckton, were never left short of ammunition. And it was not only the big and important cases that took up time and energy – some of the smaller firms to be broken up and compensated could make heavy going indeed. Pick had to decide, first, which particular services operated by a firm should be taken over and, secondly, what price or compensation payment should be offered or agreed. There was a good chance that the firm would reject the proposed arrangement and take the matter to the three-man London Passenger Transport Tribunal established under the Act.

The task was not made easier by the dissimilarity in character of the various parts; it was not as if you were dealing with businesses belonging to a single species such as railway companies or manufacturers of equipment. As Pick looked at the heterogeneous collection he found himself distinguishing between three distinct types. There were the local authorities which, he said, were 'composed of elected representatives of the people of a particular district and had been concerned only with that district and its interests'. Then there were companies like those of the Underground Group which had had to think of their shareholders. 'They were compelled to have a selfish outlook though they knew they must not interpret this selfishness too narrowly or it would react to destroy them.' With the small independent bus companies the selfishness on the other hand was 'unmoderated and undisguised, the only object was to secure as much profit as possible in order to stake a claim which might eventually lead to compensation'. A couple of months later he was served with a round dozen writs for alleged slander and the London Passenger Transport Board with another dozen for libel allegedly committed in the printing of Pick's paper. When the case came up in the King's Bench Division Court counsel for the plaintiffs produced a letter from Pick explaining that the use of the expression 'selfish' did not connote in his mind anything dishonourable on the part of the companies and that it had not been his intention to impute impropriety. And so the case presently was allowed to drop, subject to the payment by Pick of a substantial contribution towards the companies' costs. Though Pick had spoken with some feeling, his carefully chosen words stand in sharp contrast to the words used by other critics of the take-over arrangements both at the time and for some years thereafter. W. A. Robson, for example, writing in 1937 called the terms 'generous beyond the dreams of avarice' and drew a depressing picture of a London Passenger Transport Board condemned to start life with 'a staggering burden of indebtedness round its neck'. But there was a difference. Robson and the others were saying that the Lord Chancellor's tribunal had been too free of the new board's money. Pick had said that the bus companies had been selfish in demanding that money. To call a commercial company 'selfish' is truly inexcusable.

Selfishness, if such it was, was not however a thing to be found only in the men at the top, its presence could make itself felt at all levels in a business. The board's annual report for the year ended 30 June 1936 has a short paragraph which explains how 'The Board have endeavoured within the limits of their resources to deal fairly with the staff . . . They hope that the trade unions concerned and the staff themselves appreciate the action which has been taken.' No doubt there must have been a good many among the staff who did appreciate the action. There was, however, one particular group that found itself quite unable to do so. In the process of integrating the many different undertakings to be absorbed into the new board, Pick's policy had been the reverse of the common practice of the City take-over men: in any scheme of rationalisation of pay and conditions he would as a rule prefer the levelling-out to be in an upward direction rather than a downward one. The less well-off had first claim. The policy was not one calculated to appeal to the more privileged sections such as the 70,000 workers employed on the General's Central Area buses, as the company's red-painted buses were called. Between the end of World War I and the creation of the London Passenger Transport Board these men had worked themselves up into an enviable position. Their committee enjoyed the status of a national trade group having the right of direct access to the general executive of their union, the Transport and General Workers. Largely through the efforts of a full-time secretary, then something of a rarity in groups of this kind, its branches were run with an almost military efficiency: Sir Alan Bullock in his *Life and Times of Ernest Bevin* describes it as one of the most militant groups in the trade union movement of this country. The committee had now discovered that the Central Area bus crews were suffering from nervous exhaustion. Bus routes had been ruthlessly replanned, many changes had been made in the interest of what in those days was not yet called productivity. And all this had happened at a time when the drivers of the buses were having to contend with a steeply rising tide of traffic in the streets. The medical evidence showed clearly the extent of the injury done to their digestive and other organs by the incessant strain.

In the middle of April Ashfield became ill and was still away on Monday the nineteenth when the talks finally broke down. Among those with experience of London Transport's labour relations there were not many who really believed that his absence at that moment was accidental. They knew him as a man who in any sort of crisis would make up his mind very quickly whether to fight or make peace. Many years later Herbert Morrison recalled how Ashfield, if he had decided for peace, 'would be prepared to pay any price to avoid trouble'. But there were other occasions when he would judge a strike to be desirable and then would order his managers to stand firm; if necessary he might even arrange for a strike to be deliberately provoked. Here clearly was one of those occasions. Suppose he did want a strike; what could be its purpose this time? London Transport and the Underground Group before it had had a lot to put up with from this red busmen's committee. Perhaps the moment had come when it would be possible to secure that the power of the committee should be broken. Only one person was capable of doing the breaking, Ernest Bevin, the architect of the Transport and General Workers' Union and still its general secretary. Ashfield the superlative card player knew that there are certain hands that tell you at once that your best chance of winning is to enlist the help of your opponent. Bevin in this present game was an opponent indeed: he had spoken long and passionately in support of the busmen's claim. Ashfield, however, was one of the few intimates who were aware that beneath that great show of loyalty there lay a sense of cold disapproval – more than once in the past ten or twelve years the Central Area committee had been warned by Bevin that it must moderate its rapacity. If London Transport continued to stand firm, was it not possible that Bevin might decide that his union, like London Transport, had had enough? And that is precisely what did happen. In the fourth week of the strike the union's general executive was persuaded to withdraw the powers that had put this predatory committee in its position of strength and the committee, thus shorn of its special status, was unable to prevent the union from ordering the strikers back to work.

The London Passenger Transport Board was something quite new in public service organisation; it was natural that its progress in its first years should be watched with a good deal of interest and that invitations to speak on the subject should reach Pick from many quarters. The half-dozen or so lectures that he gave from the early weeks of 1934 onwards form a running commentary upon the idea of the public corporation as embodied in the one of which he was the executive head. Among the first questions with which he felt bound to concern himself was the precise meaning of a word that was now constantly heard, the word 'monopoly' that had given him trouble ever since the days of the London Traffic Bill debates. As had happened on those earlier occasions, Pick could find no fault with the use of the word. But there were monopolies and monopolies; what he had to try to do was throw some light on the nature and significance of this particular specimen. 'In our political studies', he said in one of his papers, 'at least for those of us who were trained in the Austinian school, the question of paramount importance was: Where does the sovereignty reside? Where is the ultimate power vested?' The seven members of the board formed a governing body; to whom was this body accountable? He came to the surprising conclusion that for all practical purposes the board was, in fact, a self-governing body. 'It has no master arising out of its creation or renewal. It escapes from parental control and guardianship immediately. It bursts into full competence at the moment of birth.' Pick had always been willing to accept the principle of public control, not as a good thing in itself but as an evil necesasry to check and restrain another and greater evil – the rapacity of a profit-hungry business enjoying monopolistic power. If less public control was now thought to be required, that in itself was a good thing. 'Control is always injurious. It is like a straitwaist-coat: it involves a loss of mental and moral freedom; it is an excuse for rigid unaccommodating manners. The defects of control had to become apparent before the transition from control to organised monopoly could be made.' Step by step, the right alternative to controlled private enterprise had been found in this new kind of monopoly. 'All forms of transport are now brought together and treated alike. It is the first occasion on which this has happened. And the object of the monopoly is not now directed towards fares but towards services, to the proper co-ordination and adjustment of services so that the highest measure of efficiency may be reached. All the stock jargon about monopoly in the textbooks requires to be re-written.' He saw that if the trial were successful, if the new monopoly should justify itself, its success might help to give to London better forms of public administration in many different fields:

At the end, the patterns of local passenger transport should be clear and understandable, and the distant observer will be able to look at them with an aesthetic satisfaction, and as these patterns became clear so it will be ever more important that other patterns should become clear too. Those other functions – water, gas, electricity, sewage, will demand a corresponding treatment. Parks and open spaces, roads, watercourses – all these must become collective aims and enterprises, not of this or that local authority but of the whole 353 over which the area is now shared. So the catalogue might continue. The London Passenger Transport Board is a model for the performance and control of commercial or quasi-commercial pursuits.

When Pick, in his far-ranging comments on the new corporation, had pointed to the degree of freedom it had been allowed in the management of its affairs he had had in mind a freedom from external pressures. There was, however, another sort of freedom – the freedom from constraints acting from the inside –

and when the board got under way he soon found that this freedom had in effect been drastically curtailed. The danger now was that the threat of an external bureaucracy would be replaced by the more insidious threat of a bureaucratic spirit within the business. When he addressed the London School of Economics he said:

> The coming of the Board has in some ways destroyed the freedom of the management. The Board as a public authority must accept what may be concisely described as the rule of law. It becomes accountable to public opinion by reason of its size and importance. It must be governed by its own regulations, its own precedents. What it does for one it must be prepared to do for all . . . The Board has been asked to take a sympathetic interest in certain hard cases among its staff. Its constituent undertakings were able to temper their administration of pensions, grants, and allowances with leniency and charity because they were always able to stop or withhold their hand whenever they thought fit. Not so the Board. As a public authority it may not be lenient and charitable today and severe and niggardly tomorrow. The character and temper of its administration must be more careful and measured. There seems no avoidance of this.

There was no avoidance of this, and yet without some degree of mitigation life would become impossible. 'It is essential that somehow the management should not fall into too rigid a framework. There must be left full scope for the expression of the personal factor.'

In November 1936 London Transport held a conference of members and officers at the Mayfair Hotel. The proceedings were opened by Ashfield, who spent some time speculating upon the future of the undertaking. The financial prospect as he described it was not a cheerful one. Fresh burdens would be laid on them by the rising cost of wages and pension schemes, by the demand for additional provision for renewals, by the stock redemption arrangements prescribed under the Act, and, last but not least, by the cost of financing the railway extensions authorised by Parliament a few months before. He estimated that by the time London Transport was ten years old these new liabilities might add up to something like £3 million a year. This was the measure of the extra earnings they would need if they were to remain a going concern. He warned his audience that they must make up their minds that this kind of growth was not only necessary but possible: 'A belief in the buoyancy of our revenue', he concluded, 'is essential to the maintenance of morale.' Belief. To Pick the word was all too familiar. It was an appeal that he had heard Ashfield make to the old shareholders over and over again. The words, when addressed to the meeting of shareholders, were no doubt quite harmless but this was a meeting of management staff. When Pick's turn came to speak he admitted that the idea of high morale as something that depended on being in a condition of economic growth was one that filled him with dismay. 'It is a desperate phrase', he said. It was true that the quantity of service performed had been moving steadily upwards and that this growth had proved helpful to them in their work. But the beneficial effects of growth were accidental; growth was no substitute for vitality and when it only served to conceal a deficiency of vitality it could become dangerous. A year later, when he again addressed the same audience, he came back to the subject: 'The growth of a metropolis must slow down rapidly at some stage; if it did not slow down the city would grow to an uneconomic size, like a house so large that no one can afford to live in it.' A day would come, therefore, when London Transport must carry on as a 'static undertaking'. What would be the effect of such a change?

Expenditure on the general amelioration of the undertaking cannot then be sustained. The raising of general standards of amenity must cease. Promotion and advancement among the staff becomes limited to the filling of dead men's shoes . . . London Transport has had no real experience as yet of this distressing complaint. But the time has come when it is necessary to contemplate it, and to see whether some reasonable technique of management cannot be devised that will make the best of a static condition of affairs.

Only a couple of weeks after addressing his colleagues at the London Transport conference Pick went on to develop these same thoughts in their application to society at large. The occasion was a meeting of the Institution of Professional Civil Servants. He spoke of the 'many warning signs that this growth in magnitude and complexity which is pleasantly called progress will be arrested.' Progress was not a law of life; it was something that existed only as a particular phase, an event in time. 'The notion

162

of progress is a thing of comparatively recent origin, bred of the early nineteenth-century atmosphere. It will give place to some other notion in this twentieth century, a notion of consolidation . . . a synthesis of all that is good in the accumulated riches of living.' But stable conditions mean a new climate to which society had long been unaccustomed:

> There will be a risk of torpor setting in. One of the problems which must be faced by a stationary population is how to keep alive creative ability. Creative expression will most likely be found in the application of thought and endeavour to the better solution of existing problems, to the presentation of existing things in a better fashion than they have been presented before. Quality will supplant quantity as a measure of success . . . In the reflective phase of civilisation more attention will be given to this problem of replacements, and the accumulated improvements of the years will be embodied in them, with emphasis perhaps not so much on the physical and economic aspects as on the aesthetic aspect.

'No real experience as yet of this distressing complaint.' The words, used by Pick in 1936, were only the latest of many references to the idea of diminishing vitality in human organisations. The thought of it was with him constantly. In March 1933, the month when his appointment as vice-chairman was announced, he was speaking at a meeting of the Bristol branch of the Design and Industries Association:

> In our natural history museums we see the vestiges of the whole genera of plants and animals who developed so far and then failed and perished. Largely because their development was too specific, too precise, so that they would not adapt themselves to changed conditions. You may also see in our historical and artistic museums the vestiges of civilisation that have faded away. Indeed a whole race of men has been obliterated without a trace left if we may believe the anthropologists. We are the successors of a second creation of the human race. There are warnings throughout recorded time that fluidity, plasticity, are sovereign virtues for survival.

The following year, in a letter to Harold Stabler, he was answering some criticisms of a big art school; he said: 'The trouble is it has now fallen into a formula and I do not think fresh life enters in sufficiently. We shall have to find some scheme by which even an efficient school can be waked up from time to time by incursions from the outside. We have got to cultivate revolutionary spirits for the purpose.' 'Fallen into' a formula: the use of the old-fashioned medical phrase is illuminating. But he now knew what the complaint was really called; it was something rather more serious than the dinosaur's failure to adapt. At about this time Sir Arthur Eddington delivered his series of Messenger Lectures at Cornell University; they were later published in this country in a volume called *New Pathways in Science*. Pick found in them a confirmation of his worst forebodings. Eddington was expounding a law of nature to which the nineteenth-century German scientist Rudolf Clausius had given the name 'entropy'. When Pick was speaking to the Institute of Public Administration in March 1935 the subject of entropy was brought in at the end to form a gloomy conclusion. Entropy means that 'everything always tends to level out or average out. The sun's energy radiates abroad and spreads equally throughout the universe. The higher forms of matter like radium break down into baser forms like lead. The face of the earth wears slowly away, the mountains are converted into sandbanks. The end of all things is a lowest common denominator . . . Is not this the parallel to the process that is found in the administration of a public undertaking?' In a public undertaking accord with convention is everything, there is little chance that convention will be adapted; the formula, the system, are always there, immutable, 'the law of thermodynamics turns out to be indeed a law of death'. It was true, said Pick, that death by entropy, if it could not be avoided, could at least be postponed; it could be checked by this thing called growth. But to let yourself become dependent on growth was like being dependent on fine weather. For another delaying agent he turned again to mathematical physics: 'Clark Maxwell discovered a "sorting demon" whose function it is by some selective process to prevent that general averaging of everything. So in administration there are in the higher ranks of officials sorting demons who resist the process of frittering away resources. These sorting demons are an essential part of the organisation.' But though they were no doubt useful creatures their functions were limited; all they could do was to stop avoidable economic waste. What else was there? Only one thing. The leaders must learn to become more dynamic; the way to combat the formula, the system, was to leave off being afraid of 'a spice of vice, a spark of irrationality, a fondness for inconsistency, a flash of genius'.

164

6

DESIGN AND INDUSTRY: 1931-1937

A Place for the Designer

The economic depression of the late 1920s which the government had sought to combat with a programme of massive public works had left people looking about anxiously for other possible remedies. Among the more obvious was the boosting of Britain's faltering export trade. Pick and his friends in the Design and Industries Association had been greatly impressed in particular by the way some of our European neighbours had set to work making their achievements in the design of household goods known to the world. In government circles any interest shown in the design movement hitherto had been little more than perfunctory but these foreigners clearly meant business. One day in March 1933 Sir Edward Crowe of the Board of Trade's Department of Overseas Trade, possibly but not necessarily by accident, found himself placed next to Pick at a public dinner. He started talking about a new design council which the board was considering setting up. His colleagues were aware that the chances of securing Pick as chairman of this council were not very good; the new London Passenger Transport Board was about to be launched and for the next few years he was bound to get overloaded with work. Crowe found Pick sufficiently interested to start asking a few questions. Early in November Pick was asked by Leslie Burgin, Parliamentary Secretary to the Board of Trade, to call upon him at the House of Commons. A small interdepartmental group appointed to advise on the proposed Council for Art and Industry had decided to place Pick's name at the head of their list. He had, they said, 'probably done more for industrial art than any other living industrialist'. Of him alone was it felt that the choice would have the full support of both the business community and the world of art and design.

In his book *Design in British Industry* published in 1937 Sir Nikolaus Pevsner wrote: 'In contrast to so many councils and committees, this one has almost immediately begun to act with great energy . . . During the first year such a comprehensive programme was worked out that a long time will be required to complete the task the Council has set itself.' A large part of the programme was in fact worked out at the very first meeting which was held at the end of January 1934. The meeting was opened by the President of the Board, Walter Runciman, with a welcoming speech in which he described what was meant to be the council's main task, an exhaustive study of the system of training for designers in a wide range of industries and the manner in which their services were being used for the benefit of those industries. In the course of the meeting a detailed plan was drawn up for a first committee to examine 'design in the jewellery, silversmithing and allied trades'; terms of reference were agreed for a pottery committee and a committee for cotton textiles; individual members were deputed to make preliminary enquiries in two more industries; agreement was reached on exhibitions of silverware and pottery to be held at the Victoria and Albert Museum in conjunction with the two committees dealing with these matters; and it was arranged that a programme for the council's other major task, the education of the man in the street or consumer, would be finalised at the following meeting. It was in truth a most vigorous start.

At the end of 1934, when the council had put committees to work on four more industries, there came a piece of news that caused it to make a sudden switch in its plans. The Board of Education had decided to appoint a departmental committee to report on advanced art and design training in London. The board's decision was a delayed response to much prodding from Pick and his friends in the Design and Industries Association at a time when they had begun to despair of the Board of Trade. At its meeting held in February 1935 the council, having listened to an account by a member representing the Board of Education, went on to nominate three of its members to sit on this new committee which was to have Lord Hambledon as chairman. But then it also became necessary that the council should organise itself for a new and complicated task. The Board of Education was concerned with training, but it was the responsibility of the council to declare just what sort of training would best fit designers to play a worthwhile part in industry. At this same meeting, therefore, the council arranged to start work at once on a single parallel examination of all the relevant industries throughout the country. So that this work might be pressed forward with the required speed Pick said he had regretfully declined an invitation to sit on the Hambledon Committee. The study was finally completed in a total of thirty-five meetings at which the the full council, assisted by a small drafting committee with Pick as chairman, received the evidence of more than seventy witnesses from trade associations, manufacturing firms, education authorities and schools of art. The report *Design and the Designer in Industry* appeared in print in January 1937. The speed at which Pick had driven his team, not without an occasional murmur of protest from exhausted members, may be judged from the fact that the report was ready at the same time as that of the group for the silversmithing and allied trades, which had had a twelve months' start. The report of the committee for the cotton and rayon industry turned out to be a short one and it was decided to print it as an appendix to this main report, that of the pottery group appeared later in the year as did two reports from Scotland dealing, respectively, with printing and woollen goods. To these five documents, which form the whole of the council's published work on the subject of designers up to the outbreak of war, a sixth dealing with the light metal trades was added in 1944.

When the subject of advanced art training came up for discussion in the Design and Industries Association there was one statement on which everybody had always agreed: 'The great neglected subject of industrial design must at all costs be restored to its rightful place.' There were, however, many arguments about such matters as the proper relationship between industrial design on the one hand and painting and sculpture, the so-called fine arts, on the other. B. J. Fletcher was one of the spokesmen for the all-or-nothing school who held that industrial design would never be able to hold its own in the educational system until these two were completely divorced from one another. Pick did not agree; there was no need, he said, to go as far as that. 'I am satisfied', he wrote to Fletcher, 'that it is due to bad organisation of the school that the fine art side claims a preponderance of attention.' Separate schools, each under its own head, were doubtless inevitable, but there was everything to be said for bringing the separate schools together in a single college of superior status. A few years after the end of the war the Board of Education was moved to take up the subject again and the reforms proposed in the council's unanimous report were then carried through in a most thorough manner. The Royal College of Arts having been reconstituted as an independent national college of art and design, a number of specialist design schools were set up each of which enjoyed the same status as the schools for painting and sculpture. Gradually the bias towards the fine arts started to disappear in college teaching; in the new university-style degrees which were presently introduced the balance again was scrupulously kept. Pick might have had his misgivings about some later developments but at least it could be truly said of them that what he had described as the 'great neglected subject' was restored to the place which had so long been denied it.

At its second meeting, held on 8 March 1934, the Council for Art and Industry spent some time discussing a paper submitted by E. M. O'R. Dickey, the staff inspector for art in the Board of Education, on the position of art teaching in primary and secondary schools. There was some talk about the visual environment in the school and it was agreed that a start should be made on this study by collecting information about school buildings in different countries. This was a subject in which Pick had taken a most lively interest since his tour of northern European countries with Charles Holden in the Summer of 1930. When the printed report of their tour comes to the much-admired Dutch town of Hilversum it points out how 'Great attention has been paid to the influence of the environment on the child mind. The classrooms are admirably lit . . . and considerable use has been made of bright colour. In one room, for instance, the doors were painted green and the desks were treated in a number of harmonising colours.' The whole subject of visual education for the ordinary citizen had, however, been occupying Pick's thoughts for many years before that. As he pondered Lethaby's complaint that 'we think in words, and we talk of architecture and fine designs and art and style and so on, but we do not seem to notice with our eyes how little of these things we get in the real streets of the real towns we know', Pick felt he could cry with Lethaby: 'I want to get people to see, really to *see* with their eyes.' In 1922 he had gone down to West Ham to speak at the municipal college.

In some notes he made for the occasion he wrote: 'Man's rapid progress based on words, we think in words, our minds string words like beads . . . Pictures, visions, memories of things seen, are neglected. Children see the visions more than grown-ups. We teach them the craft of word-spinning. The damage is done, we should be teaching them the art of seeing.' Whitehead put the matter very neatly in one of his lectures at Harvard in 1925: 'In the Garden of Eden Adam saw the animals before he named them.' Much of Pick's time since then had been spent teaching the art of seeing and following his own precept he had striven to teach not in words but in the actuality of things seen. When Steen Eiler Rasmussen wrote 'The moment you enter the London Underground you feel, though you may not be able to explain exactly how you feel it, that you are moving in an environment of order, of culture', he had in mind precisely what Sir Nikolaus Pevsner meant when he described London Transport as 'the most efficacious centre of visual education in England'. The effect of this education provided by London Transport was necessarily limited; most of the beneficiaries were grown-ups, people in whom as Pick said, the damage had already been done. But now his council had been told to consider the whole of education in the formal sense; this would mean concentrating on the younger people who had not yet suffered that damage, whose eyes were still unenfeebled and uncorrupted. It was a splendid opportunity.

The two reports, for England and Scotland respectively, were published within a few weeks of each other in the early autumn of 1935. Both start by agreeing that the British could not be accused of being less sensitive to beauty than people in other countries. They were, however, liable to take a more conservative view; they were also more uncritical, more ready to be pleased. They would recognise good design in the end, says the report of the main council, but recognition 'is often slow in coming, and frequently neither the manufacturer nor the distributor can afford the financial sacrifice involved in waiting for demand to develop. Accordingly, what is required of the consumer is, first, conscious realisation of the possibility of beauty in things of everyday use, and, secondly, quicker understanding of it when it is placed before him'. The subject was indeed included in the curriculum of our elementary and secondary schools, but the effectiveness of the teaching was diminished by the severance of visual education from the other subejcts taught. The problem was less in the infant and junior elementary schools, where the children's natural talent for drawing and painting was as a rule given adequate scope under a single teacher responsible for all subjects. It was when the children passed into the senior elementary and central schools that the real trouble started. Aesthetic experience here was strictly confined within the four walls of the art room where lessons in drawing and painting were given by specialist teachers; at no time were these lessons allowed to impinge on the curriculum generally. An exception was found in a few schools where instruction in the weaving and printing of textiles had recently been introduced. In the older wood and metalwork classes ideas about good and bad design were non-existent. This was hardly surprising since two-fifths of the handicraft teachers were ordinary cabinet makers and carpenters whose sole qualification was the passing of a test in technical proficiency. The report suggests a number of ways in which these teachers could be made competent to teach design appreciation. At the next stage in the child's career, the grammar school, the girl's high school and the average public school showed up very badly. The whole system of secondary education was liable to treat all children as material for the universities and all education as a process of conditioning for university entrance. 'There is an emphasis', says the report, 'on those subjects . . . to which the universities generally attach importance as being their own most favoured fields of education.' It is the universities, in other words, that decide what boys and girls who will never go near a university are to be taught at their school. The result is 'a lop-sided curriculum calculated to develop lopsided minds'. The ideal no doubt would be to dissociate the school leaving test from the university admission test, as was suggested in a report prepared in 1932 by a panel sitting under the chairmanship of Dr Cyril Norwood. But perhaps the universities might yet be persuaded to recognise art education as belonging to 'their own most favoured fields'? And better still if they could, at the same time, permit that education to be made less narrowly academic, help pupils to become intelligent and discriminating citizens instead of mere repositories of information about matters having little relevance to their adult lives.

There is nothing highly original about the council's statement on the practical aim of a sound visual education. All children should have opportunities for learning to 'observe, understand, appreciate and describe the appearance of well-designed common objects'. But from this simple statement there flow some far-reaching conclusions. The report quotes a sentence from the evidence submitted by the National Union of Teachers: most children, it says, can 'appreciate, say, a beautiful garden which is something remote from their own world, but not the difference between a good and a bad breakfast mug. It is a mistake to think that the extraneous object wrapped in fantasy, conspicuously labelled BEAUTIFUL, can contribute anything to a child's visual education. What is needed is the homely object existing here and now in the child's 'own world'. And this 'own world' is of course during the hours spent in school and the school itself. In some of the newer schools the authorities had been at pains to produce well-designed buildings, but what about the older ones? The report wastes no time commenting on their architectural demerits: bad architecture, it says, 'is no excuse for neglected paint work and dingy walls'. Information received from Geneva, Copenhagen, Lausanne, Rotterdam, Lyons and Stockholm 'suggests that considerable attention is paid to school decoration abroad'. Here at home standard colour finishes seem to have been specially chosen for their depressing effect. But the use of colour was only a beginning. 'There can be no better way of teaching design than by making the actual school an object lesson', and the object lesson should include 'all the details of the furniture, equipment and material brought into it'. A few education authorities had started to collect examples of well-designed products of local industries for use in their schools; not only should this practice be adopted everywhere, but the children themselves should also be encouraged to bring objects to be studied and discussed at lessons. The report of the Scottish Committee makes the further suggestion that the parks department should supply schools with plants and flowers for these collections.

Among the first local authorities to show an interest in the reports when they came out in the autumn of 1935 was the biggest of them all, the London County Council. The LCC's education department prepared and printed its own summary, which was later circulated to all its teachers. Next came a request for help in organising an exhibition illustrating the suggestions made in the report about teaching material for schools. The Pick council started work at once but there were many delays and its ideas had a way of growing more ambitious as the business pro-

171

ceeded. When the exhibition was finally opened in the main exhibition hall at County Hall in January 1937 visitors found exhibits relevant to practically every subject taught arranged under fourteen headings, from music, dancing and drama to history, science, geography; for the mathematics section Pick had secured the collaboration of Walter Gropius. The council's sympathy with the aims of the exhibi.ion was clearly shown in the short speech from the chairman of the Education Committee, Mrs E. M. Lowe, who presided at the opening ceremony. 'For quite long enough', she said, 'we have put too much stress in education on learning from books and books alone. Something much more is needed if a child is to have a chance of all-round development.' Of the 11,000 people concerned with education who came to see the exhibition, a high proportion were the elementary school teachers for whose benefit it had largely been designed; among the others were officials from the Board of Education who presently suggested that the board should sponsor similar exhibitions in other parts of the country.

It had always been expected of the Pick council that its members should spend a great deal of their time on studies and enquiries and the writing of reports. Yet the council was most anxious that the report business should not be held to be the only way of justifying its existence. Something had to be done, too, about the adult citizen, and in this particular matter little good could be expected to result from this pleading with the authorities. The trouble was that, whereas reports could be produced at little cost, these other activities, such as the holding of exhibitions, did as a rule require that some money should be spent. But the Board of Trade had laid it down that there could be no question of an outright annual grant; special application must be made for each individual project. The council made a number of such applications, none of which could be called extravagant, but it was hard going: in one case it took nearly three months to get authority to spend £150. In circumstances such as these the council came to the conclusion that it must start looking to the hospitality of other bodies in a less impecunious condition. First and most consistently helpful among these was the Victoria and Albert Museum. Its director, Sir Eric Maclagan, had been a member of the small informal group charged with the task of setting up the Pick council and was now a member of it. In the council's third year another friendly organisation, the Building Centre, then still in its original home in New Bond Street, came forward with an offer to provide space for an exhibition. It was an opportune moment, for the council was already busy with a project for which the place was admirably suited. In its second annual report to the President of the Board of Trade it had declared itself dissatisfied with the limited scope of recent design exhibitions, including its own. There had been undue concentration on goods designed to appeal to the higher income groups; the common things of everyday life had never yet received the attention they deserved. The proposal was that the council would collect examples of well-designed furniture commercially available to the less well-off. It started by defining a typical low income family and saw it as consisting of a married couple with two small children, one of either sex, occupying at the first stage a dwelling with two rooms, and moving when the children grew older and more numerous to one containing up to a maximum of five. Having made careful estimates of family income the council had to consider the economics of the furnishing plan. It was felt that a range of costs should be considered with a basic figure of £40 (later amended to £52 10s). The exhibition was opened at the Building Centre by the Minister of Health, Sir Kingsley Wood, at the beginning of June 1937, a few years after publication of the council's report *The Working Class Home*. The subject of the enquiry is described in the opening paragraph of the report, in sentences which could only have been drafted by Pick himself.

What is possible, within the limits of expenditure which such a home implies, in the way of securing furniture and equipment in which industrial art can find fit and appropriate expression? . . . Is the material sound, is the construction strong, is the workmanship (whether of man or machine) thorough? Again, is the purpose properly served? Again, are the form and colour pleasant, and is the surface or texture satisfying to eye or hand? Is the added decoration (if any) apt and gracious? If these questions or a majority of them cannot be answered in the affirmative, does industrial art mean anything at all to the bulk of consumers?

The report gives a complete priced inventory of all purchases down to black-lead brushes, wire-mesh meat-covers and chopping boards, all of which were displayed in three of the rooms. Other rooms showed how improved amenities might be obtained by buying more or better articles up to a maximum of £100. The most interesting thing about the report is the practical, down-to-earth approach to the human problem. This was a problem of people, real people with private lives bound together by intimate personal relationships. 'It was thought that something should be done to give each member of the family a place for his own individual possessions, whether clothes, toys or articles of personal use. Only in such circumstances can personal respect be properly developed, and the elements of a tidy manner of life secured.' A tidy manner of life meant good upkeep as well as good planning; it is noted with approval that the average council-house tenant regards a good floor covering as 'a sign of financial competence'; good curtains are 'a signal to the whole street'. A piece of advice that would appear to have made a deeper impression than most is the one that calls for the occupier to be 'encouraged to make himself handy with carpenters' tools, paint and varnish brushes, and putty knives'.

The exhibition consisted of nine fully furnished rooms with two extra rooms: one for alternative pieces of furniture and one for kitchen equipment. It was well received by most of the Press. *The Times* gave it a long and thoughtful article; the *Manchester Guardian* hoped that it would be visited not only by householders but by people living in furnished rooms who should urge their landladies to come and see it. The *Journal* of the National Society of Art Masters described it as 'a memorable object-lesson in adequate, unpretentious and beautiful furnishing', and urged that schools of art in different parts of the country should arrange similar exhibitions to be taken into the heart of the working-class areas. The only unfavourable views were those expressed by people who had formed a mistaken idea of the purpose of the show. It was a pity that one of the most intelligent accounts, Geoffrey Boumphrey's radio broadcast, should have been based on such a misunderstanding. Pick had to write a letter to *The Listener* patiently explaining what the council had been trying to do: 'The object is to direct attention to an artistic problem, the furnishing of a home for £50. If, as the Committee hopes, thought is put into this, if the trial and error of many exhibitions is added to our first one, a tradition of good furnishing for a working class home will begin to grow up.' The misunderstanding went on. A week later a reader wrote in comparing 'the jumble of odd pieces shown' with the high standard set by the council's chairman in

174

London Transport. Pick came back once more to explain. 'London Transport is not providing facilities on a minimum basis. It is more generous to its passengers. The comparison is scarcely just.' Finally, answering Anthony Bertram, who said that he 'did not believe it is possible to furnish a home with really well-designed furniture at the prices to which the Council for Art and Industry has limited itself . . . The selection committee had an impossible task', Pick pointed out that 'the majority of homes in the country must be furnished within these limits. Is there not a duty to see what needs must serve?'

Britain in Paris

Among the various writers who had helped Pick over the years to clarify his ideas about good design there were one or two who lived in a world far remote from that of man-made objects. One of the most unlikely of these was a scientist who had risen to fame as a leading authority on birds and fishes, D'Arcy Wentworth Thompson. Pick had come across his book *On Growth and Form* during World War I; Thompson's descriptions of design in nature, of the perfect adaptation of the different parts of an animal to the work they had to perform had filled Pick with a sense of thrilling discovery. Thompson had made him go back to look again at the article that Lethaby had written for the magazine *The Imprint* in 1913: 'Fortunately people are artists who know it not – bootmakers (the few left), gardeners and basket-makers, and all players of games. We do not allow shoddy in cricket or football, but reserve it for serious things like houses and books, furniture and funerals.' Again and again Lethaby brought up the subject of games; in a lecture he gave in 1916 'boy-scouting and tennis in flannels' were added to his list of 'our best forms of modern civilisation'. Pick had never changed his views about the over-stressing of the 'fitness for purpose' element in design; in his 1937 paper to the Royal College old students, for example, we still find him pleading for a kind of design that would endow objects with 'grace and charm, some overplus of care and love, which find expression in added decoration'. Only in this world of tools, tools for work and play, could it truly be said that 'fitness for purpose' was the road to complete fulfilment.

It was a pity that most of the people in the design movement should have been of the earnest type that has little use for

175

the frivolities of sports and games; Pick's inclinations might be much the same but he was not thereby prevented from seeing the truth of Lethaby's words. His earliest attempt to present Lethaby's argument appears to have been made in an article he wrote for the *Nineteenth Century and After* review in 1922. After a reference to the design of old weapons he goes on to say:

> If we have no weapons in the strict sense, we have tennis rackets, cricket bats, croquet mallets and so forth for the strife of sport. We know good from bad, toys from serious tools. We retain a sound critical judgment in this connection. Size, shape, weight, quality, substance, workmanship, all are considered, so that in the result there is beauty sprung from soundness of material, from elegance of form, from perfection in use . . . Then we have sailing yachts. It is strange how all the things that matter turn on sport. The lines of hull and sails are not artist's lines, are not really designer's lines. They are found in seeking spread of canvas and speed. They have the beauty of significance.

A couple of years later he was working with Peach on a programme for a series of lectures on design; his suggestions included an introductory paper by a biologist on design in nature, followed by others on tools ('the chief characteristic of man is that he is a tool-using animal') and goods for leisure pursuits ('man in the round or the complete man'). And presently we find him urging Peach to consider putting on an exhibition of 'all the various balls used in sport and all the implements that are fashioned for knocking balls about. If at the same time', he added, 'you could get some of the older examples of golf clubs, cricket bats, etc. it would be even more amusing to see how these implements had developed. I think if you can put together a collection of balls, bats and racquets, you should add labels to explain exactly the governing factors in the design of the ball, the weight and size, as prescribed by the rules of the game. The whole thing should be an interesting study.' 'I received your suggestion', Peach wrote back. 'Can you find someone to carry it out? It is no good doing it without making the points as you say, and I do not feel I personally can undertake it.'

At its thirteenth meeting, held on 13 June 1935, the Council for Art and Industry was informed that the government were considering an invitation from the French government to take part

Tooting Bec, 1926. All the station buildings illustrated in this section were designed by Charles Holden; the date given in each case is the date when the station was opened.

Sudbury Town, 1931.

Rayners Lane, 1933.

Southgate, 1933.

Arnos Grove, 1932.

Oakwood (formerly Enfield West), 1933.

Cockfosters, 1933.

Boston Manor, 1934.

Northfields, 1932.

Osterley, 1934.

Hounslow West, 1926.

Chiswick Park ticket hall, 1932.

A platform shelter on a surface line.

An automatic booking office, photographed in 1933.

A tube train.

A surface line car of the Hammersmith & City Line stock, photographed in 1937.

55 Broadway, Westminster: the headquarters building of the Underground Group (now London Transport), designed by Charles Holden and opened in December 1929.

'Day': sculpture by Jacob Epstein on the headquarters building.

Subway entrance to Manor House Station, 1932.

Subway entrance to Green Park Station, 1933.

A standard bus shelter.

A canopy bus shelter.

Two views of the RT-type bus, introduced into service in 1939.

in an international exhibition of industrial art due to be held in Paris in the summer of 1937. The council would be expected to take responsibility for the British pavilion, for which an important site had been provisionally allotted. The council at once got busy with its preparations and when, at the October meeting, the government's acceptance was confirmed, Oliver Hill, the architect member of the council, was ready with a detailed sketch plan. But his plan proved of little use for in the following month the council were told that there had been some misunderstanding and that the site would be only one-third as big as had been anticipated. Members must have felt that perhaps this was just as well, for the Treasury had decided that this Paris exhibition could not be regarded as falling in the 'first category' and the money available would be strictly limited. When the show finally opened on the third Saturday in June 1937 there was put on sale a handsome *Guide to the Exhibits in the Pavilion of the United Kingdom* in which Oliver Hill explained how the Pick council had laid it down that 'the pavilion building should be treated as simply and directly as possible, as a shell, without extravagance or irrelevant features.' The enforced plainness of his building was not, however, calculated to impress British visitors to the exhibition. One of them, Alfred Bossom, a one-time architect who now was MP for Maidstone, thought the building dreadful; 'it might be anything,' he said in a letter to *The Times*, 'a riding school, an aerodrome, or a factory on or off the Great West Road.' A vice-president of a well-known furnishing business confessed that he 'could never have imagined that Britain could have been let down so badly'. The members of the Pick council were not disinclined to agree with those who deplored the poverty-stricken look of the pavilion, and in their concluding report to the Board of Trade they suggested that 'it would be better not to participate in future international exhibitions unless adequate sums are provided to maintain to the full the prestige and dignity of this country.' Yet quite a number of people were heard to speak up in the building's defence. One of these was another architect, Charles Reilly, the leading person in the field of architectural education. He was no admirer either of the Russian pavilion, he said, 'with its colossal chromium plated figures', or of the German one 'with its cluster of giant columns crowned by a very Imperial eagle . . . Before the exhibition closes these pavilions, so striking at first sight, will be laughed at by most people.' Oliver Hill on the other hand seemed to him to have achieved 'exactly the right attitude for a democratic country which still cultivates free and open discussion'; it was to be hoped that we British, learning from the experience, would 'keep to our quiet way of doing things and leave the vulgar shouting to the totalitarian States who are experts at it'. Reilly's comment was echoed by one of Pick's fellow-members on the council who wrote to express his sense of relief when he first caught sight of a pavilion where, as he put it, 'the pipes of peace and civilisation fall gratefully upon the ear.' Unfortunately it was already beginning to look as though those expert shouters were unlikely to continue much longer to stick to mere shouting. When Kingsley Martin was writing about the Paris exhibition in his *New Statesman* he suggested that the pavilion 'represents a phase of Britain. In two months' time we shall be building another exhibition of destroyers, big guns, Hawker and Fury aeroplanes, munition factories, and regiments of cannon-fodder.'

Inside the building the causes for complaint about the Pick council's 'quiet way of doing things' were more numerous. In the House of Commons George Strauss wanted to know why 'the three chief exhibits which the visitor sees on entering the British pavilion are a large model of people hunting, another of people shooting, and a large picture of the Prime Minister fishing? Does the Secretary to the Department of Overseas Trade', he asked, consider 'that this arrangement is either suitable or dignified?' Whereupon Ellen Wilkinson jumped up with another question: 'Is it not possible in the exhibition to suggest that the British people occasionally do some work?' The Board of Trade, while making it clear to the Pick council at the outset that it would be given an absolutely free hand, had nevertheless dropped a hint that the council would do well to 'concentrate upon those sections of industrial art in which this country is pre-eminent, e.g. sports goods and certain types of clothing'. And so when Pick in the *Guide to the Exhibits* explained that his council had 'decided to attempt to picture to the world those elements of the curernt civilisation of Western Europe which have been contributed mainly by Great Britain, or might fairly be said to be specially represented by that country', it is hardly surprising that he should have put 'our sports and games' at the top of his list. Yet the proportion of the total space allotted to that section was not unduly great. The first thing the visitor would see on entering the building was a homely little dining room with wall panelling of British Columbian maple and furniture made of English yew. In the main hall the greater part of the space was taken up by displays of household goods, furnishing fabrics, books and general printing, graphic design, and dress with dress fabrics and accessories. There was, however, a second reason for the great prominence of sports and games, the difficulty namely of finding subjects for the wall panels and other decorations that served as a background to the exhibits. The idea was that these decorations should illustrate typical exhibits in actual use, but since you could not well expect an artist to make a mural painting of a family eating its dinner or father relaxing with a book the temptation to look to sports and games for a subject must have been very strong. The loudest complaints, however, came from those interests in the country that felt they had been less than fairly treated. As had happened in a number of recent design exhibitions the exhibits had been assembled by selection committees without any consultation with the industries concerned. But this was not a privately organised exhibition. This was HM Government putting British industry on display to the world; by what right had the Pick council presumed to tell HM Government which products of industry should be put on show and which should be denied that privilege? Week after week spokesmen for different industries came up with questions in the Commons. Was the Secretary to the Department of Overseas Trade 'aware of the deep resentment which exists in the pottery industry at the way in which the exhibits had been chosen?', and there followed a clear hint that the Council for Art and Industry had been 'got at': 'The industry are of the opinion that certain influences have been at work.' On another day the Secretary was asked whether he had 'considered the resolution adopted at a meeting of the Council of the Birmingham Jewellers' and Silversmiths' Association which expresses concern at the adverse impression created abroad'? Other bodies such as the British Toy Manufacturers' Association chose to air their complaints in the columns of *The Times*, where another correspondent warned that on any future occasion 'the Treasury should be advised by a committee of competent business men instead of by cranks out of touch with either art or industry.'

The Great Society

When Pick found himself at variance with friends like B. J. Fletcher, who wanted to see design training kept separate from training in the fine arts, he was voicing a conviction to which he had been firmly committed since his early days with the Design and Industries Association. In 1916, in a lecture to the Art Workers' Guild, he spoke about the kind of art that

> thinks of itself in works of art as distinct from articles of commerce. It thinks of itself in high prices, as though cheapness were unworthy of its pride. It thinks of itself as something that exists as an entity, when it is really nothing more than a process, a mode of expression. Because a piece of sculpture or painting has acquired a separate and valued being by reason of its art, art has claimed to be sculpture and painting. Art is described as 'applied' where it has not this separately valued existence. This is a false notion, for all real art is applied . . . In its finest periods great art is the flower of the lesser arts. It grows like a flower, unconsciously and without striving.

And again: 'Art is a living thing. It must be joined to all other living things. What we must seek is a revival of art in relation to all the things of life.' Twenty years later he was still sounding warnings about the great break-up of cohesion and continuity. In the winter of 1937 he was invited by the Royal College Old Students Association to read a paper to which he gave the title 'The Creative Purpose Leading up to Art and Industry'; in the following year it was the turn of the Cambridge meeting of the education section of the British Association. The subject is brought out strongly in both these papers. That vital element in all education, the synthetic view, was present, he said, in the old-fashioned classical education, but where would you find it in any of our existing departments concerned with the arts? He asked:

> Has anyone seriously examined the prospectuses of the fifty leading art and technical schools? Smatterings of everything in them all. Not one without its range of departments to cover all crafts and trades, printing, weaving, metalwork, dress, furniture, leather work, commercial art, drawing, architecture,

196

building, and so on . . . It is more like a dismembered jig-saw puzzle than a pattern of education; education in the arts and crafts has become a matter of bits and pieces. No one is able to put it together, to give it a completeness, a wholeness, that would allow it to have a purpose or goal, that would add understanding to knowledge.

To the old students of the Royal College he spoke of the world of today as being more and more at the mercy of the scientist:

Nature must largely do as she is told by physicist, engineer, chemist, biologist. It is a fair question therefore to ask: what are they going to make of the world? . . . It is an even fairer question to put to you who as artists in some form or other are chosen and called to be the creators: what are *you* going to make of the world? . . . Our civilisation for a century or more has been busy pursuing ends like wealth, knowledge, mastery over nature, mastery over man. There is much that is good. Everywhere there is an endeavour after order, grace, beauty. What is needed is someone to sort out the pieces and turn the jig-saw puzzle into something whole and plain.

He reminded his audience how the expression 'common sense' had been used by philosophers ever since Aristotle's day for something that had been defined as 'the sense that is common amid the confusion of specific cases'. The significance of all art lay in the fact that it was the perfect medium for this 'common sense'; 'only art', he said, 'can pull all these bits and pieces together into some kind of unity. But we have neglected art, and our civilisation reveals that neglect.' Men and women afflicted with a sensitive social conscience might perhaps

find some release in the preaching of socialist doctrine, but how much better to seek release in practising its principles in your daily work, in directing those principles towards the realisation of design in industry, suffering many martyrdoms as you will from so-called industrialists, suffering many disillusions as you will from so-called commercial designers, suffering little appreciation as you will from an ignorant market. But if you believe, as you in your profession surely must believe, that beauty is the right of every citizen, however mean or lowly his station and capacity, then you will remember that every right begets an obligation, and the obligation to bring home to him the beauty of whose enjoyment he is capable will be yours, the obligation to open his eyes to still greater beauty will be yours. Through the industrial arts you will be able to act socialism instead of talk it.

Pick had always seen art and beauty as things reaching far beyond the visual world; again and again he had talked to different audiences about art 'permeating' all departments of life, about the 'pursuit of art' as the great adventure of business. In November 1920 he had given a lecture at the London School of Economics in which this view was treated at some length. The example he took was the design of a system of fares in a public transport service. He described the complexity of the traditional fares systems of the railways, riddled with anomalies and veiled by the heavy curtain of obscurantism with which the experts had always been careful to surround it. He explained how the Underground Group had striven to bring forth some order out of this chaos, to design a simple system founded on clearly stated principles. Behind that simplicity lay a whole world of complicated facts which had only been reduced to simplicity by a great expenditure of thought. He wound up with a quotation from one of his favourite papers, A. N. Whitehead's 'Technical Education and its Relation to Science and Literature', the 1917 presidential address to the Mathematical Association which was reprinted in the same year in Whitehead's *The Organisation of Thought*.

It sums up my address far more ably than I could myself. 'Finally', says Whitehead, 'there should grow the most austere of all mental qualities; I mean the sense for style. It is an aesthetic sense, based on admiration for the direct attainment of a foreseen end, simply and without waste. Style in art, style in literature, style in science, style in logic, style in practical execution have fundamentally the same aesthetic qualities, namely, attainment and restraint . . . Style, in its finest sense, is the last acquirement of the educated mind; it is also the most useful. It pervades the whole being. The administrator with a sense for style hates waste; the engineer with a sense for style economises his material; the artisan with a sense for style prefers good work. Style is the ultimate morality of mind'.

It was John Austin who many years ago had first revealed to Pick the true meaning of sovereignty in its various manifestations, and later Ruskin and others had shown him what great things management with its 'powers of subtle but gigantic beneficence' could achieve if properly directed. Subtle but gigantic. Working alongside the political governments that rule by law were the business governments that, ruling by management, put men and women to work, build the cities in which they live, work and play, mould their environment, direct their lives. He had something to say about this comprehensive activity in his presidential address to the Railway Students' Association in the autumn of 1930. In his first rough notes for this paper the two words 'government' and 'management' are bracketed together, and when he was speaking he made it clear that he could see no material difference between the two. The London Midland & Scottish Railway Co, for example, governed a body of people twice as great as that which had been regarded as a suitable population for the city states of ancient Greece. He said:

A railway has a constitution, an organisation for the purpose of its administration and operation. Call it a management if you like, but it is in fact a government. It has a civil service for the execution of its clerkly work, and the establishment of this civil service on a flexible and enterprising basis is one of the major difficulties to be overcome today. It has courts of justice in which discipline is judicially maintained. In its agreements and arrangements it creates administrative laws . . . You are told about all these things, but are they woven together with thought so that they become a fresh pattern in the web of political science?

'Are they woven together with thought?' This was the question he was driven to ask whenever he started to examine the various forms of social machinery. 'Is there present in them the sense for style that manifests itself as beauty?' When, in one of his earliest papers, he said: 'I believe the true, the godlike function of art is to give direction to the evolution of civilisation'; when in his pamphlet *This is the World that Man Made* he defined art as 'the attempt of man to secure some semblance of beauty and harmony throughout his civilisation, to introduce order and meaning into the world he has built and fashioned for himself', he was seeing form in administration, form in business, form in things seen, as different approaches to a single aim, the attainment of this supreme virtue, style, 'the ultimate morality of mind'.

In September 1938 the education section of the British Association met at Cambridge to discuss the problems of 'Education for a Changing Society'. Pick was one of the leading speakers. Our greatest need, he said, was a bringing together of three related institutions: the *universitas literarum*, which was the traditional literary and clerical university, the university for the study of the visual world, and the university of business. 'I skip science because it already commands more than its fair share of attention and support.' Having spoken at some length about education in art and design he came to the subject of business training. Our existing business schools accepted the view prevalent in business itself that business is conducted

almost solely for gain and only incidentally for service. Students go into commercial schools not to learn the living principles and vital policies of commerce but to learn how business is being carried on at the present time. Our educationalists have failed to find for business that broad philosophical basis on which a structure of knowledge should be built up . . . No one has yet done for commerce and industry what the Greek thinkers did for politics and ethics, or what the Roman lawyers did for jurisprudence. Economics had a bold, brave career at the start but it has never attempted to cover the whole field. Law and medicine have their institutions in and out of the universities. Commerce and industry, though much more important, have given birth to no equivalent institutions.

He recalled how Sir William Beveridge had written to *The Times* a few weeks earlier deploring the shortage of scholarships that denied so many promising young people the opportunity of a university education. If Beveridge had in mind our universities as they were at the present time Pick said he would be forced to disagree. 'I somehow feel that universities such as this of Cambridge in which we meet are supplying the country with too many candidates for employment. Are not enough clergymen and authors and civil servants and critics and teachers and repertory actors being supplied from here already?' If Beveridge were willing to accept his view about the missing universities then Pick would certainly agree about the need for more scholarships; 'the country could absorb many more candidates to work in the fertilising and liberalising of the wide deserts of commerce and industry as of those of the arts . . . Is is not strange', he asked, 'to find that in a commercial nation like ours no serious attempt should yet have been made to turn its knowledge and experience into something transcending its pedestrian everyday pursuits?' When he was lecturing to the Institute of Transport in January 1933 he had quoted with approval Newman's statement that 'a man of well-improved faculties has the command of another's knowledge; a man without them has not command of his own.' He said:

> The seven liberal arts of Aristotle, which certainly affirmed the many-sidedness of man, the variety of his aptitudes, sought his education as a harmonious whole. With the rising influence of the clerkly profession in its several manifestations these seven arts had woefully shrunk, so that when the controversy over a liberal education revived in the nineteenth century it was seen as strictly confined to the classics. It meant an intensive study of Greek and Latin writers.

What modern business lacked was the concept of a liberal education, of an education 'which permeates and liberalises the life that is now lived, which takes all the manifestations of the life that is now lived and transforms them into parts of an ideal life, or shall we say the "good life" if "ideal" is too frightening a word. Business must find its place in the good life.' It was the same phrase that he had used when addressing the students: 'The school . . . must be linked with the good life at all points, it must be a part, an active part, of civilisation.'

7

DESIGN AND LONDON TRANSPORT: 1935-1938

Man at Work

Among the many letters that reached Pick in May 1933, when news of his appointment to the London Passenger Transport Board got around, were several from some of his oldest artist friends. 'I have felt in recent years', he wrote back to one of them, 'that the standard of publicity work generally has fallen off again, which is regrettable. With the coming of the new Board we shall have to make a forward movement to see whether we cannot establish once more a higher standard. This is but one of the labours which the Board opens up.' But this particular labour was one that would almost certainly mean bringing in from outside a new person having the right sort of experience. Pick, who had his hands full sorting out and assimilating so many people, held strong views about the prior claims of existing staffs and was not prepared to act in a hurry. A month or two after the appointment of the board one of his fellow members wrote asking him to see an acquaintance who he felt might be usefully employed in the new undertaking. Pick wrote back admitting that it would be desirable for London Transport 'to have certain fresh staff in order to strengthen its stock of brains, but I am afraid', he said, 'that we must deny ourselves the advantage, at any rate for a couple of years.' The letter was written on 20 May 1933. It was on the first of May 1935 that I joined him. 'A couple of years.' There was nothing slipshod about his assessment of the task that lay before him. His formal definition of my duties as the new publicity officer had however been deliberately left somewhat vague; it just said that I was to 'have responsibility for the visual presentation of the undertaking to the public'.

I got my first sight of Pick at work when I started on my regular attendance at his two big weekly management meetings. It was an unexpected privilege. The meetings were an instrument perfected over years of trial and experiment; their purpose was to enable the greatest number of decisions to be taken promptly and yet very deliberately, with all the chief officers concerned, in a given time. To assist him in the working of this machine and to record the flow of decisions he had a small personal staff of two or three young men. It was one of the things he had learnt from Sir George Gibb in York, the art of strengthening management by bringing in graduate trainees. As soon as he judged them ready for junior management posts they would be sent off and others would take their place. This constant turnover of his staff was an inconvenience he suffered the more gladly because it enabled him to choose the best people knowing that they would never be allowed to stagnate and run to seed. Alec Valentine, who later rose to the position of chairman, Anthony Bull, who became vice chairman, and David McKenna, later a member of the British Railways Board, were all passing through this school in the years when I was there. The work at these meetings was planned in fortnightly cycles that started at about half-past five on the Saturday evening, when Pick would sit down in the study of his house in Charmouth with the papers for Monday's engineering meeting. On that day he would eat a high tea instead of dinner; this made it possible to put in five or six hours of continuous work and still get to bed at a reasonable hour. He would spend the greater part of the Sunday going about the countryside and then catch the afternoon train back to town. The following week-end he would stay in London where he would find the Saturday morning a useful breathing space to be employed in clearing up the odd things he had lacked the time to attend to in the week.

At half-past ten on the Monday morning he would take his seat in the meeting room with the secretary of the engineering meeting on his left, and on his right the general manager of the railways. Arranged round the semi-circular table that faced him were the chief engineer with the civil engineer and the architect. There was the chief mechanical engineer of the railways, the chief electrical engineer, the chief engineer for the trams and trolley buses, the estate agent and myself. Charles Holden and other outside architects would attend when their jobs were under discussion. The agendas as a rule were long. Sheets of drawings would be unrolled and put aside, and followed by other sheets, so that by the end of the morning Pick, leaning back in his chair, would sometimes be almost invisible behind a heap of drawings rising in half-unrolled coils. A difficult job could bring half-a-dozen officers to their feet, their heads almost touching as they crowded round the chair in which he sat deep in thought, his eyes fixed on the cornice of the room, tapping a pencil against his teeth.

It was in February 1937 that he accepted the invitation to address the Association of Old Students of the Royal College of Art. The paper started off with something like an apology: 'When I reflect upon my position', he said, 'there is little reason to justify my coming here to speak to you.' He went on to tell the students something about the kind of person he was:

> I suppose I am what is called a man of action. Day after day I have to find answers to a continuous stream of questions about staff, finance, traffic, engineering, publicity, supplies, all the various elements that combine to build up the business of a large public utility undertaking. In no sense am I an expert. I have and can obtain advice whenever I want it. I merely have to decide, but in deciding I become responsible for my decisions. And while they are all separate decisions it is necessary for me to try and fit them together into a consistent whole. I must have a plan, a policy. This is not always easy. The mind tends to become something like a daily newspaper, a jumble of headlines and paragraphs about everything in particular but nothing in general. And time for reflection is short.

Of all the decisions he had to take those concerned with engineering works were the most difficult. In a paper read at one of his conferences of officers he compared them to decisions about birth and death. To have to make a decision about the birth of a new asset was a serious matter. He said: 'It is easy to say that the aim of these discussions on Mondays is to provide the Board with the finest physical equipment that we can possibly have. We have a reputation for good design, and now we have the pains and expense of keeping up that reputation.' A standard had been set, but it was necessary in the observance of a standard always to keep an open mind. 'It may not be good enough. It may, in certain circumstances, be too good.' A standard must not be allowed to become a substitute for thought. 'Nothing can be repeated.

Nothing repeats itself in nature, and nothing can be repeated in the undertaking of the Board. Those who think they will just replace what they had before are greatly mistaken.' When the assets had been created there was the problem of an increasing rate of obsolescence, of an expectation of life which was continually falling: 'The funeral costs of an asset, in the way of amortization, are far too heavy. I dislike the taste for costly funerals.'

One day Charles Holden was talking to me about Pick's engineering meetings; he said:

They always struck me as a model of what good government ought to be. All the persons involved are present, there is an expectation that each one will have something to say or some question to put, and that something will come up that will turn out to be important. Pick is a marvellous listener. Decisions are taken in such a way that you go to a meeting knowing that it will take you a step forward in your work. And it does, you come away with a clear picture of the next thing to be done.

Sir Ernest Clark of the old Underground companies felt that the secret of Pick's ability to make good technical decisions lay in his early legal training.

He would never fail to apply that legal mind to any matter that came before him. Where was the evidence? And evidence for the other side would have to be heard, too. The lawyer's approach to his work enabled Pick to combine two qualities that are not often found together in a manager: an ever-open mind, and a passionate regard for continuity and stability in the conduct of every sort of business.

But this method of working depended for its success on people being made to bring up their plans at the earliest moment, before they had time to become set. Holden had discovered that there was nothing that put Pick off more than elaborate presentation; in a letter to a technical journal published after Pick's death he wrote: 'He was suspicious of large and impressive perspectives but often a small freehand sketch would set us going on an important scheme.'

About the next morning's meeting, which started at eleven o'clock, Pick had this to say in his paper to the officers' conference. 'One week we have accounts and the following week staff and stores. Now what is Tuesday's policy? You leave behind the trial and error of the engineer and arrive at the exact mind of the accountant and the statistician. You find it a considerable strain. Accountancy is a cold and unaccommodating pursuit.' On the Monday 'if you think you want a certain result you may almost persuade yourself that that result will happen, but after you have met the accountant on Tuesday you know that it will not'. Nevertheless it had to be remembered that to fail to give attention to the last merciless detail 'is to disregard all the maxims that should govern our conduct and form the basis of a satis-factory life. The £5 job is as full of revelation as the £10,000 one. We should not therefore complain when on Tuesday we are asked by the audit officer to examine what has happened in quite minor matters in the discharge of Monday's works.' The staff and stores meeting, which came on alternate Tuesdays, was very different. 'Here the real problem is to give decisions that are consistent. You must give consistent decisions or perish. Staff questions in particular are full of traps for the unwary: the favourite word at these meetings is "repercussions". I often find myself quite unequal to maintaining a rightful standard of virtue in dealing with the Tuesday agenda.' He went on to talk about the con-troversial temper that meetings on staff matters were liable to generate, the ever-present fear of industrial trouble that became 'a subtle influence towards compromise . . . But compromise may become a vice. If you are not able to see both sides clearly, that is a dangerous thing. If on the other hand you are able to see both sides clearly, that again is a dangerous thing, for it may lead to a paralysis of decision. One has to wear a harder temper and not take the generous way, which is the easy way'; especially must this be done 'in those debatable matters – and there are many – that are open to judgement. For he who would sit in judgement needs, alas, all the virtues.'

Tuesday night would bring the heaviest stint of homework; it seldom took less than three hours to get through. First came the reading of the draft minutes of the engineering meeting which had always to be on his desk at 5.30 pm on the Tuesday at the latest. These minutes were scrutinised more closely than those of other meetings because of the size of the capital investments that were so often involved. And they were as a rule of considerable length; they would record not only up to a couple of dozen deci-sions made round the table but also a number of observations arising from Pick's tour of inspection of the previous week. But, whatever their length, the need for clarity and precision were never forgotten. A typical minute put down for my personal benefit dealt with a request from the Ministry of Transport for permission to put up notices at some of the new subway station entrances designating them public subways:

The Vice-Chairman directed Mr Barman to consult the Parliamentary Officer and obtain his certificate that the subways are in fact public subways. He further directed that only on those subways which the Parliamentary Officer certifies as public subways should the notices be exhibited, and that the Ministry be informed of the principles governing the decision, and, further, that they be informed that while the Board are not prepared to exhibit the notices in subways which are not strictly public subways, they have no intention of prohibiting the use of such subways by the public at this time although they may not be travelling by train.

There was no room for mistakes with that sort of minute in front of you.

The other Tuesday evening job was that of studying the agenda and the papers submitted for the traffic meeting which started at eleven o'clock on the Wednesday morning. At this meeting, facing the chair in the middle of the semicircle, there would be the managers for the various services, each with his assistant manager; next to them, on either side, sat the commercial manager and the two officers responsible for public relations and publicity. When Pick talked about his traffic meeting at the conference of officers he said:

On Wednesdays we reach the root of the matter . . . Altogether there are 593 routes of road transport, and there are the six principal railway lines. We have opportunities for making the right adjustment here and there, and the cumulative result of these adjustments may be enormous. Why cannot we make them? There are a thousand opportunities, but we cannot take them all at once. One of the financial papers has described this undertaking of ours as a 'razor-edge' type of undertaking, meaning that our success or failure depends upon a very fine point. I have the sort of mind that continually relates incongruities together, and so this comment reminded me that I recently saw in an illustrated paper a photograph of a snail climbing over a razor.

207

He paused to contemplate the image of the snail on the razor's edge. He said:

Apparently a snail can do this without injury to itself because it has co-ordinated controlled musculation. This co-ordinated musculation in relation to our system of fares, of routes, of services, should be able to provide that 0·166 of a penny, or whatever it is that we want. To hold down any increase in mileage; to look carefully at any new proposal for development; to watch the average receipts closely, knowing that if we reach that slightly higher level we can then release more miles and give more satisfaction, that is the arithmetical frame of mind in which we approach Wednesday's business.

Wednesday was chosen for this particular business because it was the time when all the statistics for the previous week were available for study; train miles and vehicle miles, and revenue earned by the different railway lines and road services. The receipts per mile for all these and many other figures were pondered and discussed. After that came the week's reports on failures and delays: causes were unravelled, responsibility fixed, ideas for remedial action agreed upon and recorded. Great care was taken always to treat statistics as a highly perishable commodity; they had to be consumed quickly or they would turn bad on you and all they were good for then was the wastepaper basket or the history book. In his lecture to the Railway Students' Association Pick had some illuminating things to say about the 'environment of facts' in which work at his meetings was carried on:

When you enter the railway service you should come into contact with facts as living, changeable things, you should find, as it were, an environment of facts fluctuating, extending, contracting, like the mists on mountain sides as the sun rises and shoots his rays upon them. The heavy, sluggish belt of mist seems suddenly to be drawn up into a waving tongue. It breaks into patches which rise and fall and creep along the mountain sides (very like statistical graphs), growing thinner and thinner until at last the sun's bombardment bursts through and scatters them. When you understand and appreciate your environment of facts you will find just the same pleasure in your business outlook as you find when, in the mountains, the cloud-hung day suddenly clears and becomes fine and sunny. But if you fail to understand and appreciate your environment of facts, then your surroundings, like the unilluminated mists, remain inert. There is a pall stretched over the whole of your outlook, your standards become fixed, you lose your most precious gift, your adaptability.

Nearer View

Pick's Thursday morning meetings would alternate between a mixed-up sort of meeting called 'claims and estates' one week and 'publicity' the next. The first of these was not very congenial to Pick. In his conference paper he said about the claims part of it that 'our heart must be suitably hardened. The justice that we are to administer must be strict justice. There is an aspect of gloom about these meetings, for the picture that cannot always be shut out is one of suffering and misfortune. Let us therefore turn', he went on, 'to publicity which is much more amusing and interesting.' The publicity meeting would start off on the unoccupied tenth floor, the lowest of the four top floors that had been found to contravene the London County Council fire regulations and were not therefore permitted to be used for offices. The ban was later lifted, but in those days the great empty space made a splendid private exhibition hall. Half-a-dozen screens were kept there on which were displayed the posters and bills produced in the previous two weeks. The output of printed publicity during that period was greater than ever before; the number of full-size posters ran at an average of some 700 jobs each year and in addition there was the steady stream of smaller bills such as the ones produced for the draught screens in the Underground carriages at the rate of a dozen or so a month. These minor items, most of which had not been submitted at the design stage, would now be studied and commented on. As soon as Pick had done with his inspection of executed work we would go down to his seventh-floor room for the meeting proper. I can still remember the impression made upon me by this room one morning when I was first shown into it. Why had he chosen to place his private office on this side of the building, on the north side where the steady north light would fall over his left shoulder as he sat working at his desk? You know where you are with a north light, you can see the shape of things, the facts stand revealed in their true colours. Then happening to look out I noticed the trees of the park. Was it the cool unwavering never-varying north light that had made him put himself there? Or was it perhaps the piece of lovely green perspective framed in the gap between the Anglo-American Oil building and the little house on the corner, the house designed by Detmar Blow, William Morris' architect friend, the man who had driven Morris' body to the grave in an old harvest waggon? It must almost certainly have been a bit of both.

At these meetings he would sit with his personal secretary at his side facing the three of us, the public relations officer and myself with my assistant, across the conference table. I can still see the broad, youthful-looking face with the shy smile playing at the corners of the mouth; the keen blue eyes flutter slowly up under their deep lids; the strong, broad-tipped fingers stretch towards the corners of the blotter on which there lies a small sheet of paper, half covered with green writing. I see the wide forehead framed in fine unsmoothed hair once of that dull, reddish-fair colour that you find in East Anglia – the pale Huntingdon red, as I once heard Sir George Beharrell call it – but now sharply turning white on the temples where it grows long and curly because he can never remember to have it cut, almost covering up the small, flat, delicately formed ears that might have been a woman's. And all the time there are those clear blue eyes looking full at you from under the lids on which the lashes spring long and thick, feeling you, probing you, measuring you up. The mouth? The lips? They could be many things. They could be hard and scornful, flashing with wicked irony, if he was talking to somebody big and self-important. They could be angry and sulky and obstinate if there was any fighting to be done, and he rather enjoyed a fight if it was about something he cared for. They could be shyly self-conscious, struggling to hold back some feeling he found it hard not to betray, a bubbling inward laughter, a movement of pity or love or tenderness, a sudden sense of uncertainty and helplessness when people around him started the kind of talk that was meant to act as a smoke screen, hiding what they were really thinking or to draw off the enemy with decoy thoughts. But however they might respond and change, however they might curve or melt or stiffen, there was a quality in those short, straight lips that was always there, in all weathers and all moods, a quality in which the demure gravity of the Puritan was mixed with the artist's passionate fastidiousness, a quality that you will only find among the kind of people our parents used to describe as the 'pure of heart'.

The business of the public relations officer was taken first.

He was the person who at that time kept open the lines of communication with MPs, local authorities, the editors of a couple of hundred newspapers and periodicals, public bodies of every kind – not to mention the man in the street whose letters of enquiry or expostulation would descend on his office at the rate of a thousand a week. Pick had a way of saying that the volume of the public relations officer's work was a measure of the inefficiency of mine: the better my publicity the less there should be for him to do. His was a personal job, predominantly ad hoc, and his work when he came to report on it was almost all of it past history.

His half of the meeting therefore took up but little time. My own inquest had already taken place upstairs and this second half of the meeting was concerned with forward planning and with the more important projects and designs which had to come up for approval. Special attention was always given to the designs produced for the poster panels round the station entrances. To Pick, these panels were something like a stage for a continually changing performance in which the more important posters followed one another in colourful procession. While the sites on the inside station walls were thrown open to beginners, to the young men and women from the schools who walked into the office to show their work or submit ideas, these entrance panels were kept for the masters, the ones it was the ambition of the young to emulate, men of the status of Sutherland, Wadsworth, Bawden, Paul Nash.

In these later years with the public board Pick's estimation of the role to be played by publicity was still as high as it had been in the old days when he had been required to give it so much of his personal time. To one of the London Transport officers' conferences he declared his belief that it was its publicity that had endowed the undertaking with something like a human personality. He said: 'The Board lives and works quite apart from the whole of us who carry on its life and work for it. It will go on when we have all departed from its service. It has become something which has a life and being of its own and that life and being of the Board are best expressed through its publicity.' My colleagues indeed were often surprised to see what immense trouble he would take over his posters. He had long been reconciled to a way of working that involved a wastage of some 15 per cent; if over a period of time something like one design in seven had not been thrown out, rather than feel pleased because we had got better work done, he would begin to wonder whether perhaps we had been negligent in our scrutiny.

The posters were changed at monthly intervals and the change was carried out to a drill almost like a military operation. There was a day in 1936 when it occurred to me to put this drill to a test. It was the morning when the BBC announced the death of King George V. The instructions went out from the bill store in the Charing Cross station building; by noon every site round the entrances to the 250-odd stations had been stripped of its poster, the dark-coloured enamelled panels were washed clean and left bare. Then, on the day before the lying in state, an announcement about this ceremony went up. Twenty-four hours later the poster was covered with a sheet of plain white paper edged with black, which remained till after the funeral. No exercise quite as elaborate as this had been tried before, yet everything went through like clockwork.

Among the various qualities that Pick expected to find in a poster design the first and most important was the quality he called 'directness'. Words like 'fumbling', 'confused', were meant to convey a sense of sharp reproof. 'Posters', he once told an audience of students, 'must give a unitary or single impression.' In a Swiss travel poster he criticised the use of objects such as flowers, an ice axe, a water trough with a landscape reflected in the water; though the job was skilfully executed the designer somehow had not been able to hit the nail on the head. About a slide of a well-known design by the Frenchman A. M. Cassandre he said: 'The artist has given his impression of England as a land of parks and houses, and having once conveyed that impression he has stayed his hand and the poster remains simple.' But Pick's ideas about 'directness' did not mean that he expected a design to make no demand on the viewer's intelligence. He could see nothing wrong in a poster being 'difficult'. In an article he wrote in 1927 he said: 'those who decry posters which require some pains and thought for their understanding underrate the urge to stretch the mind a bit more than usual, underrate indeed the intellectual level of an urban population. It is foolish to descend to an elementary treatment of a subject on the grounds that there should be nothing above the heads of the public. The public like something above their heads, if only it is attainable.' So long as the meaning was there to be grasped it was not necessary that the grasping should be made too easy.

In the early months of 1937 a war of words on the subject of modern art was raging in the columns of the magazine *The Studio*. It had been set off by an article signed 'Layman' and printed under the title 'Modern Art is a Sham'. Pick was one of a number of eminent people who were invited by the editor to make some comment. The debate was a lively one. 'Layman should have a medal' said the artist Tom Purvis; Sir Julian Huxley protested that 'the theoretical basis of modern art is wholly justified'; an article by John Betjeman was headed 'A Spiritual Change is the One Hope for Art'. Pick wrote a longish letter which appeared with about a score of others in the February 1937 issue. He admitted to finding himself on the side of the majority who sympathised with the hostile view expressed by the anonymous author. He could not, however, 'exactly agree with him'; he was not prepared to find fault with modern art in general, only with some of its 'more extravagant manifestations'. For some modern painters he had words of warm praise. As he contemplated a picture by Cézanne the artist, he wrote,

> seems to say: 'How can I represent this tree, these rocks, to convey their meaning and purpose?' and he seeks after a simplification through which they become not this tree, these rocks, but tree and rocks in general. The later Picasso says: 'Follow my train of thought as I work out the formulism of this abstraction'; he will give it an intriguing title as a clue and watch to see whether we can appreciate his mental experience. It all turns on whether the train of thought, the mental experience, is worth while.

How did one decide whether a mental experience was 'worth while'? Pick had a very simple test. First, an idea was worth while if it was genuine, if it was held with conviction. But conviction was just what so many modern artists lacked. Too often the artist

> seems to live on the surface of things. He is a dabbler in almost any current notion. He reflects the insincerities, the frivolities, the enfeebled coloured-shirt politics of the social group in which he lives. It is not therefore surprising that he has nothing very much to express. A dominant passion must possess him before he will be able to turn out anything worth while.

The 'dominant passion' theme is found further developed in his lecture to the Association of Old Students of the Royal College of Art a few weeks after that letter was printed in *The Studio*. Pick's sense of its importance was if possible even stronger than that of Tolstoy who treats 'the impelling force of an inner need' as the quality that does more than any other to make the artist an effective communicator. This time it is a painting by Van Gogh that is held up as an example:

> I must have seen a hundred or more of his pictures and not one fails completely, because throughout them all you can feel his intense fervour, his passion in paint: he is compelled to set down what he sees, whatever it may be; he is compelled to reveal some secret life in what he paints. In Munich there is a picture of some gardens and houses sweeping down to the banks of a river. On the near side there are three pollarded trees. It is a place of no special beauty or significance yet you are arrested by it, there is a sense that life is still running its course beneath the surface of the picture.

Here was an artist who knew what he wanted to say. And moreover he was fiercely determined to say it. This brought Pick to the second part of his test. There was nothing wrong with an artist considering himself as belonging to a kind of priesthood, but the priest if he wants to work as an artist must not retreat behind a private language, a curtain of exclusiveness. Art by definition is something understandable by the common intelligence and the artist must want to be so understood. 'Abstruseness', he said, 'denies common humanity', but common humanity was denied not only when the artist addressed his work to a small caste of initiates; the mere fact of having any kind of special audience in mind could not but be harmful. An artist has no business to try 'to flatter the intelligentsia or shock the bourgeoisie', still less to 'play down' to an audience thought incapable of receiving the real thing. There followed an illustration from Pick's own experience. A group of young artists had recently been 'persuaded to produce autolithographs for circulation to schools. They had obviously said to themselves: "This is meant for children, we must play down to them." It is the last thing a child wants from an adult artist. If you go and look at any exhibition of children's drawings you will see that this is the kind of thing they are very good at producing for themselves.' An artist who felt a genuine desire to communicate with children would never try to do so by aping them. Because the special value of the non-verbal arts lies in their character of a universal language, the painter, unlike the writer, can afford to forget about special audiences. More than that, he is in truth required to forget. The freedom conferred upon him cannot with impunity be rejected. Whenever an artist does not fully accept this freedom from language barriers and make proper use of it 'the spontaneity and inevitableness of good art will be lacking in his work'.

The deep-rooted ambivalence of Pick's reactions to the work of the surrealist school was fascinating to watch. If he felt that a picture was concerned with the freakish, the fantastic, with what Goya so percipiently described as *capriccios*, his sympathy was immediately aroused. 'Nature herself', he told his audience at the Royal College of Art, 'had her freakish outbreaks long before man; she has left a trail of extinct monsters, dinosaurs, megalotheria, pterodactyls for our reproof, descending to a few oddities that still survive in axolotl, duck-billed platypus, toucan, and so forth. But with Nature we know that these are not in the great tradition of life, they are by-products, chances, sports.' He could find pleasure in 'sports' so long as they were avowed and could be seen to be such. 'My memory', he said, 'turns not ungratefully to Georges de Chirico; he gives a conception of space which he partly fills with objects capable of relation but leaves it to the imagination to interpret them.' Pick did not particularly care for the later works of Paul Klee, which he quickly brushed aside as 'fatuities'. There was, however, another kind of surrealism that he would criticise with some vehemence, not for its craziness but for something that he took to be an act of regression from the present world, a desperate act, not just a backward glance but a flight into unreality from a present filled with fear. In one of his lectures he spoke about artists who, like Peer Gynt with his onion, peel off 'cover by cover the meaning of their dead selves until the final horror is disclosed'. But there was always something unreal about this 'final horror'; the attempt at escape could never succeed. 'It is not possible to go back. It is indeed impossible to stand still.' Man was doomed to live in one direction only, he might stumble and fall, he might stray into false paths, but there was no alternative to the forward movement in time. The impulse to retreat must always end either in self-delusion or in the artificiality of deliberate pretence.

Certainly Pick did believe that the public should be encouraged on occasion to 'stretch the mind a bit more than usual', but the encouragement was not to be given in tones of too great earnestness or solemnity. To be human meant being simple, relaxed, when necessary perhaps even light-hearted. At the time when I was working with him he could still amuse himself at his old game of putting together pairs of contrasting photographs that years before he had started to play in his lantern lectures. The game was regularly played each year in the editing of London Transport's desk diary, one of his best-loved hobbies. The idea had first come to him when he was collecting photographs for the 1924 *Year Book* of the Design and Industries Association and writing odd notes on the subjects illustrated; the sequence arranged under the heading of 'Costume', for example, started with an aerial photograph of Wembley stadium packed with spectators and ended with a street scavenger wearing the clothing provided for him by the Westminster City Council. A couple of years later Peach sent him for Christmas one of those German calendars displaying a series of photographs chosen and arranged with great skill. It fascinated Pick. He wrote back at once: 'I will produce a similar calendar for you for the year 1927 on behalf of our Underground Group, dealing with our own railways and with London. I think that with a little pains I could beat the German one.' Twelve months later he sent his own 'calendar' to Peach. It was, in fact, a desk diary bound like a book; two pages of diary were interleaved with two pages of pictures so that whenever you were using the diary there were always a picture or two in front of you on the facing page. In his covering note to Peach he said: 'Next year I am going to try some design propaganda in our calendar. I am going to illustrate our wonderful century at large.' When he had finished his second diary he knew he must go on; there was no way of stopping now. He was careful to see that the diaries were made to serve more than one purpose. They did something to tell the story of the Underground, its services, its people; at no time, however, were they allowed to dwell on these subjects too long. They helped to propagate the ideas of the Design and Industries Association and more especially the idea that the critical examination of the man-made world was among the citizen's first duties in a modern community. But perhaps their most important function was to act as a constant reminder that this critical examination was a part of the spirit of the

Underground Group, that the management cared deeply about the human environment, that it was always ready when occasions arose to direct this examination upon itself, upon every part of its business that was visible to the public.

Magnate and Manager

There was in Pick an awkward blend of the teacher and the administrator and as you watched him at work with his subordinates you would often see the one at odds with the other. A teacher is expected to know. His pupils, if his knowledge is not constantly seen to be greater than theirs, will think but little of him. The good administrator is careful not to appear to know too much. But with Pick no matter how painstaking or how excellent your work there was usually something to be added, some part of it to be done better still. Its solid merits had a way of dwindling and melting away under that penetrating gaze. 'His own efficiency has a bad effect on the efficiency of others' was the judgement of his old colleague Sir Ernest Clark. 'How can the housemaid', he asked, 'take pride in a job to which the mistress will insist on putting the finishing touch?' And certainly there were those who would gradually give up the unequal contest and come to lean more and more on Pick's strength. Pick had a way of being at the same time too soft-hearted and too impatient and a point would come where he would carry off the papers and have a go himself. I am sure he knew this was bad for the man, an incitement to laziness; it was just one of those little weaknesses that he had never been able to correct. But what was worse was when the man instead of giving way to laziness was overcome with nervousness and fear. The strain of trying to keep pace with an intellect so quick and so searching would be too much for him. If Pick was liable to feel a little guilty over his effect on the lazy man, the man who became afraid would cause him real distress. It is a common thing for the head of a business to have to inspire fear in order to assert himself; fear is the magic that clothes him with authority and when people cease to be afraid of him he becomes like the emperor in Andersen's tale. Ashfield had something of this in him; with Pick it was the other way round. To see a man go in fear of him would make him miserable. Then there was the kind of person who would meet his thrusts with evasions, retreating behind half truths that could be worse than outright bluff.

217

For such he would have no mercy; to run away was to invite pursuit and when in pursuit he was capable of hitting hard. There was also the sort who considered that a chief who insisted on knowing so much was taking an unfair advantage. They would feel their authority assailed, their dignity would be hurt. If Pick was talking to one of these there was likely to break into his voice a note of gentle mockery and if you watched closely you might perhaps detect a suspicion of something uncommonly like a wink.

Sometimes people might feel that thinking them mediocre he looked down on them, he despised them. But he never despised mediocrity: it was too dangerous a thing to be despised; it was like some kind of disease or disablement; there was nothing to be done except to give what help you could to the victim. What he did despise, and he never minded your seeing it, were the more complacent forms of stupidity. When he thought he detected this weakness he would often prefer to say nothing. One day his old friend Fred Phillips, the printer, sent him a design asking for his comment. 'Why', wrote Pick 'should we proceed to intelligent criticism of non-intelligent work? Silence would seem to be golden upon occasion.' It was only when he was striking out at someone who knew what he was doing and was capable of hitting back that criticism became really worthwhile. It then became a dialogue, something interesting that he could enjoy. The trouble was that this happened too seldom; he would complain to his friends about the difficulty he found in getting people to stand up to him. It was not enough for a man to know his job; he must have the ability to let it be seen that he knew he knew it. He had to stick to his guns. I myself was one of the fortunate ones who managed to sustain that kind of relationship with him. 'I like your open critical mind', he wrote to me at the end of our first year together. 'I like your disagreement with me and my old-fashioned notions. I like your bad arguments. I intend to go on struggling with you for my own and, I trust, your profit.' Some years later H. P. Shapland told me about a train journey he had made with Pick at about this time. My name happened to come up in their conversation and Pick, telling him about some of our joint enterprises, said: 'He has just been giving me ten good reasons for doing the wrong thing.' That was the way he really liked being talked to.

A proper dialogue, however, means more than just argument meeting counter-argument, it is a situation where criticism is exchanged, being contributed equally from both sides. I soon discovered that to take your turn in criticising Pick was to do him a favour. When in his lecture in Edinburgh in 1917 he used some words from the Gospel of St John he was guilty of a misquotation which cannot have been accidental, changing the second person into the first: 'The truth shall make *us* free.' That is what he really meant. One day his Danish friend, the architect Steen Eiler Rasmussen, sent him a copy of a magazine to which he had contributed an article. The article had a few unkind things to say about London's Underground. Pick wrote to him: 'I always find the outsider's point of view extremely refreshing and interesting. He sees things that we do not see who are too closely concerned with the detail. You should come and criticise and appraise our efforts more frequently.'

His attitude to his colleagues was the same. One of the first visits of inspection on which I accompanied him included the newly completed Leicester Square Station. The layout of the station ticket hall seemed to me disappointing. It was a smaller version of the highly successful Piccadilly Circus plan, but the conditions at Leicester Square were altogether different: instead of a great common escalator shaft serving both railway lines there were now a pair of shafts going off at an angle and separated at the top by a flight of stairs coming down from the street. There were five of these street entrances all told; people coming from one of them had to break through an eddying stream of passengers and sort themselves out again in order to proceed by one or the other of the escalators. The architectural design of stations was no direct concern of mine but having gone back later for a second good look I decided to put down my misgivings in writing, adding a few diagrams to illustrate my point. The answer came back at once: 'I have read your notes and I agree with you. I think your design No. 6 is a very good one for a station like Leicester Square and it is a pity that we have not adopted it.' He went on to ask me to look at the plan for the new St Paul's Station that was then under discussion and 'consider it in the light of your memorandum'.

The noticeable predominance of the teacher over the administrator had one great advantage: the constant sense of high expectation that will bring out the qualities of a person as the sun encourages the flower to realise itself in fruit. As with the sun the heat of his criticism could scorch, but if you were able to brace yourself against its action there could soon spring up something very like the creative partnership between the teacher and the taught, as if a musician tackling a new and difficult piece were playing it together with one who had already formed clear ideas about its form and meaning. Thomas Griffits the lithographer once said to me: 'Pick's personality was such that you would come away from his office absolutely resolved to do your very best for him. You simply had to produce a first-class job: you knew that nothing less would do.' The point was elaborated by Dora Batty whose first poster for the Underground was accepted by Pick in 1920. She said:

That gift for getting the best out of people was really amazing. He would immediately come down to your level, but he never forgot his standards which were the highest. When by way of comparison or illustration he referred to some other artist's work it was always the work of a master. His memory was extraordinary; he would say: 'If you go into the something museum in Düsseldorf, into the third gallery, and go up to the first case on the right-hand wall, you will see . . .' And so on. It would take your breath away. And his references somehow were always apt ones. He could discuss your work and a detail in a Botticelli picture in the same sentence in such a way that you felt yourself piercing through one of the secrets of Botticelli's greatness; you felt yourself almost on the verge of discovering a little touch of that greatness in yourself. What made it such an extraordinary experience was that he spoke with absolute sincerity. He meant every word of what he said.

Pick's first rough notes for the address to his officers' conference in which he described his weekly work routine start off with a glance at himself: 'Not a politician. Only developing a casuistical mind. Meant for a student. Became a man of affairs. Hasty, impatient.' As so often happened this little exercise in self-depreciation was afterwards scored out in red ink. But the real interest of the passage is that it contains not only one portrait but two. Just as a photographic film when you hold it up so that the light strikes it at a particular angle will suddenly change from a negative picture into a positive, so this self-portrait when read in reverse is seen to change into a portrait of Ashfield: 'A born politician, an agile casuistical mind, a man of affairs gifted with immense patience and powers of cool deliberation.' Ashfield's friends knew, for with them he made no secret of it, that he had spent many years assiduously building up his impressive image. Among the stories he was fond of telling about his early struggles some of the best were concerned with the close study he made of the ways of his betters. One such story was quoted by an old colleague of his, C. W. Reeve, managing director of one of the Underground's subsidiary companies that had to be sold off under the 1933 Act. Young Albert Stanley, as he then was, had one day walked into a drug store and got himself a cup of coffee. Suddenly he noticed his chief sitting at the counter a few places away. As he looked at him he saw him take up a salt cellar and carefully drop some salt into his cup. 'I had never before', said Ashfield, 'seen anyone put salt in his coffee, but I thought it was the kind of thing that perhaps one ought to do. I tried it. Somehow it didn't appeal to me, but for a while I kept on taking salt in my coffee, thinking I would get used to it and might even come to like it.' Some months after that, Stanley was in his chief's office when suddenly he said to him: 'Tell me, Mr Stanley, do you always take salt in your coffee?'

'I have been doing it since I saw you, sir, take some in a drug store one morning.'

His chief looked surprised. He said: 'That wasn't coffee I was drinking. That was Bovril.'

The habit of modelling himself after some admired person remained with him all his life. The object of his admiration would change from time to time and the strength of the feeling could vary greatly with the man and the circumstances. His friends had the impression that a person on whom it was concentrated with special intensity was Lord Beaverbrook. Though I had for some time been aware of his feeling for the little Canadian wizard it was not till the middle of World War II that its full significance was brought home to me. I found then that what was needed to give him full satisfaction was not just to succeed in doing as the admired person, it was to do well that which the other had managed to bungle. Among Beaverbrook's little misadventures during that period which is still remembered was the 'Saucepans for Spitfires' appeal of July 1940. To make up for the loss of bauxite supplies from abroad the housewives of Britain were asked to give their old aluminium saucepans to the nation: 1,600 receiving depots were set up by the Women's Voluntary Services to take them in. It was a stirring appeal. But when newspapers other than those owned by Lord Beaverbrook found out about the thousands of tons of scrap aluminium waiting to be used, and calculated that all the saucepans in the country would not keep the aircraft factories going for more than a couple of days, Beaverbrook's plan was made to look like a slight case of dottiness. Ashfield however knew better: the plan had been conceived as a morale booster and had indeed been a very good plan. And presently Ashfield decided to try his hand at an appeal of his own. On Thursday 24 October 1940 a number of buses belonging to the town of Halifax suddenly appeared in Victoria Street and Bond Street and other places, and an announcement went out that bus undertakings in all parts of the country would be sending up a couple of thousand buses between them to take the place of buses lost or incapacitated through enemy action. Londoners were moved by the thought that their friends had remembered them; the native of Glasgow or Huddersfield would shed tears of nostalgic pride as he saw the reinforcements from his homeland come cruising down a London street. My friend Theodore Thomas, London Transport's general manager (operations), told me the rest of the story a year or two later. 'I kept on protesting to Ashfield. I said people were bound to find out that it was not buses we were short of, it was the men to drive them. For every bus lent to us there would be another one of our own added to the buses standing idle in a garage. But it was no use. He was not interested, he was determined to go through with it.' Certainly Ashfield was not a person of the stature of Beaverbrook but there were some things lacking in Beaverbrook that Ashfield possessed in full measure. One of these was the art of not being found out.

Underneath that manufactured persona, the benignant brow, the Henry Poole suits, the aroma of expensive cigars, there lay all the inborn mental equipment that goes to make the successful political manipulator. When difficult negotiations looked like heading for a breakdown he was able, as Lloyd George had been on some famous occasions, to bide his time, watching and listening, always a master of the difficult business of inaction, till suddenly, as by the twitching of a magic wand, the crisis was seen to be no longer there. Some mysterious organ peculiar to him would tell him precisely at what moment to spring into motion and how much to give away. He had something, too, of the actor's feeling for the sudden unexpected gesture that can thrill an audience with surprised delight. This particular technique was one utterly foreign to Pick; having watched it in operation for many years he yet had never got over a mild sense of dislike. At the Reform Club one day Sir Cyril Hurcomb, the Permanent Secretary of the Ministry of Transport, was gently teasing Pick whose face seemed to him to be wearing an unusually glum look. 'It's the chairman', said Pick, and he went on to explain. A few days earlier a bus driver with a side movement of marvellous quickness had saved a man in the street from almost certain death. Pick had been with Ashfield just before lunch; as he was leaving the room Ashfield said: 'By the way, Pick, what are you doing about driver X?'

'Why, nothing in particular.'

'Why not?'

'He was only doing his duty.'

'I think', said Ashfield, 'that we should buy him a gold watch and chain.'

'A gold watch?' said Pick in astonishment. 'Very well.' He made his way to the door.

'Just a moment, Pick. I really ought to have him in. Arrange for him to be invited. He will have tea with me here in my office.'

Pick sighed. He nodded his head, saying nothing. He was halfway through the door when Ashfield leant forward over his desk and asked: 'By the way, is he a married man?' Pick, who knew many things, had no idea. 'Find out whether he is married. If he is, don't forget to include his wife in the invitation.'

'I am afraid' said Pick to Hurcomb, 'that made me rather cross. It really was *too* much of a good thing.'

If some of Ashfield's qualities could make Pick feel uncomfortable, there were others that he genuinely admired. Perhaps the most important of these was a gift of prescience, almost a kind of divination, to which Ashfield himself would deprecatingly refer as his 'hunch'. The ordinary person when coming face to face with another hears only what that other person chooses to say. If he is especially observant he may be able to read the thoughts behind the words, to sense what the other is really thinking. Ashfield could tell not only what a person was thinking but what he was going to think. In a discussion on business matters he knew even before opening his mouth to speak what his opponent would presently be saying in reply. 'I sometimes flatter myself,' said Pick to a colleague one day, 'that I can see five years ahead, but then I get talking to the chairman and I realise he is able to see not five years ahead but twenty-five.' And there was another quality which he may not have admired without reservation but which he knew to be indispensable in their business, and indeed it had made possible its survival, for it was a quality in which he himself was altogether lacking. The people on whom Pick was liable to make a bad impression were of many kinds but on no kind could he be relied on to make an impression so disastrous as that which he habitually made on the great and the powerful. It was with people like these that Ashfield was seen at his masterly best. One of his chief officers, who had felt obliged to resign over a disagreement on a matter of policy, was still able some years later to describe him as 'the most skilful commercial diplomat in London'. Ashfield indeed might well have taken as his motto Beaverbrook's favourite epigram from Edmund Burke, 'The world is governed by go-betweens'. Cyril Hurcomb, who in his long career as a civil servant saw a great deal of him, used to say that he had never known anyone to equal him in the art of approaching a Minister.

When Sir Ernest Clark became a member of the Underground's board of directors he was much impressed with one particular trick of Ashfield's that used to fill him with astonished admiration. Half-a-dozen questions would be put at a meeting and Ashfield at once would see that among those questions there was one the answering of which was liable to give some trouble. Pick, if the questions had been addressed to him, would almost certainly have taken the awkward one first and striven valiantly to give an answer that was fair, comprehensible, and true. But not Ashfield. Ashfield, with a brilliant show of confiding artlessness, would take his time answering the easy questions one by one, speaking at considerable length; when he paused to turn to some other matter that unanswered question would have gone from the minds of all persons present. On the rare occasions when he judged it necessary to bring the full force of his personality to bear on some controversial point, he could make his listeners feel that, though it might appear desirable that his view should be rejected, such action would be utterly unworthy of them, it would be unthinkable. Pick well knew how much had been accomplished by the use of this magical gift: how much, for example, it had done to help bring the London Passenger Transport Board into existence. In the succession of battles over the form of the government take-over which had gone on from 1927 to 1933 Ashfield again and again had won the day by a swift last-minute resolution of a stalemate. Towards the end, when the government Bill was going through Parliament, there had been at least two such occasions. The first was a mass meeting of stockholders and shareholders of the Underground Group held at Caxton Hall in the spring of 1931. A state of open rebellion against the terms agreed between Ashfield and the Minister was quenched by an impassioned speech that swung a majority of votes to Ashfield's side. Snatches of his highly charged emotive language were recalled by Frederick Menzler, his personal assistant at the time, in a lecture he gave a couple of years after Ashfield's death. 'I used to tell you: "Believe in me . . ." You have been very loyal to me . . . I have pledged my word to the Minister. You may fail to support me; in that event you will have to find someone else to carry on for you.' Two years later the government suddenly found its Bill in grave danger of being thrown out in the House of Lords. The opposition this time was perhaps less determined than it had been at the Underground meeting, but Ashfield had staked his reputation on the successful completion of the plan. No one who heard his moving performance in that debate could possibly have doubted that it was this that finally turned the scale.

The Ashfield–Pick alliance on the surface might be little more than another illustration of the useful English tradition of dividing power between two individuals: the amateur and the professional; the Monarch and her Prime Minister; the Minister and the Permanent Secretary; or the Magnate and the manager, as the American Peter Drucker calls them in one of his books. You could not say there was anything novel about the chairman and chief executive arrangement. The two men seemed to work together like the blades of a pair of scissors. But there was a difference. Whereas neither blade of the scissors will cut without the other it could not be said that Pick was indispensable to Ashfield as Ashfield was to him. The real dependence was all one way. It was a situation of which Plato shows himself to have been aware when he makes Socrates say about the philosopher: 'He is like a man in a den of wild beasts. He is not strong enough to hold out alone where all are savages.'

Pick after his first few years in London had seen his old

chief Sir George Gibb fall among the London financiers and if Gibb had not been absolutely devoured he certainly had not got away unscathed. Pick knew that he himself was even less well equipped than Gibb had been to stand up to the savages, that his hope of survival lay in such support and protection as Ashefild might be willing to afford. And Ashfield fortunately had proved willing. This marriage between imagination and power depended on the man of power putting a value on the union, on his seeing it as something advantageous to himself. Was Ashfield for all his deep amorality yet astute enough to recognise high excellence when he saw it? You simply could not tell. So far as publicity was concerned he did one day in a moment of frankness confess to me how he felt about it. He had no use for Pick's kind of publicity. No doubt it gave pleasure to some people but it was of no use to the business. A transport service needed advertising in the same way as a department store needed it – to tell passengers what was being offered in the shop; anything beyond that was a waste of time. But what about the architecture, what about the whole aspect of the undertaking as it showed itself to the world? Was there just the slightest note of jealousy in the voice that spoke in reply? No doubt the truth was that he found himself perfectly willing to accept Pick's work for the London Transport environment, and to accept the high personal reputation it had brought to Pick, simply because acceptance was but a modest price to pay for something really worth having – the marvellously stored brain, the selfless dedicated zeal.

And there was also something else the secret of which was told me one day by Pick's sister Ethel. When they were children together in York there were times when a younger brother or sister would say something in disapproval of their parents; she remembered one occasion when their mother had dismissed a maid for whom the children felt a special affection. 'You are not to talk like that about our parents', Frank had said. 'It is our business to cover them.' He would use that word 'cover', she said, when speaking of some person to whom he stood in a relationship involving a special duty of loyalty. If anyone similarly involved should venture to criticise that person he must expect to be at once rebuked, and she had noticed that the more deserved the criticism the angrier would be the rebuke. Ashfield knew well that he was one of those persons.

8

DESIGN AND CITIES: 1935-1939

An Act of Faith

On Fridays the office was forgotten. The long green Daimler, a double-six convertible whose roof folded back like that of an antique London taxi, its rear compartment spacious enough to hold a small committee of five, would drive Pick straight from home to the first point set down in his timetable for the day. His only regular companion was the secretary for the engineering meeting. They might start with a bus garage, arriving always unannounced, for a routine inspection. Pick would walk through the main garage shed, the office, the workshops, the storerooms, not forgetting mess-room and lavatory, with the secretary busy at his side taking notes. Wherever he went, wherever he looked, there was always something that could be done better, either now in this place, or some time in the future when new things were being planned. He might go on to see an engineering job in progress where the civil engineer, the architect, the head of the building department would meet him by appointment. A projected new bus route might need to be looked over, some traffic problems, inadequate service, the exact placing of a bus stop, of a mobile staff canteen, a stretch of route bedevilled by bad time-keeping, investigated at first hand. He would spend the entire day like this, moving from point to point, with the secretary keeping one eye on his watch and the other on the rapidly filling note-book; if new construction work was included in the intinerary the secretary might be struggling with an armful of rolled-up drawings while trying to write.

One of my clearest memories is of an evening in the summer of 1938 when we met at Victoria Underground Station at quarter-past ten. From there our small party travelled by train and bus to inspect half-a-dozen stations where improvements had been made in the lighting of the street entrances. This business of entrance lighting was one of the new responsibilities recently placed on my department; it was an attempt to avoid being cast into outer darkness by the ever-rising standard of illumination of neighbouring shops and cinemas. The measurements I had made surprised Pick: at a height of 3 or 4ft above the pavement the intensity of lighting under the canopy at Leicester Square Station amounted to half a foot-candle, exactly one-twentieth of the brightness under that of the Hippodrome theatre across the street. It was not, of course, thought necessary that the Underground should try to compete with a brilliantly lit cinema entrance, but Pick certainly felt that the contrast was getting too great and a reasonable effort must be made to bring down the gap. And so on that evening he went round these stations to look at the result of our work. When midnight came he had finished. We found ourselves down below in St Paul's Station, where the tracks and signalling had been re-arranged so that the old Central London Railway platforms could be lengthened to accommodate the new full-length trains. Half an hour later his car arrived to take us through deserted City streets to the new station at Aldgate East. The platforms had been built about 10ft below the level of the existing tracks, which were now supported on rows of stout trestles; the trains had been running over these old tracks for months, and that evening work had just started on the dismantling of the trestles and the lowering of the suspended tracks on to the substructure that lay ready to receive them. The first morning train was due to come through some five hours later. Pick was fascinated by the progress of this skilfully planned operation and it was with some difficulty that he dragged himself away to carry on with his tour. When we came to the end of his day's work at Holland Park Station it was getting on for three o'clock in the morning.

In one of his papers Pick described the management of a big undertaking as a state of continual warfare against an invisible enemy. But if the enemy was invisible the evidence of his activities fortunately was not. 'The eyes', he said, 'must be everywhere, and they must be seeing eyes.' There is another paper in which he drew a distinction between two ways of seeing. One way was with the use of statistics: 'under Sir George Gibb I was trained into that way of seeing.' The other was by random sampling. The trouble about this second way was that you could only see a thing after it had happened; it did not give you immediate insight into the present as statistics properly used could do. Nevertheless, seeing by sampling was just as necessary in management. He said: 'Monday, Tuesday, Wednesday and Thursday you are busy giving decisions, arriving at agreement as to what should be done, offering comment upon what is done, and on Fridays you go out and see what has happened and you find the unexpected and the unaccomplished.' And it was not just a matter of safety and efficiency; an environment was being created and in that environment it was necessary that order, cleanliness, regularity should prevail. An appearance of efficiency was not a substitute for efficiency in action; it merely made it possible for a sense of efficiency in action to exist, to be manifestly seen. Lack of order, of proper care, made a sort of vicious circle. They were the result of inattention in certain people and would communicate that inattention to others, spreading slovenly habits of mind and body like a contagious disease. Fortunately the reverse was equally true. 'How easy', he said in one of his lectures, 'to learn from what surrounds you daily! How comforting to learn virtue by example rather than by precept!'

He knew he could see through the objects around him into the attitude of mind that made them what they were: the dirty passage-way, the badly placed cable housing, the broken gas fire, the teacups in the booking office, the torn bookstall bill, the straying bag of cement, were signals that told him something about a particular person or group of persons; they were like so many windows through which the weaknesses of individual people became suddenly visible. And the same was true of the observed behaviour of men at work. In a memorandum to the chief civil engineer written after one of his inspections he says:

Coming down the Metropolitan Railway from Moor Park to Baker Street and leaving Moor Park, say, at 10.15 and arriving at Baker Street, say, at 11.15, stopping at Harrow and Finchley Road stations, and on the way keeping a general observation of the work in progress, I was surprised to find how many of the people employed upon work on the line were, so to speak, idle. For instance at Harrow station I should say fully one-third of the men employed were gossiping rather than working. At two or three points on the line I noticed signal-fitting staff doing no

229

work at all. At Northwood Park no one could say that the work was being pushed with any vigour. At Finchley Road there was a slackness pervading the whole appearance of the work. It therefore occurred to me that something was wrong with the supervision of the work on the Metropolitan Line. Will you please tell me who is in charge, who assists him, and the extent to which there is regular supervision of the work which is going on all the way down this Line.

In the last of his officers' conference papers he wrote:

I always think I can guess the quality and worth of the supervisory staff by looking at the men and women at work. I go into shops and depots where the atmosphere gives me pleasure, into others where I suffer disappointment. Nothing irritates me more than a loafing type of supervisor or than the officious person who must keep all his subordinates at a discreet distance, and you know you will get nothing out of your visit except a distaste of him.

And behind the supervisor there were still other men – a whole hierarchy with lines of command reaching down. He said: 'Between the final decision and its execution many people may intervene' and he spoke of the 3,000 officers, assistants, senior clerks, superintendents and so on, with several thousand more at the next level, responsible for supervising and checking the work of a labour force just over 70,000 strong. 'What pains must be taken to explain the way we are going, our policy, our programme, if we are to ensure that a word said at one level will pass to another level in the same spirit, in the same temper, with the same meaning. There', he reflected, 'is a problem which we have not solved, a problem to which we must all direct our thoughts if we are to be successful.'

He had at that time risen to a position in the business where most people would have felt justified in delegating to others the greater part of this task of keeping watch. But Pick never showed any sign of being tempted to feel so justified. To those around him there was only one thing more remarkable than his passion for observing at first hand, and that was his quickness to act on what he had seen. This was true not only of working colleagues but of friends in all places. One day Noel Carrington was trying to convey to me his impression of Pick's attitude to his responsibilities. He summed it up by describing a couple of incidents in which he personally had been involved. A daughter of his was being treated in the Royal Orthopaedic Hospital in Stanmore. On Sundays, visitors' day, either Carrington himself or some other member of the family circle would go to see her. The hours were from three till five. Every Sunday, soon after half-past two, a small procession of visitors would emerge from Edgware Underground Station to await a bus for the two-mile ride to the hospital. But when the bus came up there would be room for only a few and then the others would settle down to wait a quarter of an hour or so for the next. Then again they might be unlucky; on more than one occasion Carrington had arrived at the hospital an hour late, an experience that seemed to be by no means uncommon. One day, while seeing Pick about other matters, he decided to have a word with him on this subject. On the very next Sunday, 'only three or four days after our conversation,' said Carrington, 'my daughter's nurse on coming out of the station saw with amazement a string of no less than five buses waiting by the station bus stop. That is what Pick was like.' Carrington, moreover, found that Pick's compulsive inquisitiveness was not confined to his own business. He was a transport man, moving people was his job, and wherever he went there would be something to be learnt about that job. It so happened that in the summer of 1930 Carrington, on a journey back from Gothenburg, had found among his fellow passengers Pick and Holden, who had just concluded their tour of northern Europe. When the passengers were put ashore at Tilbury the customs officers had not arrived to start work. There was a long wait. Carrington was with Pick in the queue. He could not at first understand why Pick failed to do what any railway director would have done as a matter of course – make himself known and allow himself with his party to be shown through to the train. He was aware that Pick had little use for the red-carpet treatment, but the wait on the quayside was rather more than Carrington would have expected him to put up with. Presently, as he looked at Pick standing there, he saw that there was a simple explanation. Pick was too interested in what was going on: an opportunity had occurred of watching the development of this little contretemps through the eyes of the ordinary passenger and he was determined that the opportunity should not be thrown away. 'Whenever I think of him at work', said Carrington, 'I see him as the ideal inspector general.'

In a paper he read to the last of the annual conferences of London Transport officers Pick put the question:

Is it all worth while? I often sense that question being asked, when I am out on inspection. To-night you have my considered answer. You will remember the old saying: 'Seeing is believing, but feeling is God's own truth.' Behind the seen there is the unseen, behind the felt, the divined. It becomes an act of faith, an affirmation that life is worth while, muddled and anxious as it is. The Board's undertaking is a declaration of faith by the Board that its task is worth while, that its labours shall eventually contribute their appointed share to the transformation of our urban civilisation into some fine flower of accomplishment.

The date was November 1938. When he was writing that paper he had just finished a heavy spell of work on the government's plans for the evacuation of London.

The Urban Scene

As he went about his duties in the world of urban transport Pick would sometimes admit to himself that he would always remain a north-country railwayman at heart. The lives and work of the railway builders had set an example that was to him more than an object of admiration and respect; in his present environment it could fill him with a sense of secret challenge. When he was lecturing at the London School of Economics in 1927 he suddenly put on the screen a lantern slide that must have puzzled some of his audience. It was a view looking down on the railway tracks at the point where they enter Newcastle Station; the pattern made by the criss-crossing rails suggest at the first glance the meshes of a giant fishing net floating on the water. In 1933 he found himself talking to another audience to which the subject was rather more familiar. The occasion was the annual dinner of the Permanent Way Institution, the professional organisation of the railway civil engineers. Pick knew himself to be but a poor after-dinner speaker but on this evening he was unable to resist the entreaties of his own chief engineer who was president at the time. He held up the railway track as a superb example of the pioneering spirit of the early railway builders. For it was the people responsible for laying the permanent way of Britain's railways who were the real inventors of the modern road: the method of construction, the design of curves, the calculations for banking or 'superelevation' as the railwaymen called it, all of this had started with them. And as with the more glamorous steam locomotive these inventions were the work not of scientists or designers but of practical craftsmen, ordinary people whose training had been acquired by working with their hands. The Underground track that went deep into the earth and ran mile after mile through the tube tunnels was the work of a later race of men but here, too, the maintenance of order and safety depended on the same craftsman type. In an address he gave in 1929 he had spoken about the importance of this work.

When the trains stop running for the night little groups of platelayers, signal fitters, pumpmen, wiremen pour in, and for four or five hours – a brief enough interval – inspect the track and its equipment and repair the wear and tear of the day. The landscape is monotonous; segment follows after segment in seemingly endless files. The runs of cables and rails stretch almost unbrokenly in each direction, interspersed at intervals with signals and the brighter glow and greater spaciousness of a station. Yet in this landscape familiar features occur to those who walk its length night by night. Odd kinks in the tunnels, slips by the engineers who built them, special bits of track work, loops in the cables, crossings in the tracks, headings and connecting passages, it is thanks to little landmarks like these that the men who walk the tunnels know where they are . . . But more than this, they speedily learn the true craft of their work. An unexpected glint here, and they know that a bolt is loose or a chair shifting. A scratch there, and they know they must test the gauge of the track or pack up the sleepers. An irregularity on the polished face of the rail, and the time may have come to replace it with another, or to turn it. The faintest indications and they interpret them in terms of safety in operation night after night. In the old days the hunter was renowned for his woodcraft, his interpretation of the marks and signs in the forest, and here in London there are these ordinary workmen, it may be said, engaged on a subtler and more delicate tunnelcraft at this very day.

There were not many things that gave greater pleasure to Pick than seeing a railway track well looked after. Constantly in the minutes of his engineering meetings there would appear items like one written in May 1939 which says:

233

The Vice-Chairman referred to the stocks of permanent way material such as keys, chairs, etc. which were stored at intervals along the Uxbridge Line and suggested that the Chief Engineer (Civil) should arrange for a bin to be designed at Parsons Green Works to contain these materials. The bin would be a concrete unit and would be installed at appropriate intervals throughout the open sections of the Board's railways.

This interest in the appearance of the railway track was further stimulated by the discovery round about 1930 of a kindred spirit who was at work in the North Eastern Area of the LNER – as Pick's own old company was now called. His name was John Miller. The civil engineer of a railway spends millions of pounds in the course of a year and of all that money some two-thirds can go into the maintenance of track. Miller, who had more than 5,000 miles of it to look after, was the first main-line engineer to organise its upkeep as a single concerted operation. Pick, when he was travelling on the line, would note with approval the wonderful precision of the top edge of embankments, of the edges of stone ballast and trim grass verge. To make sure that the perfect edge of ballast would stay perfect Miller would reinforce it with bigger stones, handpicked, tapped in with a heavy hammer. There was no path or plot without its clean, firm kerbing of some strong and lasting material. His electric cable gear, his mile posts and other indication posts, all his various pieces of lineside furnishing would be beautifully arranged. Wherever Pick might look he would note that order and design had been brought to the performance of some simple everyday task. One day, when he was telling me something about one of his journeys north, he said: 'You know, when the train slows down to approach the Selby swing bridge I put away my papers. I always look forward to a sight of the Miller country.' His words reminded me of that day when we were picking out some photographs to be printed in the first annual report of the new board; because of the vastly complicated subject matter the report could not be got ready for publication till the end of 1935. Among his final choice of sixteen pictures were two views of newly built Piccadilly Line track in the neighbourhood of Acton Town Station which he insisted in putting on the first page. He asked me to write short captions drawing attention to the knife-edge trim of the ballast within the complicated pattern of the rails.

A railway, however, was something more than just a strip of ballast and rails. In the autumn of 1930, when work started on the extension of the Piccadilly Line to Hounslow, Pick found himself landed with a new problem in design. On the last lap west of Northfields Station the old District Line tracks, which were now to be used by the trains of both lines, ran over low-lying ground; for a distance of just under three miles they were carried on a high embankment. The neighbourhood had become familiar to Pick before World War I when he was planning new bus routes to link the District train services with such places as Windsor, Maidenhead and Staines. And he could hardly have failed to retain a mental picture of the way this great embankment dominated a pleasant landscape in which clusters of little houses lay nestled in well-tended greenery. The embankment had been built in the 1880s and after this interval of time it was not a pretty sight. Work was about to start on half-a-dozen new station buildings to the design of which Pick and Holden had given painstaking thought. How could this conspicuous piece of semi-derelict landscape stretching between the stations be allowed to remain in its existing state? Pick knew little about gardening, but it so happened that among the directors of the Underground Group were a couple of gardeners of considerable reputation: one was old Sir Herbert Jekyll, a younger brother of the famous Gertrude, one of the great figures in the history of English gardening. When Pick spoke to these two men about his problem they at once volunteered to join him in forming a garden committee of the board; the three started to hold regular meetings with the chief engineer in attendance. The next stop was to create a new post of gardening superintendent in the chief engineer's department. They were looking for a rather special sort of gardener, a man with a sense of landscape and knowledgeable in plant ecology; after they had been searching round for a while the director of the Royal Botanic Gardens put the committee in touch with a young man in his middle twenties called B. J. J. Moran. Moran had been trained at Kew and was now employed by the Middlesex County Council. He was put to work on the Hounslow job with a small hand-picked staff and before long they had found a way of producing quantities of gardener's top spit soil at a surprisingly low cost. Trees and shrubs began to appear; experiments were made with the acclimatising of English wild flowers – coltsfoot, ox-eye daisy, wild daffodil. After the Hounslow Line they moved

235

on to other surface lines in need of attention and to open spaces round London Transport works and other premises, constantly trying out new plants and new ways under varying soil conditions. As the work went on John Miller, who had been watching Pick's activities with a keen reciprocal interest, decided that he too must try his hand at planting and gardening. His work in the grim industrial environment of the north-east proved even more rewarding than had Moran's efforts in suburban London. The local citizens were impressed: a long article printed in the *Yorkshire Post* in the summer of 1933 spoke with something approaching enthusiasm about the new trees, shrubs and flower beds that had made their appearance by the lineside in places round Newcastle, Tynemouth, Durham and Whitley Bay. The idea had begun to spread.

On the streets and roads traversed by its vehicles the status of London Transport was only that of a user; its responsibility was limited to the placing along the road of certain items of equipment. Yet the matter was one that Pick felt to be deserving of the same close attention. It had always been the duty of the publicity department to deal with the supply and fixing of incidental street and roadside furniture and now the creation of the new board had brought a sudden increase in the demand for these things. The route mileage operated by the buses alone was more than two and a half times as great as the mileage served before 1933. And the ban on the casual stopping of buses now made it necessary to put up a vast number of those fixed stop signs for which Pick had made provision in his 1919 plan. If ever the publicity department had needed a qualified designer, this was the time. My appointment caused a good deal of surprise when the news went out – 'a particularly interesting event' the *Manchester Guardian* called it. In 1935 a first lot of experimental signs were put up along a route picked for the purpose. The experiment met with strong approval from every responsible public body, and not least from the Ministry of Transport and the police; in the next few years new stop signs were being fixed in all parts of London at the rate of a thousand a year. Pick held strong views about road signs. He was one of the first to lay down that all information that could be conveyed through symbols rather than words should be so conveyed; people in the streets should not have to stop to read things if there was a simpler, quicker way of delivering the message. But the symbols must be clear, unmistakable, to the point. Nothing was more odious to him than a symbol designed as an eye-catcher and devoid of useful content. The opportunity had now come to introduce this method on a scale never possible before. There were two kinds of bus stop, the kind where the bus would pull up anyhow and the one where the passenger waiting to board or alight had to make his wishes known to the driver. Both signs were identical in appearance and only the word REQUEST distinguished the one from the other. In the new series of signs the 'request' design was a reverse of the 'regular' one with the bull's eye symbol in white on a coloured ground. The colour told you whether the stop was one for the red buses or for the country services.

It often happened, of course, that Pick was able to take a strong line with other people's ideas about good appearance; but there were also times when others would rise in protest against his. There was that memorable occasion in the summer of 1939 when the ratepayers of Pinner in Middlesex signed a petition asking to be spared the horrors of modern architecture and suggesting that their new station building should be given a medieval look in keeping with the surrounding properties. The new steel roadside shelters, too, were often liable to call for this particular kind of protest. Pick had not been altogether satisfied with his first experimental design – he never was – and soon after I arrived we got to work developing a new model. It had a long seat facing towards the roadway, standing room at the rear, and at one end, also under cover, a small space where maps and time-tables could be studied without incommoding other users. As this shelter, which was built of slim steel tubes, started to appear in the villages of Surrey and Sussex there were some who com-plained of its appearance; it was said to be out of harmony with its surroundings, and so an alternative version was produced in which the steel columns were replaced by substantial oak framing. I can still see Pick's questioning look when one day we stopped to inspect one of these timber shelters and found it surrounded by late Georgian and Regency houses whose porches had slender painted columns very similar to the steel shelter columns that local opinion had condemned as inappropriate. They made our massive wooden structure look grotesquely out of place. Pick had never ceased to be astonished at the number of decent public-spirited guardians of the amenities who were quite incapable of thinking with their eyes as well as their heads. The rustic bus shelter in its elegant Georgian setting might be a bit of a joke but it had got there through the action of handicapped people who had lost the power of seeing.

There was on the other hand little wrong with the vision of those people who would rise up in anger against another type of roadside equipment, the kind used for feeding electric power to the trolley buses. In the late 1920s the Underground Group had had to make a difficult decision about its hundreds of miles of badly worn tram tracks. Pick and his engineers had no wish to see large sums invested in a form of transport so ill-adapted to the conditions then prevailing in London's crowded streets. Would it not be better that the life-expired tracks should be taken up and scrapped and that the six-wheeled rubber-tyred trolley bus should take over? And so the trolley bus was introduced into the Kingston area in the spring of 1931, just thirty years after the electric tram made its first appearance in this country. The new vehicle at once became popular with passengers; it had most of the advantages of the motor bus without any of its disadvantages. Like the bus, it was able to draw up to the kerb so that people could board without having to cross a busy traffic stream. It would glide away, accelerating smoothly without noise. There were no exhaust fumes to pollute the air. But other sections of the public took a diffeernt view. Where the trams needed only two overhead wires, one for each direction, there now had to be four, with suitably stout supporting gear to carry them. The wire nuisance was seen at its worst in those streets where the old trams had been made to run with the costly underground conduit installation because the local councils had refused to authorise overhead wires. The turning loops presented a similar problem. A tram has no front or rear end. It can be driven in either direction; when it has completed its journey all the driver has to do is to take up his station at the other end and drive away. The trolley bus was able to move in only one direction, but unlike a motor bus it could not reverse in a small space: it had to be made to go round a wide loop, wires and all. It was inevitable that people living or working in streets affected by developments such as these should deeply resent them; if there were a danger of spoiling the appearance of streets where the trams were already established, how much greater was the danger to those other streets in central London in which no tram had ever been seen.

In the summer of 1933 Pick took part in a broadcast talk

about design in the street. John Gloag, his interlocutor, brought up the subject of 'all those posts and wires tangled above its surface'. Pick said: 'There is no need for the wires to be tangled. They can be tidy. Really well designed suspension is beautiful as a spider's web is beautiful.' He started a few months later by commissioning Charles Holden to produce a design for a pole. 'It may', he wrote Holden, 'have to carry litter baskets, street notices, stop plates, and, above the trolley wires, street lighting fittings. The point is to secure a satisfactory design which will carry all that is required in the way of street equipment.' With the letter went a batch of papers giving all the technical particulars and at the bottom of the sheet a short hand-written postscript gave the warning 'I want a good design.' A note to the general manager of trams and trolley buses said: 'I shall want to see the scheme of suspension to be adopted. Very considerabe importance attaches to our making this suspension as pleasing as we possibly can.' Anthony Bull remembered a stormy meeting with the chief electrical engineer about a year later. The floor of Pick's office is covered with junction units and other components used with the wires and Pick in his quietest voice says: 'It's no good, we have *got* to make this stuff lighter.' In January 1935 Pick wrote to the Ministry of Transport about a plan for a prototype installation. The Whitechapel trams in East London with their underground conduit system would, he said, provide 'a convenient occasion for reviewing the whole of the poles, signs and lights in the street'. He asked whether the Ministry would agree to call a conference of all those involved in the fixing of street equipment 'in order to see how far a consolidated and agreed scheme can be settled'. The Ministry showed little enthusiasm for the suggestion but Pick went on using every opportunity to induce or, if necessary, bully local authorities to take advantage of the new trolley bus installations to improve the look of the streets. And he was not content to ask for tidier arrangements, he was determined to use his influence to get individual items better designed. It was an uphill battle. I remember to my shame how one morning in 1937 he found among his Press cuttings one which mentioned that the East Ham Council had arranged to fix litter baskets to the trolley bus poles in its area. He at once sent me a note: 'I presume you have agreed the pattern.' I told him that the litter baskets were not very good but the council had a considerable stock of them; I had not felt that we could reasonably ask that they should be thrown away and a new lot purchased. Pick was not pleased. 'We cannot agree to the old-fashioned type of litter basket being fixed to our new poles. I am sorry that you have done this in the case of East Ham. You should be more careful.'

The planning of the turning loops was the most serious worry. At the time when this note to myself was written, nearly eighty applications for consent had gone to the Ministry and of these no less than ten had been treated with all the portentous formality of a public enquiry. The amenity aspect came up with particular strength at the enquiry into the case of Bedford Square, which was held in 1934. At the junction of Hampstead Road and Euston Road there was a terminus for the trams coming in from Enfield and North Finchley. Many of the passengers arriving by these trams had to complete their journeys by changing to a bus going east or west, but these main bus routes lay half a mile to the south of the terminus and the tram passengers had first to take another bus to get to them. It was a perfect example of the kind of situation that Parliament had had in mind when it accepted the principle that the trolley buses might travel a little further towards the centre than the trams did. The plan here was to make them continue southwards the full length of Tottenham Court Road. The little narrow streets on the west side of this road were quite impossible for a turning loop and so the engineers had no choice but to turn to the east side, where Bedford Square seemed almost to have been laid out for this very purpose. If the local shopkeepers saw their Tottenham Court Road as a virgin territory about to be invaded by the barbarians, the householders of Bedford Square felt rather as though a small volcano was about to erupt in their midst. Their joint cry of protest, signed by famous residents like Margot Asquith and Sir Johnston Forbes-Robertson, the actor, then an old gentleman of eighty, and reinforced by eminent sympathisers like Sir Edwin Lutyens, made a great display when it appeared on the correspondence page of *The Times* in January 1934. A few weeks later the signatories put in a petition against London Transport's authorising Bill in which they were supported by the Duke of Bedford, the ground landlord, and by the trustees of the British Museum.

There were times when I could not resist an impression that Pick had been a little lacking in respect for the very special quality of Georgian Bloomsbury. No doubt his thoughts were

240

concerned rather with London as a whole, with the effect on that whole of the streams of traffic crashing round in it. The electric bus, an improvement on the tram running on steel rails, was offering a means of escape from something worse than the tram, the nastiness of the internal combustion engine. It was a civilised vehicle; the loss of amenity at a few isolated points like Bedford Square was but a modest price to pay for the gain to London. Yet if the whole of London did mean more to him than the parts he was never unwilling to make most strenuous efforts to do the best thing possible for the parts. Among the many quarters from which appeals came to him was a committee of the Royal Institute of British Architects. Three poles had been put up in front of Staple Inn to carry wires for the trolley buses coming down the Gray's Inn Road; it was claimed that they spoilt the view of the old half-timbered houses that had been so carefully preserved in that rapidly deteriorating environment. Pick wrote back the same day: 'I am going to visit the site next week to look at the problem.' A fortnight later the owners of adjoining buildings were being beseeched to allow supporting stay-wires to be fixed to the walls of their premises; in September 1937 the newspapers announced that this work was being carried out and that the poles would shortly disappear. I think it was the Bedford Square incident that did most to help me understand some things about Pick that, like a number of other people, I had found a little perplexing. Behind this obstinate wrestle with the trolley bus overhead gear there lay a feeling that must have sprung from his deepest beliefs about the works of man. He had never lost his sense of man's responsibility for the totality of his creation. And he was convinced that most of the hideousness of the man-made world was caused not so much by those who had tried to achieve beauty and failed as by those who said that some particular works of man are ugly by nature – if you find you cannot do without them you just have to accept them as they are. No doubt the adverse Bedford Square verdict must be deemed to have been in the public interest but it cannot have been easy for Pick to see the decision as other than a denial of this central part of his faith.

A Green Belt Now

Pick's eager interest in the arts of planning and urban design was first fully aroused in the early 1920s when work on his big development programme got under way. The completion of the work would be setting off new, powerful forces, forces that must inevitably change the size and shape of built-up London with a speed and thoroughness such as had never been dreamt of in the past. It was right that the reformers of the later Victorian age should have pinned their faith to the 'diffusion' of the population, but this mass movement of people needed a plan.

In 1919 there had come a moment when the outlook seemed a little brighter: Neville Chamberlain's Unhealthy Areas Committee was at work and had let it be known that it was seriously concerned about this failure to plan. And its report when it came out was found to make a most urgent plea for the preparation of a comprehensive plan for London and the Home Counties and the setting up of a statutory authority to watch over its execution. But nothing had happened – only more committees and conferences, more talk, more well-meaning reports. Pick's programme had been based on a number of carefully framed assumptions but he knew these assumptions were no sort of substitute for a plan. It was clearly necessary that he should try to learn something about the planning of cities, about the meaning of the work in which he had allowed himself to become absorbed. The course of his studies can be traced in a series of about a dozen lectures and addresses spread over a period of some fifteen years. Among the first was the one he delivered at the London School of Economics in March 1925; it was published in the Year Book of the Design and Industries Association for 1926–7. Having tested the ground he was able to get down to some serious research. The little team of hand-picked members of his staff appointed to help him let themselves go; sometimes the result of their labours took him by surprise. His 1927 paper to the Institute of Transport had already been tried out on the students of the Leicester College of Art and Technology and in the intervening twelve months it had suffered considerable expansion: he confessed to this second audience that he had been 'having a very bad time trying to digest some part of my material into an intelligible form' and went on to apologise for inflicting on it a printed paper which set a new record in the institute's proceedings by running to a length of nearly 14,000 words of text with half-a-dozen statistical appendices. He came back to the same institute four years later with a sequel which was only a little shorter. He went on to give more lectures: to the Marshall Society in Cambridge, to the Royal Society of Arts, the Institution of Professional Civil Servants and other bodies of diverse kinds, ending up in 1939 with an address to the seventeenth International Housing and Town Planning Congress.

In one of the earliest of this series of papers he goes back to consider the origins.

> The English village started with a group of small farms and cottages for those who tilled the soil and pastured their cattle on the surrounding waste which they held in common. The houses usually stood round a green or on either side of a wide grassy lane. There was little distinction among them until the church came, and then from the heaths and wilds the Christian God entered and dwelt in their midst. Later the foreign conqueror arrived and the big house of the manor was built and thenceforth church and hall shared the domination of the village . . . If the village were advantageously placed, at some ford of a deep river, or at some bridge across it, or at some starting point of a trackway over the hills, or at some meeting place of frequented ways, it would grow into a town.

Transport increasing in intensity had 'created a new unit of life'. He went on to describe the slow growth of the town beginning with the little market; the inns that came clustering round it; the emergence of the market square which in its turn would attract 'the workers in wood and iron and leather, the clothiers, dyers and fullers'; the building of the market hall, of the guild hall or town hall:

> the creeping network of streets and lanes, of houses and gardens . . . There would be little organic change over several centuries. The development would be so slow that each addition would seem to fit its place and match its neighbours, without disharmony or disproportion. Out of the fires that frequently destroyed parts of the old towns, in which wood was so largely used for building, minor improvements would spring, but everywhere there would be no more than the steady and continual adaptation of means to ends. In these old towns of natural growth everything seems in its right place.

The growth in those early times had been the result of a creative response to local circumstances; it had been of the same kind as the growth we see in nature. But today we were living in a new world:

Now man is master of the forces and influences that used to beset his work; he can command them, and they therefore command from him conscious design to take the place of the unconscious design which hitherto they had drawn out of him. He must shoulder the responsibility, and while he may seek guidance in watching and interpreting the early unconscious stages, he must now go forward, more and more compelled to justify his mastery, and to prove his ability, in building cities which will proclaim the beauty and splendour of his city life.

The coming of the new age first made itself manifest in London when a little local railway line was opened which connected the suburb of Bermondsey with Greenwich. Speaking to the Institute of Transport in 1927, Pick reminded his audience how London's first suburban railway had been a sort of early warning of the great 'Victorian flood tide. Rows and rows of mean houses in mean streets filled in all the gaps for which the suburban network of railways supplied a ready means of transport . . . Cheap fares for the working classes produced the vast and dreary expanse of north-east London, a district without a redeeming feature in the way of plan or building or object of interest.' In Walthamstow, the standard example, a population that had numbered 5,000 in the middle of the nineteenth century had leapt up to 95,000 at the century's end and reached 131,000 in 1925. The railways had been responsible for most of that. And then, after the railways, there had followed other developments in transport in the design of which one might have expected that our present century would have learnt from the experience of the last. But in fact it had learnt nothing. Arterial roads, on which express coach lines soon started to circulate, had produced mile upon mile of sprawling ribbon development; the ubiquitous motor car had gone

planting villas sporadically over all the countryside without any reasonable economy in the employment of land so that the distinction between town and country around London is almost wholly breaking down. This is an even worse abuse than beribbonment but it has attracted less criticism . . . So it goes on, each means of transport creating its own pattern of development, one overlying another until all is confusion. The cells multiply without any organic framework, without differentiation of function, without the discipline of any control.

'Our forefathers knew how to grow a town', he told a Bristol audience in 1933; our own contribution is described in a sentence found among some notes he wrote a couple of years later for a lecture which cannot now be identified. 'We live in cities and towns that we dare not look at.' Pick's unhappiness about the continuing filling-up of outer London was most certainly genuine. At the time when the new London Passenger Transport Board was about to take over he had arranged to address the Bristol branch of the Design and Industries Association; when he was asked about the subject on which he proposed to speak he told them the title would be 'Plan or Perish'. He had borrowed the title from a report by the architect Clough Williams-Ellis on a recent visit to Russia which had impressed the author with the possibilities of effective planning. The communists had got the wrong idea but, said Pick, 'I could only wish we had a tithe of their passion, for then I should look to the future with greater hope.' But if you were going to plan something you needed more than just passion, you must know the purpose and scope of the plan. Were you planning an ample ten-roomed house or a labourer's cottage? 'When the structure or framework is complete any growth too large for it to bear or carry may be malignant', he said in his paper to the 1937 annual conference of the Municipal Transport Association. 'The human frame may serve as an analogy. Useless flesh only impedes the movement, an unexpected growth may be a tumour or a cancer. Because it is hard to set a limit to size, that is no reason why the problem should not be faced. Indeed, there can be no plan without a limit set to size.'

In those autumn months of 1938 the two of us were busy examining and arranging a stack of photographs for the London Transport desk diary. We neither of us had any idea that this would be the last time. The diary was called *London's Country*. It was laid out with exactly one hundred pictures from places up to a distance of twenty to twenty-five miles: Hertford, Gravesend, Tunbridge Wells, Guildford, Amersham. The choice of photographs shows Pick in one of his sunniest bucolic moods: some of the captions were still full of the old fun. Below a barn owl caught by flashlight as, mouse in beak, it makes for the shelter of its hole is a second picture in which a brood of baby greenfinches extend huge open beaks towards the mother bird. 'Grace before Meat' he wrote under these. A view of Haileybury College described as 'Public School' appears above one of a typical village school for which his caption is 'School for the Public'; at the end of the book a flock of turkeys and a pair of sows with their litter ('Christmas Store') look nervously across at the diary page for Christmas week. But he insisted on using as a frontispiece a grim air view of the Kingston bypass with, at the bottom, the words 'We Make a Desert'. His collection would have been incomplete without this reminder of a world of ugliness and despair. The diary had only just been got off to the printers when my assistant who had worked on it with me was switched to another publication. Pick had persuaded the London County Council to join with London Transport in producing a shilling paperback called *Open-Air London*; it was described on the title page as 'an illustrated guide to some 480 open spaces in and around London, including the Green Belt'. Both these publications had been planned by him as a sort of celebration of a great event, the passing of the LCC's Green Belt Act. The proposal for a ring or belt of open land round the built-up area of London was not a new one but it was only recently that it had shown signs of coming to life. This latest news from County Hall brought great comfort to Pick. He had been having grave doubts about his old assumption that the duration of the journey to work in the centre would place a natural limit on development round the outskirts. One of his last references to that comforting view was made in his 1931 paper 'The Growth of Cities':

There is a time limit set to the length of daily journey for most people; this limit is round about thirty minutes travelling time with a short walk at either end. The size of the city depends largely upon the area which can be covered within this time. The speed of local railways in London has crawled up from 14 to 25 miles per hour by gradual advances, and with each advance has come the possibility of a larger city. By express trains with limited stops it has become possible to stretch the city out to the 25 or 30 mile zone, not by good fortune with solid housing but with scattered groups of housing about the stations.

But what if this good fortune should fail to hold? We were entering the new age of the people's motor car. How long would it be before the alliance between the fast main-line train and the motor car caused all the little local groups to flow together into continuous building?

246

The idea that the Outer Ring, his Greater London, might be in danger of losing all its open spaces filled him with a sort of horror which cannot but have been further chilled by a sense of personal involvement. When he spoke to the municipal transport people he reminded them that 'in the old days a green girdle was essential for the defence of a town . . . The idea is revived again in a fresh connotation. Now it is a means of definition; the town is set in a ring of fields and woods so that it can be seen, grasped, appreciated.' A few months earlier he had been telling the Institution of Professional Civil Servants how

the Green Belt, which would serve to define London geographically much more clearly, has become a popular notion. The London County Council's munificent offer has stimulated activity all round. Middlesex has made a definite approach to a settlement of its open spaces for all time on as liberal a basis as the opportunity and financial resources of these years will allow . . . With the discontinuance of expansion and growth it will become much more possible to conceive of London as a whole and to grasp what it means. It will therefore be much more possible to proceed to an integration of the various parts of London so that that whole is a social unit effective for the living of a good life.

'A vast conception' is how he described the Green Belt to another audience eighteen months later – '28,500 acres secured'. The acreage in fact was going up very quickly. The chairman of the Council at the time when *Open-Air London* was published was the same Mrs Eveline Lowe who a couple of years earlier, when she was chairman of the Education Committee, had presided at the opening of the Pick council's exhibition in County Hall. In an Introduction contributed to the little book she says:

This great scheme was announced by the Council in January 1935. Grants were offered up to a maximum of two million pounds to assist local authorities in the six Home Counties to preserve beautiful country within reasonable distance of London. By December 1938 the Council had approved and provisionally agreed schemes covering over 70,000 acres, an area almost as large as the County of London itself.

Just how much the Green Belt meant to Pick can be seen in a short dialogue that took place on the final day of his examination by the Barlow Commission earlier in that year. It happened to come at the moment when the LCC was working hard to get its Green Belt Bill through Parliament. One of the members of the commission, Patrick Abercrombie the town planner, had been impressed with the references to the Green Belt in Pick's written evidence and at the end of the formal examination he went on to put a number of questions. 'There comes a point', said Pick in reply to one of them, 'when the size of London could become its undoing. You cannot pile up people on one site and think they can live efficiently on it.' If the expansion of London were allowed to go on the city might, he said, start to decline, and if that should happen there would be 'no controlling that decline. London may crash in and cause a much more serious problem than you have to-day with the distressed areas.' No doubt this language must have sounded somewhat more sensational in 1938 than it does to us today, when terms such as 'urban decay', 'subtopia', 'exploding cities' have become as familiar as 'oil slick' or 'inflation'. But Abercrombie persevered and after a while he brought up the subject of the purchase of land for the Green Belt. 'How urgent is this problem of acquiring land?' Pick replied that if there was going to be a Green Belt within twelve to fifteen miles distance of the original Great London they must get busy now. 'It must', he said again, 'be *now.*'

In Pick's writings about the works of man the imaginative use of analogies from the natural sciences was not confined to his treatment of industrial design problems; his papers on the various aspects of town planning have at least as many to show. Such words as 'organism', 'organic', 'arteries', 'tentacles', would come readily to his mind. His fullest exploration of these biological parallels is found in the 1927 lecture to which he gave the title 'Growth and Form in Cities', a direct borrowing from D'Arcy Thompson to whose book he owed so much. He drew a picture of a city functioning in the same way as the human body.

There is the alimentary system concerned with the provision, use and clearance of those things which are requisite for the support of the body. To it corresponds, in the city, the markets with their machinery of collection and distribution, their control of price in which most often demand plays the leading part. There is the respiratory system, which bulks next in importance, to which correspond the parks and open spaces of the city; and as, with the expansion of the body, the lungs must also expand or activity decline, so with the expansion of the city must the parks and open spaces also expand . . . The arteries and veins may be taken to represent the passenger circulation . . . The arteries must be capable of delivering a full supply of blood to all parts and extremities of the organism . . . As in the human body there are arteries varying in capacity, so in the cities there should be streets of varying width. The latest contribution of those expert in town planning has been the scientific employment of diversity in streets. Then, after the circulatory system, there is the nervous system. The network of nerves that covers the body corresponds closely to the network of telephone wires.

But in any living organism the most important part is the brain and it was in the failure to develop 'an adequate brain' that he found the cause of most of the city's troubles. When he was talking to the Holiday School of the Middlesex County Council ten years later, he went into considerable detail describing the multiplicity of little brains that shared responsibility for the London Transport area: 10 county councils, 182 local authorities of various sizes; the purveyors of public services numbered 154 for highways, 39 for water, 137 for sewage. 'There is no single coordinating authority except Parliament, and Parliament can only rarely give a little time and attention to it.'

'Directing intelligence. Where?' asks a lecture note jotted down sometime in 1924; speaking at the London School of Economics in the following year he pointed to the need for 'an effort of the mind to express something in cities in an orderly, purposeful way'. Man the maker of cities, he told the Institute of Transport, needs above all clear ideas about

what it is he does, what it is he seeks, what it is he intends . . . Our cities must proceed by a differentiation of parts to realise a whole which is a novel creature, and it is the form of this novel creature which must engage the attention and the endeavour of its inhabitants. A distinguished exponent of church organisation, Paul, when writing to the Corinthians made use of this same analogy and what he said in relation to the church is equally applicable to the city. Both should be concrete shapes worn by an idea. Paul had the advantage of a clear notion of what he, at least, meant by the church. There is no such clear notion of what is meant by the city. To ascertain the form of a city it is first necessary to resolve the purpose for which it is assembled.

He came to the subject when addressing the Marshall Society five years later: 'The metropolitan city is still in the experimental stage. It is full of accomplishment but it is not accomplished. It serves many purposes but it has failed so far to serve one great overriding purpose. If it is to endure it must find that overriding purpose.' All through his remaining years this failure of the city builder to find the idea, the purpose, was always in his thoughts; the failure was not only on the part of the builder or planner, it was something for which all of us must share the blame. When he spoke to the Royal College of Art Association of Old Students in 1937 he made this search for 'the idea, the purpose' the main subject of his paper. He said,

The outward form and show of civilisation are of moment only in so far as they express, or offer opportunity to express, the good life. The content is more than the form, the play must be conceived before the settings, costumes, action are devised. What is the good life to-day? Only when some answer to that question is possible can we proceed to design its setting in cities and buildings and gardens, to fashion its implements and modes in costume and furniture, its things for everyday use and enjoyment. Do you know what is the good life to-day? The answer can only come from within. From within: how strange that to-day we should think of this looking within only as the probing of our sub-conscious to its dark and secret recesses. The spirit that is in man must be likened to a spirit that is in the universe. If we can arrogate a spirit to ourselves, surely the universe, too, may be accorded one. Nature so far as we can judge is uniform throughout and our spirit can be no more than a manifestation of a spirit immanent in the vast scheme of things. Should we not then start out upon a new exploration, and try to find a way in which our small spirits may make contact with that great spirit and gather enrichment and refreshment? If only the psychologists instead of pursuing their Freudian analysis would attempt a survey of this larger country, would try, now that the priests have lost the track, to find where are the wells of the spirit at which the thirsty can drink in this desert of modern civilisation, why, they might gather a harvest of wheat instead of the harvest of tares which seems to be all that comes from their delving into the secret heart of man alone.

250

9

FINAL YEARS:
1938-1941

Way Out

In the opening months of 1938 Pick, like so many other
Londoners, found himself becoming deeply concerned about the
lack of progress in the preparations for war. Together with the
main-line railway managers he had been working with the government's Air Raids Precautions (Organisation) Committee, but little
had been done except make plans and talk about money. The
Treasury had laid it down that the railways and London Transport were to be treated on the same footing as the local authorities; the government's contribution to the cost of any works
carried out would be limited to 50 per cent. But the railways were
claiming that theirs was a special case. They were an essential
service; in addition to the workshops and other buildings there
were many vulnerable engineering structures to be taken care of
and if any were to suffer damage the country would expect the
trains to go on running regardless of expense. Pick was getting
increasingly restive sitting through the endless disputations
about who should pay what. With Easter week out of the way he
finally made up his mind; together with his engineers he drew up
some immediate plans and got the Board of Trade to agree to a
modest interim payment. After that nothing much happened till
that dark Monday in the last week of September, the day when
French and British ministers having conferred in Downing Street
solemnly announced their countries' intention to take a stand
against Hitler. On that day the war became real to the nation.
The anti-aircraft and coast defence units were called out; trench
digging began in London's parks; citizens were exhorted from
loud-speaker vans to lose no time collecting their gas masks and

later huddled round their radios were left to ponder the dark rumblings of the Führer's Berlin speech. In Whitehall ministers were calling for progress reports on air raids precautions work and a sense of alarm spread round their offices when they discovered the full extent of the delays that the bickerings about financial aid had caused.

For Pick that day, 26 September 1938, marked the beginning of the war. And he, too, however much he had laboured at the job of preparation, was now found wanting. Nothing had yet been done about those tube railways under the bed of the river Thames. Here was one of the most vulnerable danger points in the railway system of this country: a single bomb could flood not just the tubes running under the river bottom but miles of tube railways all over London. This was his personal responsibility; he could wait for no one. All he had to do was to speak to the Ministry of Transport people and get their consent. On the following day, Tuesday 27 September, an announcement went out that at eight o'clock in the evening the Bakerloo and Northern Lines would close down 'for urgent structural works'. When the trains started to run on the Wednesday morning each of the four tubes had been sealed off with solid concrete plugs, one at either end of the stretch that ran under the river; the trains stopped short at Strand and Piccadilly Circus stations on the north bank and Elephant and Castle on the south and a special shuttle service of buses ran across Westminster Bridge to carry passengers from one station to the other. That was the morning when Sir John Simon interrupted the Prime Minister in the middle of a speech to hand him Hitler's invitation to the Munich meeting. The tubes remained sealed off during the rest of that memorable week; it took the whole of the week after that to blast out the concrete plugs and clear the tunnels for the trains.

For the past couple of years Pick's colleagues seeing him and Ashfield at work had been consicous of an extraordinary change in the two men. Ashfield seemed to have suddenly resumed the old interest in day-to-day business that he had been glad to drop when Pick was made managing director. Moreover he was continually finding himself in disagreement with Pick, but the disagreement was always expressed to a third person, never to Pick direct. There were some who would remember one of Ashfield's old secretaries explaining how Ashfield 'had long been a student of Napoleon and his ways; like Napoleon he believed in

252

pitting his generals against one another'. In the summer of 1937 these dismal goings-on had worn down the two railway chiefs, the general manager and the civil engineer, to a point at which both agreed it would be impossible for them to carry on much longer. They would wait only till their sixtieth birthdays when they would become eligible for their pensions. The first retired at the end of 1937 and the other six months later. When the news of their decision reached Ashfield he at once became concerned about the state of Pick's health; he took the unusual step of calling on Dr E. S. Prior, Pick's family doctor in Hampstead, for a first-hand opinion. Next, on the departure of the second of the absconding men, he arranged for Pick to be examined by his own physician, a Harley Street consultant whose name was a household word. The report confirmed that Pick was suffering from the effects of strain. There was, however, an excellent chance of complete recovery; all he had to do was to slow down a little over the next twelve months. Could some of his duties perhaps be taken over by 'a third person of sufficient weight and capacity near the top'? But the report warned that two things were to be avoided at all costs. One was some acute 'onus or anxiety of an unexpected sort'. The other was idleness. An extended period of rest, which could have been a boon to another type of patient, would in Pick's case do more harm than good; it was not the kind of treatment to which a person of his temperament was likely to respond. There was some talk between Ashfield and Pick on the subject of this advice but it was not till some ten months later that Ashfield was able to make up his mind. His new scheme of organisation provided for all of Pick's principal management meetings to be wound up; only weightier matters involving policy decisions were allowed to be brought up for discussion in his private office. As for myself and my colleagues who had attended his regular meetings, from the beginning of April 1939 we were never again to see or speak to Pick on any matter of business. It now began to look as if Pick in truth was on the way out. For six years he had lived under the shadow of the 1933 Act, knowing that the two full-time members of the board, Ashfield and himself, had each been appointed not just for a fixed term of years but for a term of the same length, a seven-year term. And both were over sixty years old. If there had been something of a real difference of age, say ten years or more, there would have been little question as to which of them might be chosen to carry on.

But the gap was a small one; Ashfield was the older by a mere four years. And Pick's state of weariness was common knowledge; it was a weariness so great that it had driven him into a kind of half-retirement already.

All through the year 1938 Pick had been busy assisting the government with its plans for the evacuation of London; at the beginning of September the Minister of Transport had appointed him to take charge of the entire transport part of the operation. Presently, as the moment of crisis was seen to be approaching, arrangements were made for an emergency evacuation of half a million school children which was to take place on Friday 30 September. But then Chamberlain suddenly set off for Munich, the sense of crisis was relieved by a gleam of hope, and the government at the last moment decided to cancel the arrangements. It was not till a year later that the business of evacuation really got moving. When Pick left home early on the morning of Friday 1 September 1939, the car took him straight from there to Enfield West Station on the Piccadilly Line, the station which today is called Oakwood. It pulled up on the opposite side of the road and for some time Pick sat and watched the streams of women and children coming out of the station where a string of buses was waiting to carry them to New Barnet Station on the main-line railway to the north. Evacuation was in full swing; he was seeing the execution of his plan. He had with some difficulty persuaded the government that their original plan for using the big terminal railway stations as departure points was unworkable and that the only way was to take the evacuees by Underground and bus to lesser railway stations down the line. And so on this day 172 Underground stations and a fleet of buses were on the job collecting the first wave of evacuees, nearly three-quarters of a million of them, and delivering them to ninety-eight different stations on the main-line railways out of London. He drove on to the office where the reports were starting to come in. Everything seemed to be going according to plan. Anthony Bull brought in his letters and laid them on his desk.

'Anything happening, Bull?'

'Yessir. Germany has advanced into Poland. There are reports of air battles over Gydnia.'

'Anything else?'

'Just one thing. Sir Reginald Hill rang up from the Ministry to say that the government took over at midnight.'

Among the many far-reaching consequences of Munich week had been the government's decision to prepare forthwith to take control of the railways if war should break out. In World War I the Board of Trade – there was not yet a Ministry of Transport – had established for that purpose a joint committee called the Railway Executive Committee; in September 1938 the government had announced that this committee was to be resuscitated. In 1914 the Underground had had only the District Railway taken over but on this occasion it was inevitable that the whole of London Transport's railways should be brought in. The members of the committee were the general managers of the railways, with Pick representing London Transport; an independent acting chairman was brought in to deputise for the Minister. During these first months the committee worked in an advisory capacity only. But now, at midnight on 31 August 1939, it suddenly became an executive body. It was, said the Control Order, to be the Minister's 'agent for giving directions under this Order', and 'any directions in writing signed by any two members . . . or by any member and the secretary, shall be valid exercise of the authority hereby given to the Committee.' What precisely was the extent of those 'given' powers? No one seemed to know. The Minister had said that the managements were to carry on as usual, subject to the directions of the Railway Executive Committee, but no one had told them where their authority ended and that of the committee began. As the months went by, their state of uncertainty deepened until, in the summer of 1940, the railway chairmen collectively decided that they must approach the Minister insisting on a clearer explanation. Was it true that his powers were meant to cover the operation of the railways, the day-to-day management of all their departments? An exchange of long, involved letters went on through the second half of the year; the search after clarification was not made any easier by the fact that during these months the chairmen found themselves writing to a succession of three different Ministers of Transport. It was not till a few days before Christmas that the latest of them, J. Moore-Brabazon, managed to say in plain English: 'The whole detailed administration of the railways has ceased to be the responsibility of the Companies' boards and has devolved upon me.'

Moore-Brabazon's statement of December 1940 was clear enough and now for the first time there could be no excuse for any misunderstanding. The statement however came too late so far as Pick was concerned. All through that first winter of the war the other members on the board were not puzzled as were the railway directors. His colleagues knew what was the matter: Pick, they said, had got above himself. He was giving them orders. And incidentally he was also causing them much personal inconvenience. The Railway Executive Committee had first claim on his time and its business would often make it impossible for him to be present at their own meetings. At neither of the two board meetings held in October 1939 had he been able to attend. Presently there came a point where members felt obliged to remonstrate with Ashfield. All they were doing at their meetings was to receive reports from Pick on his implementation of decisions made by him and the railway managers in another place. Since their meetings no longer served any ascertainable purpose, why waste members' time calling them together twice a month? Surely twice a year would be enough? There were no doubt other places where a piece of wartime organisation hastily improvised had produced the same kind of situation. The BBC was such a case. One of its employees, A. P. Ryan, was seconded to the Ministry of Information to act as 'Adviser to the BBC on Home Affairs'. After Ryan's death thirty years later *The Times* obituary notice described his position as 'manifestly absurd'. But the members of the London Passenger Transport Board did not have quite the same excuse as the BBC for failing to understand. When in World War I the government decided to take over the direction of the country's railways Sir Albert Stanley, as he then was, had become President of the Board of Trade. It was he who as the Minister responsible for transport had set up the original Railway Executive Committee; its members had been appointed by him and had taken their orders from him. In 1939 therefore no person alive was more competent that Ashfield to explain the scope and powers of this committee and the way it was meant to perform its work.

Talks about the financial arrangements for the government take-over of the railways had been going on for the better part of a year. The proposal was that a government Control Pool should be established on a similar lines to the London Passenger Pooling Scheme but taking in the entire railway system of the country; as with the London pool, each of the member undertakings was to receive from it a fixed proportion determined in advance. The railway companies however insisted that the Pool must be confined to themselves only. London Transport's financial prospects were poor; its earnings had already suffered a greater decline than had those of the railways. And its system, being concentrated in the Greater London area, would be more vulnerable than theirs to enemy action; the burden of carrying London Transport in the new Pool would become even more onerous as the war went on. Early in January Sir Leonard Browett, the Permanent Secretary of the Ministry, asked Pick to call on him for another talk. An arrangement which would give the main-line railways a fairer deal had been set out in a draft White Paper; among its various provisions was the placing of a ceiling on the profits of each of the partners. London Transport's capital structure, as defined in the 1933 Act, included only one class of stock carrying a variable dividend. But the Act laid down a minimum rate (which it described as the 'standard' rate) and it was a regrettable fact that London Transport had never yet succeeded in paying more than a fraction of that rate. The Minister now proposed that for the duration of the war the dividend should be limited to that fraction. It was not a softness of heart towards the holders of the stock that moved Pick to disapproval; some of them had done very well indeed out of their exchange of securities; he had expressed his opinion on those transactions in public and had been duly punished for so doing. It was his lawyer's respect for the law. Of course few people would seriously believe that during the war London Transport, if it had been left to carry on by itself, would have been in a position to pay the statutory rate which it had never yet succeeded in paying in times of peace. But it was now being asked to bind itself in a formal agreement to abstain from paying it. Pick spent the weekend considering the proposal and on the Monday morning dictated a memorandum to Ashfield setting out his objections and offering some possible counter-proposals.

A special meeting of the board was called for 12 January 1940. Of all the part-time members one only found himself free to attend. Ashfield had spoken with two of the absentees on the telephone before the meeting, had explained the terms proposed by the government and told them of his own decision to urge that they be accepted. And now, at the meeting, he was able to report that both these gentlemen were of the same view as himself. The part-time member disagreed. What could Pick do but give him

257

his support? Ashfield then proceeded to close the meeting; the matter was too important, he said, to be settled with so small an attendance. When the meeting was resumed in the afternoon of the following day the two who had already signified their approval were the only part-time members present. Pick expressed his regret at finding himself in a minority of one; he said that after the previous day's meeting he had told Ashfield that he would feel bound to refrain from offering himself for reappointment next May if that should be Ashfield's wish.

It was not till the middle of the following week that he got the letter. It was written in Ashfield's own hand. 'Your decision to retire from the Board at the expiry of your present appointment in May next which you conveyed to me after the Board meeting on Thursday last and which you confirmed at the meeting on the following day came as a great surprise both to your colleagues and to myself.' The letter went on to say some pleasant things about their many years of work together: 'You have always', it declared, 'been a true and loyal friend.' Was there some faint hope on Pick's part that this loyalty might now be returned? When in July 1938 he put up his suggestions for the redefinition of his duties he had added a few words about a possible 1940 organisation, or 'ultimate' organisation as he called it. Back in 1907 Ashfield, when he first joined the old Underground company, had started as general manager and spent three or four years working in that capacity before being appointed a director. Would it not be possible for a joint general manager post to be created and offered to Pick at the end of his term of office? Pick saw no objection to such a stepping down; all the old problems would still be there to keep him usefully occupied. But the suggestion had met with no response.

Harry Trethowan could recall many years later how Pick one day broke the news of his resignation to him. 'We didn't see eye to eye on a matter of principle', he explained. 'As things are it need never have happened.' In an old notebook of mine I find an entry about a chance meeting in the street about this time. Pick had just come out from a session of the Railway Executive Committee in the committee's bomb-proof offices at the bottom of the old abandoned Down Street tube station, just off Piccadilly. He was making his way back to Westminster by way of the Park. We stopped for a moment. Suddenly he started talking about the struggle he had had overcoming a terrible impulse to step out on

258

to the old tube platform and throw himself under a train. It never occurred to me that he might be speaking seriously; it was probably just a joking reference to the tedium of those hours spent down in the shelter listening to the railway chiefs. It was not till a few weeks later that I learnt the truth. London Transport's financial years had always ended on 30 June but with the introduction of the Control Pool the board had been ordered to switch from 30 June to the end of the calendar year. Ashfield had just announced that the board was now in the happy position of being able to pay twice the Ministry's proposed rate of dividend on the stock that had been the source of all the trouble. And then Pick had written another note to Ashfield reminding him of his suggestion that he might be found a new post of the general manager sort. 'It would seem improper', he said, 'that I should retire in time of war.' Moreover the doctors had warned him that he must at all costs avoid giving up his regular habits of work. He must continue working, though it was desirable that the pressure of his work should be somewhat relaxed. He went on to make some suggestions. But still nothing happened. The board members first heard about Ashfield's acceptance of Pick's offer of resignation at their meeting of 4 April, nearly three months from the date of Ashfield's letter. The next thing was the drafting of a public statement. When the chief executive of a big undertaking decides to retire at the age of sixty-one it is usually expected that something will be said about the reason for his decision. It was only when he saw the first news cuttings that Pick learnt that his reason had been the poor state of his health. A few days after the announcement went out he was due to read a paper to the Institute of Transport. When he got up to speak he said: 'I have unfortunately been in the news these last days. I have learnt that I am older than I am, that my health is worse than I thought it was, that I am very tired, more tired than I thought I was, and also that the Government are going to find me some other job, of which strange to say I know nothing.' I was in the audience at the time and remember being conscious of the shocked silence in which this piece of unaccustomed candour was received. Pick's inability to dissemble was not a matter of more or less, it was absolute.

On 18 May there came the news that the trustees had renewed Ashfield's appointment for a second period of seven years. London Transport had run into trouble; it had lost not only

Pick but also the two other key men on whose experience so much depended, the railway manager and the civil engineer. The loss of these three men was not unnaturally seen as a grievous blow to London Transport. Happily Ashfield had been quick to rise to the occasion. Not only had he succeeded at this critical moment in doubling the rate of dividend on the C stock, but the Minister's agreement to the recent increase of 10 per cent on all railway fares, which helped to make this possible, had been largely his doing. London Transport's interests had never been better looked after. An announcement was made that the post of chief executive had been abolished; a new group of six 'heads of department' took over from Pick just fourteen days before he left.

Paths to Peace

Pick had always kept in regular touch with his sister Ethel in York but most of his letters being of merely passing interest had not been thought by her to be worth preserving. His war-time letters, however, were different. Among them was the letter dated 19 May 1940 in which he told her: 'I am now a super-annuated man. It could not have come at a worse time, with this war in a critical state . . . I shall go mad if I am to be idle. It is strange that no one has offered me a job.' Some weeks before that he had been in touch with Ashfield again. He could see that there was no hope now of his being allowed to continue with London Transport. Perhaps Ashfield would yet be willing to use his influence to find him suitable employment elsewhere? It so happened that a little later, on 12 May, a friend of Ashfield's, Alfred Duff Cooper, had been appointed Minister of Information in the new Churchill government. Ashfield was aware that one of Cooper's first problems would be to find a new director-general. The present holder of the post, Sir Kenneth Lee, was a well known businessman with an outstanding record of public service on a series of government boards and committees, but the vast ramshackle machine of this new Ministry had proved too much for him and he was known to be looking for something else to do. And so Ashfield had asked Cooper to consider Pick as a possible candidate. Cooper was doubtful whether this difficult post would be suitable for a person who had given up his appointment for health reasons. But Ashfield was not to be put off; at the end of May he wrote Cooper a letter: 'I am wondering whether you are in a position to let me know about Pick. It is probable that his services will be sought in another direction.' When he ran into Cooper a few days later Cooper told him he had called for a medical opinion which had shown that Pick quite definitely was not the man.

Shortly after this Pick did receive some news from that 'other direction'. He was commissioned by the new Minister of Transport, Sir John Reith, to make a tour of the principal ports of the United Kingdom and review their arrangements for handling ships and cargoes under the constantly changing conditions of the war. He started on 17 June by spending a week each in Liverpool and Bristol, in South Wales and on the Clyde. In mid-July he was writing to Ethel: 'I do not go to sea but I perambulate ports, which is a bit more tiring. It is however a new and interesting experience.' The work no doubt was interesting but it was far from easy. Operations were being directed by Port Emergency Committees on which all the main parties concerned were represented. Like so many defence arrangements at this time the plan for these committees had been prepared years earlier by the Committee of Imperial Defence; when brought into actuality they were seen to be somewhat imperfectly related to the needs of war. As was pointed out in a departmental report, they were constantly having to deal with 'disputes arising from the conflicting needs of Government Departments': one of their worst problems was how to settle these disputes by sensible but, above all, prompt decisions. Reith had become aware that the machinery was badly in need of an overhaul and this was the task he entrusted to Pick. He was not disappointed. In his autobiography *Into the Wind* he describes the action he was able to take on the strength of Pick's report. 'Complacency about the ports had been shaken . . . A new directive to Port Emergency Committees was issued. They were to take the widest view of their powers to secure quick turn-round, and rapid clearance . . . Above all, the chief executive of the port was to be given discretion to act on his own.' Thirty years later, in the last year of his life, Lord Reith was still able to recall 'the objections raised by the Civil Servants to Pick being given that particular work to do; how well he did it; how quickly, how fully, he endorsed the opinion I had formed of the Port Emergency Committees; and how he found to his surprise that he enjoyed working with me, and would have stayed on permanently had not someone held him to an earlier promise which I told him he would greatly regret, as he surely did, and died.'

At the Ministry of Transport Reith was busy making arrangements for Pick's next job, when suddenly there came an urgent summons. Ashfield having learnt about the imminent departure of the worn-down Sir Kenneth Lee had decided to make a final appeal to Duff Cooper. It is difficult to believe that he might already be looking ahead to that second critical year, the year 1947, yet no other reason has ever been suggested for his insistence on getting Pick away from the Ministry of Transport and switched to the Ministry of Information. The next piece of news came to him in a letter from Pick: 'Just to advise you that Duff Cooper sent for me again . . . I was given no excuse or option but to accept so now I shall, in a day or so, have the dangerous task of putting the Ministry of Information to rights. It is an unlooked-for affair and one that nobody would seek for himself. I am sorry to leave the Ministry of Transport where I was securing a satisfactory position and interesting work. However it was no good being afraid.' If Pick did not like the look of the new job, Reith, his chief, liked it even less. He himself had spent four miserable months at the Ministry before moving to his present post at the Ministry of Transport; after his departure Neville Chamberlain who had given him the appointment had agreed that 'you never had a real chance there'. Reith had done his utmost to dissuade Pick from going. 'I told him', he wrote in his autobiography, 'that I thought the work was not in his line.' He remembered Pick's reply to his arguments: 'I won't go if you want me to stay.' Pick clearly went as far as he dared asking to be commanded to stay on but this was more than Reith felt able to do. If only Pick could have got rid of the feeling that this was not a job offered to him, it was an order. 'It was beyond me', he confessed in his letter to Ashfield, 'to refuse help.' 'I went in under compulsion', he wrote to B. J. Fletcher, 'not from choice.'

The appointment took effect from Monday 12 August. I first learnt of it from the newspapers. My heart sank. When he wrote to acknowledge my letter he said: 'It is kind of you to write and wish me luck in my new job. I hope if I am a Spitfire I shan't be shot down too quickly!' I had told him that his acceptance of the post made me feel as though he were in a Spitfire heading for the English Channel. Those who have read Duff Cooper's *Old Men Forget* will remember his picture of the 'monster', as he calls it, that 'came into existence on the day of the outbreak of war and

999 officials sprang to their office chairs', of the dreary procession of 'ex-ambassadors, retired Indian civil servants, briefless barristers' – no species of clever amateur was unrepresented – who continued to arrive in a flurry of brave intentions that soon turned to a state of bewildered gloom. It took Pick no more than a couple of weeks to discover how ill-equipped he was to deal with this strange assembly. On 1 September he was writing to Ethel: 'My new job is a thoroughly bad one. It is a mess to clear up. I sometimes wonder whether it can be done. It almost drives me to despair, there is so much muddle.' His life was not made the easier by his night-time experiences in the bombing. The same letter to his sister tells how 'two high explosive bombs have demolished a house two doors from us completely. Luckily it was empty. But unluckily for us its bits blown into the air descended in a rain upon us and smashed our tiles and roof and windows; the blast blew in some windows and the door.' A week later came another letter: 'I have retreated to a service flat in town for four weeks' and he gave his address, Queen Anne's Mansions, Westminster. But he was not to stay the full four weeks. On the evening of Friday 13 September a bomb sliced its way down just behind the Petty France frontage and reduced a tall, cliff-like section of the building not far from his flat to a cascade of rubble pouring into the street below. On 22 September he wrote giving his latest address, the Russell Hotel, Bloomsbury. Here 'the bombs fell all round about us but we escaped. It seemed however like waiting until your turn came, so that the nights were far from cheerful.'

His work at the Ministry was made especially difficult by his old inability to instruct others on matters of which he had not made himself a master. It was necessary that he should always understand what he was talking about. Well-meaning colleagues who had acquired the civil servant's technique tried to reason with him: the proper way was to require the points to be set out on one side of a single sheet of paper; or, if that was not possible, to send for the man and say: 'Tell me what this is about.' They warned him: 'If you insist on going on like this it will kill you.' There were just a few people in whom he was able to feel real confidence. One of these was Cyril Radcliffe, the controller in charge of news and censorship. Many years later, when he had become Lord Radcliffe, he was still able to give me an account of the one interview he had with Pick. Having listened to what Radcliffe had to tell him about his duties, Pick said he did not understand enough about the censorship business; since Radcliffe seemed to be doing the job with the greatest efficiency no purpose would be served by his trying to understand more. But Radcliffe was an exceptional case. At the end of the war, having spent some years in Pick's old job of director-general, he was one of the very small company who managed to leave the Ministry with their reputations enhanced instead of depressed. Pick's encounters with the other civil servants were mostly of a very different sort. He spoke about his troubles in a letter to Ashfield: 'My fault was that I acted too slowly and considerately, and this they took for weakness.' And so he set himself to try to correct his appearance of weakness. The process of correction was, however, carried on in a highly selective manner. Margaret Lambert, the historian, who saw a good deal of him in the course of her duties in the Ministry, was struck by the way his efforts at rudeness were carefully modulated to suit the person to whom they were directed. 'The more important a man is', she explained to me at the time, 'the ruder he becomes. If you are a nobody you will get nothing but great patience and consideration, it takes a Cabinet Minister to make him really lash out.' Sir Harold Nicolson in his diaries describes Pick's appearance at a duty room conference. 'He throws his weight about . . . He rages . . . Pick says that he doesn't care a hoot for the Air Ministry . . . He says "To hell with the Prime Minister".' Nicolson goes on to comment: 'I think his ideas are right but his manner is really terrible.' The deputy director-general, Sir Norman Scorgie, was reputed to dislike Pick, whose mildly left-wing views and tolerance with wayward intellectuals dismayed him, yet as one of the few regular civil servants working with Pick he was probably better able than most to understand his problem. Some ten years afterwards he wrote to me: 'That impossible Ministry of 1940–1941 annoyed and frustrated him more than it did the few who were struggling to bring some sort of order out of the chaos . . . He never spent a happy day in those marble halls.' Scorgie was referring to Holden's new building for London University, which had become the Ministry's home.

The story of Pick's solitary encounter with Churchill at this time has had a wide circulation. It appears in Lord Francis-Williams' *Press, Parliament and People*; Sir Harold Nicolson in his diaries records a very similar version he heard from Lord Gladwyn. Churchill is quoted as expressing a wish, after Pick had been shown out, never to be asked to see 'that impeccable bus-man' again. A fuller account of the incident was given to some of his friends by another person present, Lord Swinton, a leading figure in the 'Invisible War', who held the dual posts of chairman of the Security Executive and of a company set up to work secretly for the Ministry of Economic Warfare. Among the items for discussion at the meeting had been the notorious plans of the Political Warfare Executive for the spreading of false news among the people of enemy countries. The Prime Minister, who was known to take a keen interest in the plans, was somewhat taken aback to hear Pick expressing passionate disapproval. There could never, said Pick, be any justification for spreading untruths, not even in war. According to Swinton, Pick then went on to say that he had never knowingly told a lie in all his life and he was not prepared to turn liar now; if these plans were to go forward he would have to ask his Minister to accept his resignation. Churchill looked at him and said: 'Mr Pick, Dover was heavily shelled from the French coast yesterday. I shall be at Dover my-self tomorrow, it is likely that the town will again be shelled, and it is quite possible that I myself may be killed by one of those shells. If that should happen to me it would give me great com-fort to know that a few hours before my death I had spoken to a man who had never told a lie.' Was Churchill's personality really as simple as these exchanges suggest? In the volume of essays presented to him on his eightieth birthday there is a little character sketch that Gilbert Murray, the author of one of the essays, attributes to 'another Prime Minister'. 'I have often differed from Winston. I have had hard tussles with him, but I will say this for him: he is a hard fighter but he never bears malice; he never intrigues; and he can't tell a lie, because I have seen him try and he turned pink all over.'

Fortunately for Pick his painful sojourn in 'those marble halls' was not to be of long duration. A fortnight or so before the Christmas of 1940 Sir Kenneth Clark, as he then was, came in to see him; his business was films. When he had spoken for a few minutes he saw Pick lean back in his chair spreading his hands on his desk. 'I'm sorry to have to interrupt you, Clark, but I've just got the sack. It's something that's never happened to me before. I've got the sack. But I will say this for Duff Cooper, he did it very nicely.' Later that day he was writing to Ashfield: 'What I foresaw has happened. I shall be quit of this Ministry

265

on Saturday . . . It causes me no regrets.' He left 'with a sigh of relief' as Duff Cooper was to write about himself after handing over to Brendan Bracken in the following year.

During his period at the Ministry of Information the great question of the meaning and purpose of the war, of what the war was about, had been a part of Pick's daily life. Of all the jobs for which the Ministry was expected to make itself responsible could there be any more important than the job of helping people to understand what it meant to England, to the world? There was a moment when he had felt he must get a Cabinet Minister to write something like a declaration of aims. Ernest Bevin was an old friend – why not ask Bevin to write? It was with some difficulty that his colleagues had persuaded him of the impossibility of getting a Cabinet Minister to make a personal pronouncement on the subject of war aims. This particular proposal had had to be dropped but the subject kept busying his mind. It had never ceased to do so since that terrible week of Munich. For to him the word Munich seemed to stand as a symbol for the great gulf that divided the meaning of the present conflict from that of the last. In 1914 a little friendly country had been attacked and we had immediately rushed to its aid. It was a simple issue, understood by all, and when Pick had ventured into the field of war propaganda all that needed to be done was to remind people of their duty and tell the world how well they were doing it. In 1939 we were fighting to make reparation for an act of treachery committed the year before. We had betrayed a friend. And the cause of the treachery did not lie in any special baseness on our part; it was simply that we had lost our way. We had failed to understand. When the inevitable war did break out Pick had seized on one or two small opportunities to improve that understanding. One was London Transport's 1940 desk diary on which he worked in the autumn of 1939. The 1939 diary had as usual been full of gay and sometimes nostalgic photographs but this diary would have to be of a different kind. No more pictures now. He would spend evening after evening copying out in his own hand passages from some of his favourite writers. They ranged from Solomon and Thucydides to de Tocqueville and Newman. The quotations were described on the title-page to the diary as 'Statements from the Past Illustrating the Aim and Purpose of the English-speaking Peoples.' The other occasion for reflecting on war aims was a little exhibition in Charing Cross Underground Station. In this station,

266

at the rear of the ticket hall, there is a space that during the period 1933–9 had been used for a regular series of propaganda exhibitions; it was there that some half-dozen government departments and official agencies had been persuaded to make their first entry into the publicity field. Pick suggested that I should at once cancel the next exhibition that had been booked and instead offer the site to the Ministry of Information for a photographic exhibition on the subject of the war. But the offer was not accepted. The only photographs the Ministry would be interested in exhibiting were photographs of the fighting in the front line when there was one; my approach had been premature. When I suggested to Pick that we ourselves might be able, without incurring any expense, to get together an exhibition of this sort he at once agreed to my going ahead. He made only one condition: I must do a short series of them, not just one. I knew my friend Christopher Hobhouse, the brilliant young biographer of Charles James Fox, had made a close study of the new Nazi Germany since he first met Hitler in the early Munich days. He had very clear ideas upon the subject. He generously undertook to write a script in the form of a sequence of picture captions round the theme 'Why We are at War'. He was killed in the raid on Portsmouth nine months later; they were the last things he wrote. The display screens, made for the cancelled exhibition, were easily adapted; the photographic agencies made us a present of the right photographs; and a friendly printer offered to set up Hobhouse's captions in type. When Pick came to see the first show, which was opened by Sir Samuel Hoare just before the Christmas of 1939, he was full of enthusiasm. 'I think it is excellent,' he wrote me. 'I hope you will be able to make an even better one when you come to the next round. At any rate your present exhibition seems to have taken on for I hear it is going into circulation in many directions.' What had happened was that the War Office had made up for the coolness of the Ministry of Information; within a few weeks the government were dispatching one hundred replicas to the Dominions and to neutral countries throughout the world. Pick went on watching the development of the story in further exhibitions with passionate interest.

At the beginning of 1941 having got clear of 'that impossible Ministry' he took up the subject again. He was back in his Hampstead house which had been made habitable after the bomb damage of the previous September. The subject was still the war, but it was not the origins that held his attention now, it was the future into which the war would be leading us. Everybody by now had pretty clear ideas about what we were fighting against. The question what we were fighting *for* was less easily answered. He wrote a couple of essays which were published in a little paperback called *Paths to Peace*. 'Someone had to write these essays', he says in the Introduction, and he goes on to explain how his 'employment this last year forced upon me the consideration of the problems of which they treat.' The first of the essays deals with the war, the conditions of victory, our attitude to the German people, the ultimate place of their country in a post-war Europe. The public's ideas about these matters were somewhat confused at this time. After years of argument about the Treaty of Versailles the voices of those who claimed that its evil effects had been wildly exaggerated were being increasingly heard. Pick was not inclined to take their side. The treaty had undoubtedly done grievous harm to the cause of peace but the harm had come less from its harsh terms than from the irresponsible manner in which those terms had afterwards been relaxed. It was right, he said, that the Allies should have had second thoughts. But whenever they tried to amend some of the conditions it was always done 'piecemeal and often grudgingly so that the mitigations became so much evidence of weakness rather than of a change of will'. The treaty might indeed have started the German nation off on the road to aggression but it was these later displays of weakness that had propelled it along the road to the bitter end. On the other hand Pick was equally critical of Sir Robert Vansittart's pamphlet *Black Record*. The author's inaccuracies and omissions had been widely reported; the real case against the pamphlet, however, was not that the diagnosis had been falsified but that it had been falsified for the purpose of supporting a doctrine that was bleakly nihilistic. Vansittart, having set out to prove that Germany was a nation impossible to live with, had traduced his own intelligence in the process. It was indeed necessary that people should recognise the existence of wrong but it was even more necessary that the recognition of wrong should be seen to spring from a strong sense of right. The trouble about *Black Record* was that this sense of right was not present. In the words of one of the Letters to the Corinthians it was 'an evil communication'. The task before us, which we had no choice but to take up, was: 'to explore how the German people may be converted,' how best to work with them after the war developing 'a common language of ideas' and realising 'the all-embaracing conception of Europe as a co-ordinated and co-operative stronghold of western civilisation, a counterpoise to the co-operation of peoples which the New World of the Americas presents to us. Let us learn of our children. We seek a peace as active as war, as determined in its purpose to achieve what each one of us really cares most about, the good life for all.'

This 'good life for all' is the subject of the second essay. It is too early, says Pick, to start speculating about the map of Europe in any detail, about the fearful problems dividing country from country that will be waiting to be cleared up. But it is by no means too early to give thought to the arrangement of our society here at home. He puts up a list of proposals, some of which anticipate the ideas developed by Sir William Beveridge in the following year and by others after him:

the conversion of a mercantile economy into a true political economy, the disciplining of money so that it becomes a tool or a servant, security for livelihood, home, family life, the widening of the scope of social insurance, a standard of living which safeguards the health and full development of all citizens and relieves the nation once for all of the shame and disgrace of the underfed, the stunted, and the deficient.

But his main interest is the education of the citizen for the society to come.

There must be a new conception of education as the art of living, or skill in living well. The pedagogues have held sway far too long, they are ensconced in the Board of Education. Education is much more than extending the years at school. It is providing one type of education for the countryside, another for the small town, yet another for the industrial city, with variants within each of these types so suit the geographical, the physical, the cultural needs of different regions. It is finding in every human activity scope for education and means of culture. It is recognising the craftsman of the hand and eye equally with the craftsman of the tongue or pen. Further, education as opportunity must be enlarged and developed. The poverty of leaders that now besets the State and that makes any reconstruction of government a mere game of musical chairs must be remedied by seeking talent and ability wherever they

269

may be, and by encouraging their unfolding and securing their training so that the highest posts in politics, in commerce, in administration, in industry, are open to all as well as the highest positions in literature, science and art, for which some provision has already been made. The right treatment of this problem may prove the most fruitful measure of any scheme or plan, for it will discover the means by which the plan may be realised and established in ever-increasing might and splendour.

At the Ministry of Transport, which Pick had left with such reluctance, there was now a new Minister, but the civil servants who had accepted Pick with little enthusiasm when he was first brought in by Lord Reith had not forgotten him. He had turned out better than they expected. Early in February 1941 he was asked to undertake an inspection of inland waterways of the same kind that he had already carried out for the ports. He found it difficult to make up his mind. There was no future for canals and other waterways in this country: 'I see no prospect in them at all', he wrote to a friend explaining his predicament. In the first week in March he was writing to Ethel: 'I begin my wanderings on Monday to see what the job is like. It is quite a disorganised industry, broken up into small pieces that must somehow be fitted together.' Then, in another letter written two months later: 'This week I may be in Wisbech and Peterborough. The job is coming to an end. The change of Ministers has left the situation muddled. I don't know where I am.' Nevertheless before the end of May he had finished a long and comprehensive report. He was critical of the war-time arrangement for managing the canals with the aid of an advisory committee of canal companies and carriers; the new regional bodies he wanted to see established would include representatives of a number of interests like other forms of transport and transport-using government departments. There were recommendations for new financial terms for the canal industry with improvement grants in special cases. All of these recommendations were adopted soon after. He also made some proposals for drastic reorganisation which were thought to be too long-term to be seriously considered at that time: the consolidation of all the canals including those owned by the railway companies into seven regional groups; the preparation of traffic surveys as a means of deciding for what kind of traffic the canals were best suited; the creation of a canals division within the Ministry. This last proposal, however, was found to be immediately feasible and at the end of the year Sir Osborne Mance was appointed Director of Canals, the government having in the meanwhile to take full control of all canals 'capable of making an appreciable contribution to the war effort'. Pick's work did not end with the submission of his report. He was continually being sent for. At the beginning of October he was writing to Noel Carrington to express his regret at having missed the annual meeting of the Design and Industries Association: 'when I called at the Ministry of Transport the week-end had produced a sheaf of troubles over canals. Duty required that I should stand to.'

One day after he had left the Ministry he chanced to run into our mutual friend Tom Griffits. 'He told me', Griffits wrote to me a few years later, 'that he had never worked so hard in all his life as he had to work on the canals and waterways investigation. He complained that he had been sleeping in a different bed every night.' Week upon week of war-time meals in provincial hotels had played havoc with his digestion. He had lost a couple of stone in weight in a few months. Yet though the work had proved a heavy burden the idleness that followed proved even heavier; he knew the one thing he wanted was some real work to do but he did not know what work. He wrote to Harold Stabler: 'Age has come upon me and made me indifferent and idle. I feel cross about myself but proceed to no cure. I just waste my life. How do you contrive to keep alive and alert in these dreary days? There seems no spiritual or intellectual sustenance about.' All his letters at this time speak of the lack of work. Only activity could cure him; the doctors had told him so and he knew now how right they had been. To Carrington he explained that what he was suffering from was 'the nervous effects of underwork which apparently can be just as damaging as overwork . . . My writing, as you will see, has deteriorated.' Carrington had wanted to consult him about some discussions he had had with the Council for the Preservation of Rural England; Pick went on: 'I shall get out of London for a few days as soon as I can, so our further talk must be carried over to the week after next at the earliest.' In the last week in October he had the satisfaction of seeing *Paths to Peace* appear in print. The book had a curiously mixed reception. The programme it outlined was, according to the *Times Literary Supplement*, 'fundamentally materialist, garnished with culture and ethical Christianity'. The *Manchester Guardian* reviewer thought the pamphlet said something that many readers were

271

feeling and added: 'it strikes me as far and away the sanest thing of the sort that I have read.' Presently Pick was busy signing a few copies for his friends. One of them was for B. J. Fletcher; with it went a short letter: 'I am become an idle and useless member of society, and so unwell. I suffer from some form of nervous breakdown for want of active life and work. I write tracts. Will you accept a copy of my latest? I feel they are mere fill-ups of my time, and possibly vanities. I am in a bad way spiritually as well as physically.' At the end of the letter he added: 'However, I am picking up and expect a job next week which may wake me up and give me fresh interest in life.'

The Ministry of Transport had recently been merged with the Ministry of Shipping in a new department called the Ministry of War Transport. The Minister, Lord Leathers, the former Minister of Shipping, had brought with him his director-general Sir Cyril Hurcomb to fill the same post in the new enlarged Ministry. As with other departments at this time, the problems of post-war planning and reconstruction were beginning to claim serious attention. Hurcomb, who still saw Pick occasionally at the Reform Club, was impressed with *Paths to Peace* and he had decided to see if he could be induced to lend a hand. An appointment had been made for Pick to call on him at the Ministry on the following Monday. Hurcomb was looking forward to their meeting. He knew that Pick, if he could be persuaded to take on the job, would find greater satisfaction in it than he had got from his other jobs with the old Ministry of Transport. The date of Pick's letter to Fletcher was 7 November. On that day he was just finishing his afternoon tea in the dining room of his house in Hampstead when, suddenly losing consciousness, he lurched heavily forward. He died of a cerebral haemorrhage a little before midnight on the same evening.

A couple of months later, in January 1942, an article called 'Re-energising Religion' appeared in the *Congregational Quarterly*. It was the text of a lecture Pick had given early the previous October. There are several references to it in letters written to Robert Best during the time when he was working on it. It was causing him considerable trouble. A fortnight before he was due to deliver the lecture he wrote: 'It seems an ephemeral effort; I doubt if it is worth printing. I may make a serious job of it later but it is a bit outside my experience.' The article is concerned with the place and function of religion in the society of today. 'What we call religion is no more than the eviscerated skeleton of it.' How could this dead thing called religion be brought back to life? He examines a number of religious ideas ranging over the history of thought from Mithras to Jung and then, at the close of his argument, he speaks about the language of visual beauty, the only language able to reveal the wholeness of life to the human mind. He ends with a short description of an experience he had had one day when he was on holiday in Switzerland; he uses it to illustrate the state of aesthetic exhilaration without which the experiences of religion can never be complete. He was on his way climbing to the highest point he had ever reached on earth. 'All at once, at about ten thousand feet above sea level, there seemed to come an extraordinary shift of colour. The blue band of the sky had come down to earth and was enveloping the land. Nature works by leaps at critical points and it seemed to me as though Heaven had come down to earth. Above, the sky had almost a hard whiteness. The whiteness of God. We were coming face to face.'

ACKNOWLEDGMENTS

When a spare-time writer of odd pieces is persuaded to try his hand at a life-size book he clearly has to lean more heavily than is usual on the kindness of people around him. For myself, I owe a special debt of gratitude to three co-operators. Among the things Michael Robbins did for me was to supply me with copies of the typescript of his official History of London Transport well in advance of its publication. Charles Lee and Nikolaus Pevsner shared between them the task of reading through the first draft and offering much-needed comment and advice. Next after them come four of my old London Transport colleagues, Sir Alec and Lady Valentine, Anthony Bull and David McKenna, and Pick's sisters Ethel (splendidly helpful) and Marion and his brothers Martin and Sisson. Among others who undertook to read various parts of the work I must mention Nigel Balchin, Bryce Beaumont, Kenneth Clark, C.M. Jenkin Jones, Sir Harold Nicolson, Gilbert J. Ponsonby and Steen Eiler Rasmussen. And then there are the illustrations, which are used by courtesy of London Transport and for which I owe the warmest thanks to the helpfulness of Michael Levey and R.J. Pigram.

Many other people came forward with information in various fields. I would like to mention the following: W.A. Agnew, W.S. Graff Baker, Dora Batty, Sir George Beharrell, T.R. Bilbow, P.S. Burrows, H.T. Carr, Noel Carrington, Clarissa Churchill, Sir Ernest Clark, Sir P. Ashley Cooper, Christopher Cornford, J.E. Cowderoy, H.C. Davy, Sir Gavin de Beer, George Duncan, George Eland, Evan Evans, B.C. Foxcroft, Ivor Fraser, Sir Robert Fraser, John Gloag, H.S. Goodhart-Rendel, W. Gott, A.W. Green, Lord Greene, Thomas Griffits, Brian Harbour, A. H. Hawkins, Christopher Heal, Sir John Hodsoll, Charles Holden, H.R. Hughes, Lord Hurcomb, Christopher Hussey, Stephen G. Jones, E. Mc-Knight Kauffer, H.W. Lamprell, Sir Alfred le Maitre,

R. McDonald, Sir Leslie Martin, J.H. Mason, F.A.A. Menzler, Esther Meynell, Herbert Morrison, F.P. Philips, R.H. Pitts, C.W. Reeve, Noel Rooke, Sir Norman Scorgie, H.A. Short, G.F. Sinclair, E. Rawdon Smith, W.A.C. Snook, Walter E. Spradbery, H.L. Spratt, W. Tetley Stephenson, R.P. Summers, J.P. Thomas, Cycill Tormley, Sir Alker Tripp, Sir Ralph Wedgwood, Gladys Winfield and Frederic T. Wood.

Another and perhaps greater problem was the one of shape and continuity. The first person I turned to here was Patrick Ryan of The Times, who showed me how to take a close look at the arrangement of what he called my four individual narrative strands. Then, after nearly thirty years of much-interrupted labour, I found I had been carried away by a fascinated interest in the flood of information and had written far too much. The length of the typescript had to be cut down by something like half. If I had managed to give some shape to the full version, this subsequent chopping about left the bits and pieces more disconnected than ever. The two people who came to my rescue at this moment were Alan A. Jackson and Priscilla Metcalf. They had to put in some really hard work, and their meticulous process of re-modelling deserves the very greatest thanks.

Perhaps a last word of acknowledgement should go to a couple of old friends who were responsible for causing this study to be undertaken. A year or two after the end of the last war a number of people were discussing the idea of a memorial in honour of Frank Pick, who had died in 1941. There was talk of a medal or other award, of an endowment for lectures, either on the ground or over the air, of scholarships, exhibitions and so on. I was at that time President of the Society of Industrial Artists and Designers and I was asked to put the problem before one or two suitable public men. The people to whom I first spoke came down heavily in favour of something quite different from any of these things — a book. But the biography must be a one-man job, not a collection of essays 'in honour', and the author if possible should be one who had known the subject, and known him well. What about myself? I had spent some years working with Pick, and I had already written a few articles about him, including one in a well-known Swiss magazine with an international circulation. And so a final acknowledgment must go to Lord Reith and Stanley Morison, to whose urgent advice this attempt owes its existence.

INDEX

277

278

281

285

use of poster space in entrances, 211
Stockwell Underground Station, 117-18
Strauss, George, 194
Studio, The
  controversy on modern art in, 213-14
  publication of Kauffer's posters, 41
Sudbury Hill Underground Station, 139
Sudbury Town Underground Station, 132, 134, 135-6
Sunday bus services, 69
Surrealist art, Pick's attitude to, 215
Surrey, posters depicting countryside, 41
Sutherland, Graham, 211
Sutton, extension of Underground to, 80-5
Sweden, influence of architecture, 132-3, 134-5
Swinton, Lord, 265

'Technical Education and its Relation to Science and Literature', Whitehead, 198
Telegraaf building, Amsterdam, 140-1
Tengbom, Ivar, 135
Thames, river, lithographed posters depicting, 37
This is the World that Man Made, Pick, 56, 64, 199
Thomas, Theodore, 222
Thompson, D'Arcy Wentworth, 173, 248
Ticket booths, 96, 113, 117, 123
Ticket halls, 96, 117, 120, 122
Ticket machines, 122-3
Times, The, comment on Underground Group headquarters building, 127-8
Tolstoy, Leo, 214
Tooting, extension of Underground to, 79-80, 84
Tooting Bec Underground Station, 119-20
Tooting Broadway Underground Station, 120
Tooting Junction, Underground extension through, 79-80
Tottenham, north, rejection of proposed Underground, 75-6
Trades Facilities Act (1921), 74, 81-2, 87
Trafalgar Square, poster depicting, 37
Traffic Development and Advertising Department of Underground Group, Pick's appointment as manager of, 27-8

Tramways
  absorption by Underground Group, 65
  links with Underground, 94-5
  phasing out, 239, 240-1
Transport and General Workers' Union, relations with London Transport, 158-9
Trethowan, Harry, 258
Trolley buses
  introduction, 238
  problem of turning loops, 238-41
Turnpike Lane Underground Station, 94, 139
Typography
  design of, 48
  introduction of 'Underground' alphabets, 41-6

Underground Common Fund, 66, 146-7
Underground Group
  absorption of other concerns, 65, 146, 147
  agreement with LNER over Underground extension to Essex, 147, 148
  Ashfield's role in, 24, 25-6, 65-6, 73
  gardening committee, 235-6
  headquarters building, 125-31
  participation in revenue pooling scheme, 66, 146-7
  Pick's role in, 22-3, 27-8, 73
  publicity, use of posters, 25, 26-34
  retirement of Lord George Hamilton from chairmanship, 73
  see also London Transport, Underground railways
Underground railways
  appraisals of visual impact, 169
  concepts of station design, 93-4, 96, 113-23, 131-41, 152-5, 219
  display of names, 30, 45-6, 119-20
  early electrification, 22-3
  extensions, improvements, 28, 73-85, 85-95, 147, 148, 152; *see also individual lines, places,*
  improved doors, 124
  landscaping, 235-6
  lighting, 94, 116-17, 118, 120, 122, 139, 154, 228
  links with bus routes, 67-8
  modernised rolling stock, 123-4
  policy on spacing of stations, 93, 94
  preparations for war, 251-2
  significance of Pick's contribution to, 12